Chandler sought to pioneer a leadership deve
generation of young vibrant leaders on the cu
In doing so, he built and unleashed a movement of high capacity, agile leaders who
are building their own movements within their spheres of influence. This book—part
memoir, part manual—shares how he did it. It is essential reading for anyone seeking to
invest in a fresh generation of leaders, and a valuable resource.

—JO SAXTON, SPEAKER AND LEADERSHIP COACH; AUTHOR, *THE DREAM OF YOU*;
CO-HOST, LEAD STORIES PODCAST

One of the great privileges of my life is to travel around the world to work with both
senior leaders and emerging leaders. After spending twenty-four hours with the Uptick
group in Virginia, I have to say that it is about the most impressive program I have ever
seen. This is the leaven of hope for the church. These are the kinds of leaders who are
going to make a difference. In a moment in the church's history when many despair
what the future brings, I wish everyone could do the same. I think the work of Uptick
in the Baptist General Association of Virginia (BGAV) is a model that needs to be
replicated and distributed as far as possible. The work of intense formation in a deeply
relational environment creates cohorts of learning that will be, for these leaders, for the
rest of their lives, the tribe of people who will help hold them faithful to the gospel, and
will continue to support them in their own leadership. I just cannot commend Uptick
and the BGAV enough for their investment in these amazing young leaders. I want to
go on record as saying that I am encouraged because I've been able to be a part of it.

—TOD BOLSINGER, VICE PRESIDENT AND CHIEF OF LEADERSHIP FORMATION,
FULLER THEOLOGICAL SEMINARY, PASADENA, CALIFORNIA;
AUTHOR, *CANOEING THE MOUNTAINS*

Uptick let me taste and see an approach to discipling young leaders that is
extraordinarily deep, rich, and acutely needed in our contemporary culture. I know of
almost no other initiative that approaches Christ-centered leadership development with
such intentionality, creativity, strategic focus, and theological depth. Anyone looking
to develop mature, Kingdom-focused disciples with humble character, wide-ranging
relational competencies, practical leadership skills, and, most importantly, a vibrant,
"fully abiding" walk with Jesus needs to read this guide. The designers of the Uptick
journey have generously given away their DNA here, offering a reproducible model
par excellence. I took pages and pages of notes—that's how packed it is with insights,
resources, tools, and practices to apply. I also took to my knees more than once, having
been convicted by a penetrating paragraph that spoke the healing "ouch" of biblical
wisdom. Chandler describes the Uptick journey as simultaneously highly invitational
and challenging—and his book is that as well.

—DR. AMY L. SHERMAN, AUTHOR, *KINGDOM CALLING:
VOCATIONAL STEWARDSHIP FOR THE COMMON GOOD*

Good books are developed by solid people, and John Chandler is as solid as they get. This book is filled with the most significant ministry lessons John has learned in over a decade of devoting himself to the development of young, pioneering missional leaders. It is experientially rich and practically helpful. If you want to help the church live the future in the present, pick up this book.

—JR WOODWARD, AUTHOR, *CREATING A MISSIONAL CULTURE*; CO-AUTHOR, *THE CHURCH AS MOVEMENT*; NATIONAL DIRECTOR, V3 MOVEMENT

I have worked closely with John since 2007 as we hosted young ministers at our mentoring retreats, and I admired the time, energy, and wisdom he shared with his Uptickers and now shares with you. I am particularly impressed with his personal interaction with them, and I am confident John's investment in these leaders will produce Kingdom-building results in churches across America. This book will equip you with many insights and ideas that will enable you to become more effective in leading your church, building a discipleship pipeline, and developing future church leaders.

—BOB RUSSELL, PASTOR, TEACHER, AUTHOR, LOUISVILLE, KENTUCKY

Many yearn for a movement of capable, godly new leaders. John Chandler actually makes the movement happen, and this thoughtful, practical book shows how others can too. Imagine a leadership factory producing the best of leaders for Christ's church in our generation. Uptick provides the manual—from blueprints to operations to outcome.

—LEITH ANDERSON, PRESIDENT, NATIONAL ASSOCIATION OF EVANGELICALS

As a guest presenter for Uptick, I have been able to see what an immersive and transformative experience it is for the emerging leaders involved. We need this kind of visionary and proactive leadership development in the church to ensure the future of our mission and engage the many gifts of the next generation. The future church will be shaped by work like Uptick, and I, for one, have hope for a church led by the kind of leaders Uptick shapes!

—MANDY SMITH, PASTOR, UNIVERSITY CHRISTIAN CHURCH, CINCINNATI, OHIO; AUTHOR, *THE VULNERABLE PASTOR*

I have seen the results of Uptick not only in my life but in the lives of many of my peers. The culture of discipleship taught through the Uptick experience birthed a vision in me to start Ordinary Men, an organization focused on making disciples who make disciples. The impact it has made in our community of business leaders is immeasurable. In society, there exists a seam between ministry and the workplace, and Uptick Entrepreneur is smoothing out this seam by teaching workplace ministry. I have seen firsthand the impact that Uptick has had on the faith, boldness, and the network of Christian business leaders in our community. I would highly encourage Uptick and this valuable handbook to anyone seeking to advance the Kingdom in their workplace and local community.

—JEREMY MCCOMMONS, CO-FOUNDER AND OWNER, FOUNDATION COMPANIES; FOUNDER AND DIRECTOR, ORDINARY MEN; 2016 ENTREPRENEUR OF THE YEAR, FREDERICKSBURG, VIRGINIA REGIONAL CHAMBER OF COMMERCE

For a decade, I've had the privilege of watching John Chandler lead up close. John's integrity, wisdom, courage, and profound compassion, all poured out so generously for the dream of equipping a generation of leaders, inspires even the most cynical among us. Though John would be the first to acknowledge his indebtedness to many teachers, Uptick really is a masterful, bold initiative birthed through the Spirit's awakening in John's soul. It's a beautiful thing to watch a true, godly leader at work—and to see so many lives transformed as a result. Uptick is art. John is the artist. And God is the fire that burns through it all.

—WINN COLLIER, PASTOR, ALL SOULS CHARLOTTESVILLE, VIRGINIA;
AUTHOR, *LOVE BIG, BE WELL*

Uptick is a veritable treasure trove, a manifesto of movemental wisdom. What you will read in this book are not mere ideas, but a wisdom born through a thoughtful and reflective leader who has given almost thirty-five years of his life investing in the development and deployment of young leaders, both men and women, from diverse class and ethnicity. John embodies the definition of a hero-maker—someone who has created the right forums for others to become everything God wants for them. *Uptick* ought to become a classic, definitive text. We give it our wholehearted endorsement.

—ALAN AND DEBRA HIRSCH (FROM THE FOREWORD)

I am grateful for the rich friendship and visionary leadership of John Chandler. I am no less grateful that John has been hard at work serving and shaping young Christian leaders through Uptick, including a number of gifted graduates from Baylor's Truett Seminary. In this timely book, John not only shares with readers how Uptick came to be, but he also helps us to see what makes Uptick tick, as it were—how we can be more thoughtful, faithful, strategic Christ-followers and leaders, and how we can be a part of transformative moments and catalytic movements that shape future Kingdom leaders. I benefited significantly from reading Chandler's "manual" and anticipate returning to it time and again as I seek to lead well and to learn from others who are learning, leading, and loving it!

—TODD D. STILL, PHD, CHARLES J. AND ELEANOR MCLERRAN DELANCEY
DEAN; WILLIAM M. HINSON PROFESSOR OF CHRISTIAN SCRIPTURES, BAYLOR
UNIVERSITY, TRUETT SEMINARY, WACO, TEXAS

I am a marketplace minister, and there's a strong message of Kingdom and discipleship work in John Chandler's book for all of us. This book calls us to have a Kingdom mindset and to be involved in intentional discipleship in our own world. Through soul work and skill work, through character and competency, it's about creating a place in our own world where we can impact our workplace, neighborhood, city, nation, and the whole world for Christ. I loved this book and pray that millions of people will hear God's voice in its message to "be Uptick" in their own world. I pray that this powerful *Uptick* book will grab your heart, spark you to listen more closely to the Lord, to know where he is calling you, and to love and follow Jesus at a deeper soul level.

—ELIZABETH JEFFRIES, EXECUTIVE COACH; AUTHOR,
*WHAT EXCEPTIONAL EXECUTIVES NEED TO KNOW:
YOUR STEP-BY-STEP COACHING GUIDE TO BUSTING COMMUNICATION BARRIERS,
KEEPING TOP TALENT, & GROWING YOUR EMERGING LEADERS!*

Thank you, John Chandler, for the wonderful telling of the Uptick story and for curating so thoroughly its fruitful history. I cannot state strongly enough how the BGAV is currently being transformed by the leadership of those who have come through the Uptick cohorts. Churches, institutions, governing bodies, and agencies, are thinking more creatively, moving more boldly, and acting more fruitfully because of these leaders. This book is a must read for any organization attempting to navigate their way into the future.

—JOHN UPTON, EXECUTIVE DIRECTOR, BAPTIST GENERAL
ASSOCIATION OF VIRGINIA

Having read this book and met repeatedly with Uptick leaders, I am encouraged to know there is such a fine resource available for helping young leaders grow into and participate in God's movement in the world. The Uptick pedagogy makes room for young leaders to discover the issues they face, acquire tools to improve their own spiritual health and that of the communities they serve, and learn to replicate networks of disciples. As someone who has worked with young Christian leaders for over twenty-five years, I found the book to be a thoughtful and practical read. It reflects the integrity, the intentionality, and the spiritual depth of the Uptick pedagogy.

—GRETCHEN E. ZIEGENHALS, MANAGING DIRECTOR, LEADERSHIP EDUCATION,
DUKE DIVINITY, DURHAM, NORTH CAROLINA

In this book, John Chandler generously pours out a powerful guide for leader development. Based on my interactions with John, I know he speaks from the authority of living what he believes. His model, Uptick, fills a necessary space by dealing with issues that too often hinder young, promising leaders. Uptick's groundbreaking approach uses various sociological principles that speak to the needs of leaders within the broader social structure. By applying the Uptick model of sharing spiritual, relational, physical, intellectual, and financial capital with young leaders, we can all participate in developing disciples who successfully build the Kingdom in connection with others. I am praying to see an increase in Uptick cohorts as readers take hold of this important work.

—ONEYA OKUWOBI, SOCIOLOGIST, THE OHIO STATE UNIVERSITY;
CO-FOUNDING ELDER, 21ST CENTURY CHURCH, CINCINNATI

This is a powerful combination of prophetic Kingdom vision and practical guidelines that can be implemented today. Uptick has a proven track record of equipping and mobilizing leaders. If you want to build and release next generation leaders who will pursue transformational ministry, this is the place to begin.

—ELIJAH BROWN, GENERAL SECRETARY, BAPTIST WORLD ALLIANCE

We live in a day of unprecedented change, in all aspects of society, including the life of the church. There is no map for the road ahead or any certain sense of being prepared "ahead of time" to lead the people of God in the midst of such dramatic shifts. Instead, what we have are wise friends who have learned the art of preparing leaders who are ready "just in time" for many of the challenges that will meet them. Having spent more than a decade of focus on honing the craft of preparing leaders for a world that is coming, John Chandler has given us a gift in sharing in these pages what he has learned. I know firsthand that this is not a book of theory, but a book of practice—one that has been practiced and found fruitful.

John's book is a great contribution to the leadership landscape in these uncertain times. The kind of leader and the type of training that has served previous generations are woefully inadequate today. The land needs plowing once again by a new breed of pioneer leaders. The skills needed by today's leaders are different. John has taken us back to the roots of Jesus' training methodology—to make disciples. Discipleship with all the attendant tools, language, and vehicles that God has entrusted to John and the Uptick program are powerful and priceless. I commend this book to you and any leaders you are raising.

Those of us who love and serve mainline protestant Christianity need all the help we can get in the present moment. John Chandler through Uptick offers a tested, proven way to energize our leaders and our communities of faith. This book is packed with the wisdom that John has gained and now shares with the rest of us.

Actors are trained to be fully present at every moment, in preparation for a role, in rehearsal, in performance and in life. Chandler has created a compelling movement which advocates for the same kind of presence among those who serve in pastoral ministry. He suggests that clergy act their way into a new way of thinking, rather than thinking their way into a new way of acting. Uptick inspires God's disciples to reframe their past experiences and future lives, freeing themselves to pioneer, create, connect, nurture, and guard, and to recognize and deploy these same gifts within their teams and congregations.

I am thrilled with what John has written in these pages. It is a monumental undertaking because my own observation is that Uptick is more a relational philosophy than a systematic methodology. Having been involved with Uptick and "Uptickers" from the beginning, I have seen the difference this relational framework can make in the ministries and lives of these young women and men. Plainly stated, Uptick is a remarkable model of an intentional, peer-based process that can make good leaders better and provide them with a support system that can sustain them for the remainder of their careers. I commend both this book and this model to any leaders who have any passion for young leaders and the future of the organization they will lead.

—DR. JIM BAUCOM, SENIOR PASTOR, COLUMBIA CHURCH, FALLS CHURCH, VIRGINIA

John Chandler understands the church, the twenty-first century, and the life of the minister like few others in my world. Uptick is not only a highly effective way to grow leaders for the coming church, it is an idea that needs to be spread. This book shares John's heart and dream for the church and shows all of us how to engage leaders and our faith communities with the transformational power of the gospel. We are all indebted to John for his work and his words.

—BILL WILSON, DIRECTOR, THE CENTER FOR HEALTHY CHURCHES, CLEMMONS, NORTH CAROLINA

In his characteristically personal manner, John Chandler has shared generously his advice, practical instructions, and inspiring guidance in this starter kit for those of us stepping aboard the forward-looking movement that Uptick inspires. A must-read for anyone focused on the formation of the next generation for leadership within the Kingdom.

—T. LAINE SCALES, PHD, UPTICK MENTOR; PROFESSOR OF SOCIAL WORK AND BAYLOR MASTER TEACHER; CENTENNIAL PROFESSOR, 2019; CO-DIRECTOR OF BAYLOR IN OXFORD

I encountered Uptick through the partnership between the Romanian Baptist Union and the Baptist General Association of Virginia. At the time I was trying to start a mentorship track for ministers starting their first pastorate in our context. Discovering Uptick existed was an answer to prayer, as it embodied something similar to the project I was hoping to start but it was more developed. What impressed me most was the dedication and quality of the people involved and the impact Uptick has had in the lives of many Uptickers I have since met. Uptick inspired me to continue the efforts to develop something similar in Romania. I am very glad that John Chandler, who enthusiastically encouraged our partnership, has been able to write this book. *Uptick* is a welcome contribution toward a better understanding of how mentoring functions and is a much-needed guide for those who want to implement its principles in other contexts. I know that Uptick will continue to contribute significantly to the lives of many who will be impacted by this inspiring formation process. As John himself acknowledges, Uptick is not just about personal development but also about developing the prophetic gift of hearing God for others.

—DR. OTNIEL IOAN BUNACIU, DEAN, FACULTATEA DE TEOLOGIE BAPTISTA, UNIVERSITY OF BUCHAREST, ROMANIA

Uptick is quite literally an answered prayer for me. My participation in the Uptick cohort came for me at an influential time. I was just starting my career and looking for ways to develop personally and professionally. Furthermore, I had identified a greater need to know how to perceive God's calling on my life and live it out faithfully. In essence, I was seeking holistic formation that would lead to transformation in not only myself but those in my sphere of influence. Participating in Uptick not only gave me a whole new set of tools (relational, organizational, spiritual, professional, etc.) but also caused me to pray about and envision what God would have me build with them. It challenged me to reevaluate my way of thinking about leadership and invited me to express it in my own context. In short, Uptick is a catalyst for impact, the scope and depth of which is yet to be seen because of its emphasis on paying it forward.

—JACLYN BONNER, UPTICKER, SAN ANTONIO, TEXAS

Uptick Voice is an amazing leadership development track that helps young adult women like me find and cultivate their own voice and leadership style in the world. After participating in intense leadership and spiritual development sessions led by dynamic teachers and practitioners from around the U.S., I departed with a sense of call and a burden to reproduce something greater than myself in the world. Participating in Uptick gave me the confidence to be the bold leader God has called me to be, not only in my ministry context, but also in the world.

—STACY DANDRIDGE, UPTICKER, MEMPHIS, TENNESSEE

Uptick isn't just leadership development but *human* development. We are better people because of Uptick. We are better friends. Not just better ministers, not just leaders of the gospel—we are better human beings. It's hard to quantify what a blessing that is. All that you can say is that you've been blessed and now you go on and are moved to bless others in the same way.

—SCOTT DAY, UPTICKER, HUNTSVILLE, ALABAMA

Wow, Uptick has been amazing. It is one thing to be in a room full of leaders and peers. It's another thing to be a part of visionaries and thought leaders and people who are here to help you be not only better believers and Christians, but truly to help you take the Kingdom mission forward. I have been inspired by the relationships built and information shared. Uptick has been life changing. It has taught me how to live a better life. I am a better husband, better pastor, better person because of this experience.

—VERNON GORDON, UPTICKER, RICHMOND, VIRGINIA

I have admired John and Uptick for years and recommend him wholeheartedly. In this book, he builds on the work of some of the greats—Bob Buford, Dallas Willard, and most importantly, of course, the lessons that Jesus taught us in Scripture. You don't have to be a pastor to benefit from this book; the Uptick process has impacted businesses and entrepreneurs already and can help you become a faith-driven leader whatever your context. In Uptick, you'll find a framework that will not only be useful for leadership but also in coming to know and serve God in a way that will help you move closer to the life that is truly life—and bring along others as well.

—HENRY KAESTNER, FOUNDER, FAITH DRIVEN ENTREPRENEUR

UPTICK

UPTICK

A BLUEPRINT FOR FINDING
AND FORMING THE NEXT
GENERATION OF PIONEERING
KINGDOM LEADERS

JOHN P. CHANDLER

FOREWORD BY ALAN AND DEBRA HIRSCH

First published in 2019 by 100 Movements Publishing
www.100mpublishing.com

Cover design and typeset by David McNeill, www.revocreative.co.uk
Cover Art by Kristen Peyton, www.kristenpeyton.com

ISBN 978-1-7333727-1-8

This book is dedicated to the hundreds who have been Uptickers and hopefully the thousands who will be Uptickers. Learning is a two-way street, and discipleship formation through you has been a big part of my own story. The book is especially dedicated to the memories of Uptickers Melissa Cheliras and Nabeel Qureshi, who fought the good fight, ran the good race, and finished the course on this earth much too early. I know that they now see what they once believed. May their joy in the Kingdom be great, and may their lives inspire us to work with urgency, wisdom, and hope.

Well, the first thing that strikes me is that God is still in action. And that's really the first and most important thing, because what you see in these dear young people is God in action. God is moving on them. And then, the other side is the hopefulness and the love that is in them, and the willingness to serve in confidence that God will be with them. And he will be with them. With young people like this, you have to be encouraged about the future of not just the church, but of the world. God has good things in mind, and these young people are part of it. I think maybe we are on the cusp of a different way of thinking about church, especially about church in our communities, and in the world. And it makes me very hopeful to know them, to listen to them, to see the kinds of questions they are asking and to see the kind of venture they are on with God. That's the main thing that comes to me: the hopefulness that you find, not just in them, but from them to the rest of us (the "over the hill" gang, you might call us!). We may be getting on the edge, but they are coming on strong. You just have to thank God, and to bless them in that.

—DALLAS WILLARD GIVING HIS IMPRESSIONS OF UPTICK,
FEBRUARY 2012, CHEVY CHASE, MARYLAND

uptick

/ˈʌptɪk/

noun

an asset that appreciates with investment.

Briefly stated, Uptick is an intentional development track that invests in high-potential, high-capacity young adult leaders, fundamentally using the lens of discipleship. It is a cohort-based, time-limited, selection-based investment that aims to grow various "capitals" in the lives of leaders who are on the front end of their ministries. It is not a program, but a process, or a "track." Uptick finds Kingdom "assets" (young leaders), invests in them at a mission-critical stage of life, and helps those assets "appreciate"—both in the sense of helping them "appreciate in value" (by becoming better leaders) and "appreciate in gratitude" (thus paying the Uptick process forward through replicating it in their own contexts).

Contents

Foreword

ALAN AND DEBRA HIRSCH

What a joy it is for us to do the foreword for this book. First, because John is a genuinely good man and a dear friend for whom we have huge amounts of love and respect. Second, we feel privileged because John is also a really smart missional leader, and the material in this book is simply outstanding.

Uptick is a veritable treasure trove, a manifesto of movemental wisdom. What you will read in this book are not mere ideas, but a wisdom born through a thoughtful and reflective leader who has given almost thirty-five years of his life investing in the development and deployment of young leaders, both men and women, from diverse class and ethnicity. John embodies the definition of a hero-maker—someone who has created the right forums for others to become everything God wants for them.

John starts out with the idea that "what is most personal is most general," which is to say that many of the defining concerns of our own lives are probably also the defining concerns of other people's lives. And how one might go about resolving these concerns will help others resolve the issues they too are facing. This certainly has been our experience. Our own struggle—grappling with deep existential concern for more movemental, missional forms of church, and a robust spirituality that thrives in the midst of this—has turned out to be the same struggle of countless others across the world. We are pretty sure that's why we are writing the foreword for this book.

One of the great challenges for movement leaders is to distill ideas down to repeatable practices that can be practically embedded in the life of a community. But the trick is to ground these practices in big ideas … ideas that have significance for our time. We call these *meta-ideas* because they are foundational ideas that influence the very culture and purposes of the organization. There are such ideas throughout this book. Ranging from issues of spiritual discernment through to the creation of super-viable pathways for the development of emerging leaders, John provides numerous well-tested models, which the observant reader can apply in ways that can lead to systemic change. These are hard-won distillations that could only have been written by a "wise old man" who is deep into legacy mode—giving it all away so that others might flourish. Pushing the metaphor even further, we can say that in *Uptick*, John is actually giving you the family treasure ... for free.

If you were to start a leadership development forum, these are excellent principles that you can invest into the system. Heck, we wish that we had been given such a treasure trove of insight when we had started out with our various local church plants—Forge Mission Training Network, 100 Movements, and the like. We believe we would have got a whole lot more right and made a lot less mistakes. Consider this book as John's investment in you, your organization, your spirituality, and your future.

If you are a leader wanting to genuinely impact your context through developing discipleship-based organizations that further the Jesus cause in the world, then John's story can indeed interpret yours and become part of your unfolding story as well. That's how manifestos work, and that's also how movements take root and grow.

If it's not obvious by now, let us come clean and say that we think *Uptick* ought to become a classic, definitive text. We give it our wholehearted endorsement.

This Book Is for You If ...

- You are a pastor in a church where more of the heads than not are bald or gray. You want to find a way to identify, equip, and deploy a cadre of young leaders who will energize your church for its mission in the neighborhood or network.
- You are a denominational executive in a context where even many of your most loyal and longstanding churches question their affiliation with you. They increasingly fail to see the relevance of denominations as vehicles of mission.
- You are an entrepreneur and want to build the foundations of your business with a discipleship ethos.
- You are a seminary graduate and local church staffer, well equipped for biblical exegesis yet thrown to the wolves in terms of how to "help reach the young people"—which the church fully expects you to do on their behalf, since they have otherwise been unable to make headway in that area.
- You have a level of influence in a vocational setting that you would like to utilize for the benefit of a generation of emerging adults.
- You have had a cadre of teenagers within your sphere of influence over the years who have now left for various colleges, travel, military, work, etc. The nature of your interaction with these emerging adults has changed as they have become geographically dispersed. Yet, while they are away, they also circle back to their hometown from time to time, and you want to leverage your relational history, trust, and wisdom for their spiritual advantage.
- You are a strategist with influence in your environment (work, neighborhood, family, etc.) who wants to create long-term impact in your sphere of influence, and you have the patience and discipline to carry this out beyond quick-fix methods.
- You are a coach of youth sports and you see a group of players within your team who have natural leadership ability and a heart for the Kingdom. You want to expedite their development and maximize their impact.

- You are a grandparent (biologically or spiritually) who wishes to see the network you have acquired over years of experience be put to use for the benefit of those who otherwise would have no access to such a robust ecosphere of relationships.
- You are a church leader who has the capacity to serve as "special forces" in your congregation and take on leadership outside of your church's "standard operating procedures." You want to create a "pioneer class" of leaders for your church and community.
- You are a Christian philanthropist and want to see your ample capitals invested in young disciples at the beginning of their leadership journey, enabling them to accelerate their impact widely and well.
- You lead in the Global South, with very few financial resources, but with the spiritual capitals of wisdom, faith, and hope. You have a cadre of young leaders who will follow you. You are looking for help in how best to develop them.
- You are someone who loves to mentor others, but who has been frustrated with the lack of time and space to do so on a broader scale. You would like to increase your influence for the Kingdom exponentially.
- You are a youth group leader who sees the potential in some of the teenagers of your church to give their lives in significant ways to the work of the Kingdom of God. You are looking for guidance about how to work with these teenagers at a critical juncture.
- You are an executive looking to build a pipeline of talent and to spread an ethos of discipleship throughout and beyond your organization.
- You are approaching the "legacy" stage of your life and are ready to reallocate your time, attention, and resources for Kingdom gains. You want to offer your life, experience, network, and any wisdom you might have to willing recipients.

How to Use This Book

As an avid motorcyclist, I would suggest treating this book the same way I treat my bike's *Rider's Manual*.

1. When I first buy the motorcycle, I read the entire manual, cover to cover. It can be a little confusing or (gasp!) boring compared to the experience of riding the bike, but I need to digest as much pertinent information as I can. An overview of the manual can be incredibly helpful at unanticipated moments once I begin riding. In the same way, there may be information in this book that doesn't seem to apply specifically to your expression of Uptick, but it will serve to orient nonetheless.

2. After getting a few hundred miles under my belt, I find it helpful to go back and reread, or at least skim, the manual. Not only does this help me identify things I could only have noticed after having started to ride, but it also helps me to take advantage of features I missed when trying to take in the whole book. I find I discover things the bike can do that I didn't realize. I've often said, "Oh, so *that's* what this button is for and how it works!" Likewise, you will be amazed how much more helpful the content of this book is once you are actually *in the process of leading* your Uptick network. If a first reading through the manual gets you in the general vicinity, the second reading, once you've started to take action, can coach you through all sorts of potential leadership crossroads.

3. When something on my bike doesn't sound, feel, or look right, I go back to the index in the *Rider's Manual* and look up the potential area of concern. In other words, I use it to troubleshoot. This has sometimes helped me figure out whether something needs to be replaced or merely adjusted and has saved me lots of unnecessary expenditure. The appendices in this book will enable you to do the same.

4. I review the *Rider's Manual* at scheduled maintenance and service intervals. For my bike, every 6,000 miles means a visit to the shop for inspection, tune-up, repair, and sometimes replacement of parts. I am tempted to lengthen the intervals in order to save a few dollars. But I have learned that a well-maintained bike means fewer breakdowns. And I have never been stranded on a bike. In the same way, this *Uptick* book can help you review and stay tuned to the discipleship process, ensuring you don't have a breakdown because you've neglected to attend to some critical areas.

To summarize, the best use of this book is for "just in time" learning while launching and leading an Uptick. My mother often quipped that if we waited until we became perfect parents to have children, then none of us would ever have children! If you wait until you feel fully equipped and prepared to lead, then you will never launch. No one memorizes the entire *Rider's Manual* before hopping on the motorcycle. But, if you launch without learning, then you risk making a lot of messes that are a lot of trouble to clean up, and you will frustrate yourself and others by being unclear and inefficient.

So, spend a few hours reading the *Rider's Manual*. But no one bothers to read such a manual unless they intend to ride! Know that your best learning will come in the times of reflection that occur *after* you have taken action. Over time, it will be in the interplay between this action and reflection that will grow you as an Uptick leader.

Uptick: My Personal Journey

Psychologist Carl Rogers famously noted that "What is most personal is most general."[1] That is, when trying to explain where things come from, people are wise to tap back toward core and pivotal moments in their own stories. As usual, Henri Nouwen puts it beautifully:

> We like to make a distinction between our private and public lives and say, "Whatever I do in my private life is nobody else's business." But anyone trying to live a spiritual life will soon discover that the most personal is the most universal, the most hidden is the most public, and the most solitary is the most communal. What we live in the most intimate places of our beings is not just for us but for all people. That is why our inner lives are lives for others. That is why our solitude is a gift to our community, and that is why our most secret thoughts affect our common life.[2]

MY STORY

The origins of Uptick in many ways emerge from my own story as a young pastor and leader.

In 1987, at age twenty-six, I arrived as pastor of Effort Baptist Church in rural central Virginia. I came to my first full-time pastoral role with an active and healthy spiritual life, having been nurtured in the church's faith from birth. My wife, Mary, and I were in the early days of our marriage and we very much functioned (and still do) as a team in ministry. We didn't have much money, but neither did we have debt. Between savings and Mary's work as a nurse, we were able to save enough money to buy a modest house.

I was equipped with two graduate degrees from one of the finest seminaries (Princeton Theological Seminary) in the country—one degree focusing on New Testament studies, the other on preaching. I had studied key church disciplines with some of the greatest thinkers

---

1 Carl R. Rogers, "'This is Me': The Development of My Professional Thinking and Personal Philosophy," in *On Becoming a Person: A Therapist's View of Psychotherapy* (New York: Houghton Miffling Company, 1961), 26.
2 Henri Nouwen Society, "Meditations," February 23, 2018, www.henrinouwen.org .

in the English-speaking world and was intellectually equipped for the regular duties of teaching and preaching the Bible.

Furthermore, I was not a complete novice as a pastor. During seminary, I had served as part-time pastor at a very small Baptist congregation just outside of Princeton. First, I had been mentored in field education by the previous pastor, who had taken me under his wing before leaving a year later for international missionary work. Then, as I was ordained and became the next pastor, I was on the receiving end of incredible patience from this loving congregation. They were accustomed to raw seminary students whose idea of good preaching was to repeat in the pulpit highly technical academic material learned earlier that week in the classroom. They gently prodded me toward preaching and ministry attuned more to the congregation, workplace, and community rather than to the academy.

I visited in homes and hospitals, baptized new believers, led children's sermons, buried the dead, and married the willing—all new experiences for me. I got to know area and regional colleagues, networks, and denominational folk. I learned the rigors and rhythms of being responsible for preaching every week, which was a steep learning curve. Most people don't have the blessing of being able to learn-on-the-fly with such a patient group of church folk as I did.

Upon graduation, I moved to Virginia and arrived at Effort Baptist Church. I found a tiny congregation of fifteen people who could not have been more eager and collaborative in their approach to ministry. The church was depleted but had energy to work and grow together. For the most part, they were my cheerleaders and fellow workers.

All in all, if one was "asset mapping," then I had a huge cache of pluses in my corner:

- Solid personal faith experience
- Harmonious and supportive marriage
- Quality education
- Absence of pressing debt
- Relevant experience in similar work
- Overwhelmingly eager and collaborative congregation

Our time with Effort Baptist Church was incredibly fruitful. Though we were in a rural and isolated community (not a single stoplight in the entire county!), we grew explosively to become a congregation of nearly 500 in weekly worship attendance. We baptized hundreds of new believers. We became exponentially more generous in service and giving. We saw hundreds of lives transformed toward discipleship by hearing and practicing the gospel. Multiple building and fundraising campaigns stretched the faith and capacity of the church. And when I left, it was with sadness but with the full blessing of the church for my next ministry venture. By nearly any imaginable ministry metric, this was an effective, joyful, "model" pastor/church experience.

Except that this was not *exactly* the case.

THE PROBLEM I DIDN'T SEE

Don't get me wrong; I recall many of our days at Effort Baptist with great fondness. The gains were real and deeply meaningful to many, and to me. It was extremely difficult but rewarding work. It bore lasting fruit and God's Kingdom advanced.

However, there were aspects to my work there that I now lament. In so many ways, I was ill-equipped at age twenty-six to lead a church:[3]

- I had no idea how to mobilize a church for its specific mission.
- I was woefully unprepared to deal with church disputes. One particular individual within the church became my "thorn in the flesh" and caused steady conflict, difficulty, and heartache for me. I had been trained in seminary for certain skills that were necessary for pastoral leadership, such as preaching and teaching the Bible, but I had received no training on how to manage conflict and stress.
- I was unaware of the impact chronic financial pressure would have on me, my family, and on the church.
- I was spiritually isolated. In terms of the growth of my own faith, I was on my own.
- While Mary and I have had a remarkable marriage, the pressures of ministry brought extra challenges in our relationship.

---

3 Similar to the experience of my friend, Alan Hirsch, *The Forgotten Ways: Reactivating the Missional Church* (Michigan: Brazos Press, 2006), 30–31: "I have to say that nothing in my seminary training had prepared me for the experience of those years [of leading a church]. Everything in my education was geared toward maintaining the established, more institutional forms of the church. The vast majority of the subjects on offer were theoretical and were taught by theoreticians, not practitioners. So, we had to learn on the run, so to speak. On reflection, perhaps this is the only way we really learn, but certainly at the time this was the way that God chose to somehow make a missionary out of me."

- Though it had many advantages, we had no idea of how difficult it could be to raise children in a high-visibility church and neighborhood environment.
- We were relationally isolated. Finding friends was surprisingly difficult. At university and residential seminary, we had been surrounded by ready-made networks of peers and potential friends. But we then became newcomers in a neighborhood of people who were very different from us in terms of background, age, education, etc. And being the community pastor surprisingly reframed how people treated us—often with respect and even love, but not necessarily as friends. Mary and I prayed achingly and for many years that God would send us soul-to-soul friends.
- I was untrained in aspects of my role. While I was highly educated in many aspects of ministry, I didn't have a clue how to select (or deselect) leaders, run a business meeting, deal with a church budget, work a room or the back door of the sanctuary after worship, work with the county supervisors when we wanted to expand facilities, raise money, or countless other skills required in my day-to-day life as a pastor. While these things may not drive the church's reason for being, if they are not handled competently, they can quickly derail a church away from its primary purposes.

Clearly, I was unprepared to deal with the administrative and interpersonal challenges of leading a congregation. But most critically, I was struggling with the dawning realization that I was ill-equipped to form and lead a robust band of disciples to live on mission in our neighborhood, county, city, and world. If the Acts 1:8 mandate of Jesus was to receive the power of the Holy Spirit to be witnesses in Jerusalem (Lake Monticello and Fluvanna County), Judea (Charlottesville and the Commonwealth of Virginia), Samaria (the United States), and the ends of the earth, then we were going to experience a serious power shortage. Not because the Holy Spirit was absent from our midst; that was clearly not the case. We were set up for lackluster missionary results because I had been formed to lead in a world that was passing away. For instance:

- I had received an excellent education in how to lead in a Southern United States Christendom context. But that cultural context was already shifting when I arrived at Effort Baptist in

1987 and would be radically different when I left in 1999. In the Christendom moment in which I arrived, the U.S. was the great *sender* of missionaries. By the time I left, the U.S. was *receiving* missionaries from all over the world; people were now coming to share the gospel with North America.

- Intuitively, I knew that "more of the same" in pastoral leadership was not going to lead our church to fruitfulness. Lyle Schaller frequently said, "The road from yesterday to today is not the same as the road from today to tomorrow." I lived with the internal discontent of that, even when I couldn't articulate it.

- I inherited expectations of how pastors were to function in the congregation. Tasks such as administering and growing a Sunday school and prioritizing pastoral visitation were non-negotiable givens. At the time, I did not understand it was not only my role to *meet* expectations, but also to *set* expectations, particularly regarding pastoral roles and our emerging mission.

- I knew nothing of how to grow ministries. As the church grew, I didn't know how to transition from a "shepherd to rancher" role in how I related to the congregation.[4]

- I learned in seminary how to exegete Scripture. I learned on the fly how to "exegete" the congregation and the county. Yet I was always behind the curve in my sense of how to exegete the larger shifts in wider culture. I had been steeped in Christendom culture from birth through my start of ministry. But halfway through my tenure at Effort Baptist Church, Christendom culture in the United States was eroding at an accelerating pace, and it was affecting our congregation. Ten years after I left, our county was largely post-Christendom. Had I stayed, I would have had to reframe ministry there entirely.

- Finally, I had little comprehension of the *movemental* dimensions of ministry.[5] While I was a good local and denominational colleague and foot soldier, I had little understanding of the larger

4 Lyle E. Schaller distinguished how the "shepherd" pastor can function well in a small congregation (fewer than one hundred people—see Luke 15:3–7), whereas the "rancher" uses different skill sets to function among hundreds or thousands. It has been a helpful analogy for pastors seeking to understand how to lead growing and larger churches. See "Lyle E. Schaller," *Wikipedia*, https://en.wikipedia.org/wiki/Lyle_E._Schaller .

5 "I will use the terms movemental or Jesus movements in a way that approximates what David Garrison calls church planting movements. He defines these as 'a rapid mobilization of indigenous church planting churches that sweeps through a people group or population.'" See David Garrison, *Church Planting Movements* (Midlothian, VA: WIGTake, 2004), 21; as quoted in Hirsch, *The Forgotten Ways*, 22–23.

sense of the Christian movement in a Western culture that was increasingly post-Christendom.[6] Tacitly, I thought "mission" was something we did in our church and neighborhood—and farmed out the mission of God to other "professionals" by paying "dues" to denominations, associations, organizations, and missionaries beyond our local setting.

MOVING BEYOND THE NEEDLESS JUNK

I'm aware, even as I write, that this sounds like whining. I hate whining. I once even had a stone sign hanging above my office desk at the church with the words "Thou Shalt Not Whine." My intention, however, is not to whine, but to outline the various ways in which I was woefully ill-prepared for the task at hand. And I believe that this experience was not unique to me but was, and still is, the experience of many other leaders across the U.S. and the Western church. Leadership is hard on its own; my hope is that it doesn't have to be harder than it already is or needs to be.

I had to learn what every pastor has to learn—that pastoral ministry is demanding. I wish I had a dollar for every time I have quoted Peter Drucker, who reputedly said, "The three most difficult jobs in the United States are university president, hospital administrator, and pastor of a local church." It is undoubtedly difficult work. How many times did I smile outwardly when people joked that I only worked one day a week (or even one hour on that one day)? In my heart, I registered them as flippant at best, and, at worst, as morons.

But this is not an apologetic for how hard it is to be a pastor. There's a reason it's called "work," and every job has its challenges. Nor am I complaining about the trials and tribulations of ministry (or life), because it is within those places of challenge that we learn who we are, what we are made of, and what comes out of us when we are pushed or squeezed. We grow when things are demanding. Our best times at the church were during seasons of extreme challenge, often involving great financial risk and sacrifice, where we submitted ourselves to God and

---

6 Mike Breen and the 3DM Team, *Leading Kingdom Movements: the "everyman" notebook on how to change the world* (South Carolina: 3DM Publishing, 2015), Kindle edition, Kindle locations 186–87. "Kingdom Movements: A community that functions as a portal to the new world that God wants for all his children. A Kingdom movement is a community of disciples who passionately seek the expansion of God's reign here on earth through the reproduction of disciples, seeking the transformation of whatever places they inhabit."

to doing what was not easy. As we often quoted, "we also boast in our sufferings, knowing that suffering produces endurance, and endurance produces character, and character produces hope, and hope does not disappoint us, because God's love has been poured into our hearts through the Holy Spirit that has been given to us"(Romans 5:3–5).

I'm all for the character growth that comes through necessary suffering. However, I'm opposed to unnecessary and preventable suffering. I'm opposed to the junk that I (and the church) went through *needlessly* that did everything except build character. It built frustration, distraction, discouragement, disillusionment, and disgust. It led people—including me—to take a long hard look at whether to leave the ministry, leave the church, and/or even leave the faith. I didn't, but those thoughts did cross my mind. And many other leaders *have* left the church.

How different might this ministry chapter in my life have been if there had been wise guides alongside me to help in areas such as:

- Keeping my relationship with Christ vibrant in challenging seasons;
- Finding and building a network of mentors, peers, and protégés to keep me supported and sharp;
- Learning best leadership practices, and having conversations about where the Kingdom of God was breaking through in the U.S. and around the world;
- Keeping a healthy rhythm of life to attend to my family and my own body; and
- Planning financially so that money did not become an obstacle to ministry, or to my own soul.

This is not to understate the countless church members who helped me as they could, often sharing useful and wise guidance about some of these matters. Nor is it to discount my own deep hunger to learn, know, and grow as a leader.

But in many ways, when I sat down in the tiny office on the first day as pastor of Effort Baptist Church with nothing but my books and a blank sheet of paper, *I was on my own.*

And that's a dangerous place to be.

A HINT OF A BETTER WAY

Fortunately for me, two critical experiences helped me to see that being a leader did not mean I had to live on an island.

First, in 1989 I attended a "How to Break the 200 Barrier" conference in Virginia Beach, headlined by Peter Wagner, whose work I had come across in seminary. He brought two then-unknown speakers with him to the seminar: Carl George and John Maxwell! These presentations opened a whole new world to me. During those three days, I learned how to address many of the ministry challenges I was facing that had not been addressed in my very fine seminary education. The seminar gave me some concrete skills for casting vision and building a ministry team that I was able to implement as soon as I got home. Because of this experience, I would eventually enroll at Fuller Theological Seminary for a Doctor of Ministry degree, which helped continue this development in immensely helpful ways.

Second, in 1994–95 I was selected by my denominational family, the Baptist General Association of Virginia, for what was then called the "Young Leaders Program." Taught by a former seminary professor, Bob Dale, who would become a personal mentor and eventually pave the way to my employment with the same organization, the Young Leaders Program gave me a peer group, some self-analytical tools, and concrete instruction around managing power dynamics, organizational change, and leadership styles/teams. It was not without its flaws, but it was fantastically helpful.

The long and short of it is this: Uptick began out of my very personal conviction that intense but time-limited "communities of practice" could be tremendously helpful to young leaders. Other twenty-six-year-old pastors shouldn't have to endure some of the avoidable and unhelpful suffering that drives so many out of ministry. I never left ministry, but on occasion I was certainly at risk of doing so. Young leaders will always suffer because the work is challenging, and being stretched, pushed, and bruised is an integral part of growing stronger. It is necessary suffering.

However, what I longed to address is the unnecessary suffering young leaders face, the "needless junk" I referred to earlier that comes from being ill-equipped to handle the life of ministry for which seminary could not prepare them. It's good to learn from our own difficult experiences. It's great when we can learn from the difficult experiences of others, and bypass avoidable suffering for ourselves and those we lead. In doing so, the hope is that we can stand on the shoulders of others and move further, deeper, faster, and more beautifully into redemptive ministry.

Today's pastors not only experience many of the frustrations and difficulties that I faced as a young pastor but also face the added challenge of a shifting cultural context—we have moved even further away from Christendom. Even though many seminaries and training programs now acknowledge this cultural shift, most emerging leaders are still ill-equipped to know how to navigate and lead in our current landscape.

Let's go back to Nouwen's statement: "What is most personal is most universal." My very personal experience as a young pastor struggling in a decidedly good but needlessly painful pastorate is perhaps not unique. What the hints did not yet provide were clues that Christendom was eroding, and that making disciples and leading a church to bear witness in a *post*-Christendom world would require a serious reframing of what it meant to lead well.

INTRODUCTION
Leadership for a New Landscape

While Christianity is exploding in the Global South, in North America it is becoming increasingly difficult to serve a congregation, and more and more challenging to live as a disciple in what is now firmly a post-Christendom context.[1] The Religion News Service reports that:

> In a shift that stands to impact both religion and politics, survey data suggests that the percentage of Americans who don't affiliate with any specific religious tradition is now roughly the same as those who identify as evangelical or Catholic.[2]

It is even more difficult to lead a disciple-making movement in this context—especially when most leaders have been formed in a system attuned to helping them navigate a world that increasingly does not exist.

I have commonly described the shift from leading in a Christendom context (challenging) to leading in a post-Christendom context (even more challenging) akin to moving from a "home game" to an "away game." It's still the same kind of ball game, but the odds are steeper and the challenges greater.

As a minister in 1987, unwritten rules of Christendom were clearly in effect in the United States South. For instance, it was generally understood and accepted that the local pastor:

- Was a central community figure (sometimes historically even called the "parson" or "person");

---

1 See the work of Philip Jenkins in relation to the growth of Christianity in the Global South, *The Next Christendom: The Coming of Global Christianity* (1st ed.) (Oxford: Oxford University Press, 2002). This was the first of three books Jenkins wrote on the changing face of Christianity, and it deeply influenced my perspective. Professor Jenkins has been a great help to Uptick, for which I am thankful.
2 Jack Jenkins, "'Nones' now as big as evangelicals, Catholics in the US," *National Catholic Reporter*, March 22, 2019, https://www.ncronline.org/news/people/nones-now-big-evangelicals-catholics-us .

- Could show up on the doorstep of people in the community unannounced;
- Would set the moral tone for key neighborhood decisions;
- Would be consulted in important conversations in church and community;
- Was deemed a respected public figure until proven otherwise; and
- Would be treated favorably by local officials, who assumed that the well-being of the church was tied to the overall welfare of the community.

Within five years, those unwritten rules had seriously deteriorated, and by the time I left my first ministry position at the end of the twentieth century, they had virtually disappeared. Two decades into the twenty-first century, they now seem quaint relics of a past era.

I didn't know it at the time, but some of the struggles I faced in leading a church were not related to *internal and institutional* factors of personal and congregational growth, but to *external and contextual* factors of major cultural shifts.

What, then, would help young leaders understand the changing cultural and congregational contexts, and the shifting view of ministers and the church in both? What would be helpful for a congregational leader, whose church has expectations from a Christendom era, when in fact the church (whether it knows it or not) is now in an "away game" of post-Christendom?

WHAT'S NO LONGER WORKING

A church which pitches its tents without constantly looking out for new horizons, which does not continually strike camp, is being untrue to its calling ... . [We must] play down our longing for certainty, accept what is risky, and live by improvisation and experiment.[3]

HANS KÜNG

There was a day, in Christendom, when a new pastor's leadership questions could largely be answered by denominational resources, books, conferences, widely available networks of mentors, and a local network of

---

3 Hans Küng, as quoted in Hirsch, *The Forgotten Ways*, 15.

easily accessible colleagues. Very rarely do those provide the path forward anymore. They exist, but are a form that "is passing away"[4]—they are Christendom resources that are ill-suited for post-Christendom leadership.

This became clear to me as I began working for the Baptist General Association of Virginia (BGAV), in 1999. I began with the title of Director of Evangelism and Church Growth. One of my responsibilities was to lead large how-to conferences that helped pastors and churches share the gospel effectively with their communities. I would also preach, teach, and consult with congregations and Baptist networks on this. Almost all of the training was framed in a set of Christendom assumptions that were disappearing. We sensed this disappearance intuitively, but because we were in the middle of the cultural shift, it was difficult to adjust the denominational work accordingly.[5]

I tried to use the opportunity to interact with many of our 1,400 congregations to, as Ronald Heifetz has put it, "get off the dance floor and step onto the balcony overlooking it."[6] We began to understand that the world was changing, and the denomination had a responsibility to signal those changes for the congregations and leaders in their care. Part of the role of a denomination is to report prophetically back from the frontier with a wider perspective about the challenges that congregations are facing.

In 2002, John Upton became the executive director of the BGAV, and his background as a missionary in Taiwan brought a new and helpful framework to this prophetic challenge. My work became part of a newly framed "Courageous Churches" team. The name was instructive. "Church Growth" or "Church Health" were appropriate Christendom-era challenges. But, as we were on the cusp of a massive culture shift, the virtue that was called for from churches was missional *courage*. Brad Smith captures this nicely:

> In talking with hundreds of church leaders each year, I've seen two movements of God that seem to cross all boundaries of denominations, geography, and church style. First, we see church

---

4 See 1 Corinthians 7:31.

5 Speaking of his own similar experience, Alan Hirsch says, "Guiding a denomination while being engaged on the margins at the same time served to accentuate my increasing conviction that the West had to change and adopt a missionary stance in relation to its cultural contexts or face increasing decline and possible extinction. It also created a lot of angst, and it was in this place of tension that I really transitioned from seeing myself primarily as a pastor to being a missionary to the West." Hirsch, *The Forgotten Ways*, 50.

6 Ronald Heifetz and Marty Linsky, "A Survival Guide for Leaders," *Harvard Business Review*, June 2002 issue, https://hbr.org/2002/06/a-survival-guide-for-leaders .

leaders progressing beyond the church growth movement of the 1980s, which opened up a new awareness of the culture around us. They're also moving beyond the church health movement of the 1990s, which created a new emphasis on intentional discipleship. We've worked so hard to get people inside the church and on a path to maturity; how do we now move them back outside of the church to serve in the marketplace, the community, and the world? Church growth and church health really don't make sense without church dispersion, yet that may prove to be the most difficult task yet. We like comfort. We like safety. It is a daunting task to change church from a place that serves consumers to a place that creates servants.[7]

The church needed to figure out how to distribute courageously into the world, because (as would become apparent) the Western world was rapidly losing interest in finding its way into churches.

Organizing big conferences began to fade, and the emphasis shifted to church planting, discipleship focus, and leadership development. But old habits die hard. Compared to other denominations, the BGAV was ahead of the curve in this transition. But leading a Christendom-focused organization to help Christendom-focused churches meet the opportunities and challenges presented by a post-Christendom culture was still challenging. It is somewhat like trying to teach basketball to a group that believes that it is playing (and will always play) football.

Conversations with Tod Bolsinger in 2018 provided a post-mortem on this struggle. Denominational defaults had been to recommend:[8]

- **More preaching** (talk longer);
- **Better programs** (improved versions of old tricks); or
- **Pastoral care** (try harder).

These, however, are technical changes to challenges beyond the realm of technical adjustments. Technical leadership adjustments don't address massive adaptive challenges. Tweaks to current practices generally don't work when what is called for is new practices in new paradigms. We can (and should) attempt to make our Sunday services dynamic and attractional for non-Christians, with insightful teaching, lively worship,

---

7 Brad Smith, quoted in John P. Chandler, *Courageous Church Leadership: Conversations with Effective Practitioners* (Missouri: Chalice Press, 2007), 8.

8 These are notes taken from Bolsinger's "Church and Beyond" conference and also small group, personal, and Uptick group conversations with Tod Bolsinger in Virginia during March and November 2018.

and a warm welcome. However, this ignores the cultural reality that most non-Christians won't even contemplate going to a church service, however entertaining we make it.

We must address the root issues of our culture, equipping ordinary Christians to become missionary disciples in their everyday lives. As Tod Bolsinger puts it, "Yesterday's successes are the seedbed of today's failures. We were good at sending money overseas but terrible at dealing with the Spanish speaking people across the sidewalk from our church." According to Edwin Friedman,

> Members of highly reactive families wind up constantly focused on the latest, most immediate crisis, and they remain almost totally incapable of gaining the distance that would enable them to see the emotional processes in which they are engulfed. The emotionally regressed family will stay fixed on its symptoms, and family thinking processes will become stuck on the content of specific issues rather than on the emotional processes that are driving those matters to become "issues". [...] When any relationship system is imaginatively gridlocked, it cannot get free simply through more thinking about the problem. Conceptually stuck systems cannot get unstuck simply by trying harder. For a fundamental reorientation to occur, that spirit of adventure which optimizes serendipity and which enables new perceptions beyond the control of our thinking processes must happen first.[9]

It is clear that systemic change is required, but it is important that we understand how and what will bring this change about. On a purely emotional level, in the face of major systemic shifts, Bolsinger noted factors which *don't* produce positive and helpful change as:

- **Fear** (which leads to reactive rather than proactive responses);
- **Facts** (most of us know the truth about diet and exercise, but don't do anything about it); and
- **Force** (try harder; our church would be better if our pastor simply worked longer hours).

To that last point, Bolsinger describes pastors who are blamed for "stuck" churches:

9 Edwin Friedman, *A Failure of Nerve: Leadership in the Age of the Quick Fix* (Revised Edition) (New York: Church Publishing, 2017), 32.

If only you could preach better! If only you were more pastoral and caring! If only our worship was more dynamic! Please, pastor, *do* something! (That is what we pay you for, isn't it?)[10]

No wonder "reportedly, upwards of 1,500 pastors leave the ministry *every month.*"[11]

Better denominational iterations of current programming is not going to help. Slightly improved seminary curriculum is not going to change the world. Tweaking your Sunday school is fine but will have limited upside. Yelling at churches or chastising pastors will be an exercise in futility.

And so, for the BGAV, what was called for was not fear, restatement of facts, or force, but an adaptive new expression of the core BGAV story; a new kind of missional courage.

LEARNING TO LEAD ADAPTIVELY IN A NEW DAY

I can no more live in the church I grew up in than I can now live in my mother's house. Both the church of my childhood and my mother's current house are lovely; but I must leave, cleave, and birth.[12]

—TOD BOLSINGER

There are things about my upbringing that I love, but I realize that everything I like will not attract this next generation. It's sort of like composting. I realize that I'm trying to take resources of a dying system and repurpose those resources/beliefs as the soil for the new to go forth. So now I'm in the tension of what traditional things do I hold on to and what do I let go of? One of Howard Thurman's favorite poems says, 'I'm tired of sailing my little boat, far inside the harbor bar. I want to go out where the big ships float, out on the deep where the great ones are. And should my frail craft prove too slight for waves that sweep those billows o'er, I'd rather go down

---

10 Tod Bolsinger, *Canoeing the Mountains: Christian Leadership in Uncharted Territory* (Illinois: InterVarsity Press, 2015), 12–13.
11 Ibid., 12–13.
12 Ibid., 12–13.

in the stirring fight than drowse to death at the sheltered
shore.' I'm ready to launch out into the deep![13]
—TIONT WILLIAMS

Just as confession of sin is an integral part of worship and discipleship, so it became instrumental for me as a pastor and denominational leader. I have confessed and repented many times for the things I have counted as ultimate and immovable that were simply products of a particular cultural moment—a temporary application rather than a foundational tenet. If the central jobs of the leader are discernment and wisdom, then I must be able to determine what is core and unchanging, and what can (and must always) adapt over time. As Alan Hirsch has often said, "If you fall in love with your system, you lose the capacity to change it."[14]

Churches and denominations are not alone in needing new systems of leadership for a new landscape. I would argue that most major sectors of North American life are in the same boat of needing what Ronald Heifetz and Marty Linsky call "adaptive leadership."[15] This includes government, health care, business and industry, military, the non-profit or social sector, education, etc. The church is not alone in these post-Christendom, postmodern challenges. In fact, the great missionary hope of our day is that if the church can get ahead of other major social sectors in making adaptive leadership changes, it will be "first to the front" and become an agency of great impact and influence for societal good.[16]

Having been gifted with a world-class education, I have frequently been tempted to believe that I can "think" my way beyond being stuck and move into adaptive leadership. Would more precise theology get us to a new day? Debra Hirsch claims, "You don't change systems by changing your theology but by changing your posture around proximity to Jesus. We need to be very concerned about the lack of a quality Jesus-core at the center of the evangelical church." We can't change through better education or theology alone. *Strike one.*

Are more preaching and Bible study the answer? Well, these are certainly not bad, but in and of themselves, they haven't moved the needle of the church observably as it engages with post-Christendom culture.

13 Upticker Tiont Williams, Richmond, Virginia.
14 Alan and Debra Hirsch's comments included here were made at an Uptick gathering in Alexandria, Virginia on March 14–17, 2018.
15 Ronald Heifetz and Marty Linsky, *Leadership on the Line: Staying Alive through the Dangers of Leading* (Massachusetts: Harvard Business School Press, 2002). See also Bolsinger, *Canoeing the Mountains*, 87ff.
16 www.thegreatopportunity.org .

Alan Hirsch observes, "We have tried to be 'People of the Book' (a name given to us by Muslims) rather than 'People of Jesus.'" Many church leaders and members are educated beyond the level of their obedience. They know what the Bible says to do but don't do it. *Strike two.*

And how about better programming, pastoral care, technology, etc.? Again, these are technical responses to adaptive challenges. A bigger choir? More emphasis on Sunday school? Increasing pastoral visitation of shut-ins? As Einstein quipped, "We cannot solve our problems with the same level of thinking that created them." *Strike three.*

By 2007, having worked in denominational life for eight years, I had worked with hundreds of churches up close and personal. Many had "put in stone" things that never should have been fixed as permanent. Elaborate theology, more Bible drills, better curriculum, bigger and more exciting celebrity-driven conferences—there was nothing intrinsically wrong with any of these things. They just weren't going to get our churches where our churches needed to go, namely, to the fulfillment of their missionary callings in their communities. Something else would be required—something spiritually and relationally rich, focused on the front end of the key-leadership pipeline. Our churches needed something that would form people for adaptive leadership. We especially needed this formation to impact young leaders who could potentially influence the wider network for decades to come.

THE BIRTH OF UPTICK TO ADDRESS THE CHALLENGE

When the solution is simple, God is speaking.

—ALBERT EINSTEIN

In his inaugural "Kingdom Advance" address of 2002, John Upton highlighted a crisis in the BGAV leadership pipeline. Responding to dozens of focus groups around Virginia, Upton revealed research of an accelerating shortage of pastoral leaders. "For every three pastors who are retiring," he said, "only one is entering ministry leadership." He elaborated that half of those who entered ministry leadership after seminary had dropped out within the first five years.

Combine these statistics with a shrinking pool of seminary graduates who want to lead congregations, the breakdown of historic denominational collegiate "feeder" ministries, and a sharp decline in young adult participation in local congregational life in general, and the BGAV faced a leadership shortage. Absent of a proactive strategy to mobilize and equip bright young leaders for the mission of God, this shortage would rapidly escalate toward crisis and denominational irrelevance. We have since discovered that what was and is true with the situation within the BGAV is replicated across many denominations and churches across the U.S., Canada, and much of the Western world.

To help move the BGAV out of crisis mode, Upton and a strategic team launched what was then called the "Spence Network" in 2004. This was an entrepreneurial venture, designed as a research and development arm to address declining social capital in BGAV life through network building.[17] In 2007, Upton appointed me to become its first full-time leader.

Within the first year, our leadership team focused on the strategic pathway forward. As a first step to address the hemorrhaging of the leadership pipeline, evidenced by the alarming decline of young, capable, congregational leaders, I designed and led the creation of the first "Uptick" network that year. It was a small cohort of six young leaders. Two years later, my friend and colleague Laura McDaniel rightly challenged, "Where are the women?" We would quickly move to double the size so that future Uptick cohorts would consist of six women and six men.

The BGAV needed (and needs) the native intelligence of these Uptickers to take it into its future as well. Our hopes for that first Uptick cohort were that they would pioneer a movement that would help the BGAV travel toward where it wanted to go.

"How do you change a church's [or denomination's] culture?" Bolsinger asks:

> How do we change any DNA? Through sex. You have to birth something new [...] the new birth won't be all you or all them but a new creation, a new living culture that is a combination of the past and the future that you represent. For change to last, it has to be a healthy adaptation of the organization's DNA. But you have to communicate that you really love them, or they will never let you close enough to them to take in the different perspective, experiences and vision that you bring ... Love precedes change.[18]

17 Originally named "The Ray and Ann Spence Network for Congregational Leadership," this network went through several name changes over the course of its first decade (e.g., "RASNet" and "Spence Network"). The network today is simply known as "Uptick."
18 Bolsinger, *Canoeing the Mountains*, 72, 82.

It's in the mixing of the old and new stuff, in love, that the magic happens. The BGAV narrative began in 1823 as a missionary movement of churches collaborating to evangelize the West. They appointed the "Bedford Plowboys as evangelists."[19] Now, nearly 200 years later, Uptick leaders would adaptively carry on that Bedford Plowboy tradition to advance the Redeemer's Kingdom in the twenty-first century. It was an act of love by the BGAV, sacrificing for the next generation, in hopes of going places and reaching people those of a previous generation would never reach.

In 2007, my first year, we developed Uptick as a targeted leadership investment for innovative young leaders to engage in an intensive process of mentoring and development over the course of one year.[20]

Of course, "there is nothing new under the sun."[21] While the name "Uptick" was new, it was simply a new iteration of the story of the "Bedford Plowboys," the touchstone missionary story of the BGAV since its founding in 1823. Uptick would be a denominational "Fresh Expression" of that missionary impulse to help churches move into pioneering territory with the gospel.[22] Just as the 1823 convocation of the BGAV signaled a willingness of churches to collaborate in commissioning young missionaries for the Western frontier, so Uptick represented that same desire to devote sacrificial attention to the deployment of feisty and willing young leaders for the missional frontier.

STANDING ON THE SHOULDERS OF GIANTS

In 1989, Bob Dale created the "Young Leaders Program" as part of the Center for Creative Leadership, housed in BGAV headquarters in Richmond.[23] For twenty years, this author and former seminary professor of leadership selected annual cohorts of fifteen pastoral leaders, typically in their thirties, and worked with them over the course of a year on a vast array of leadership topics. While Uptick would later

---

19 www.bgav.org/bgav/history .
20 Initially, the track was to include a second year of "residency" within a healthy congregational system; that second year was tabled as the network attempted to raise money for the Uptick initiative.
21 Ecclesiastes 1:9.
22 See www.freshexpressionsus.org , a similar initiative intertwined in many ways with the origins of Uptick.
23 For additional history on BGAV initiatives to create momentum in deploying young missionaries, see Robert Dale, *Memories of the Future: A Memoir of Virginia Baptists Young Leaders' Program*, Center for Baptist Heritage and Studies, www.baptistheritage.org , 2009. This monograph focuses particularly on the lineage of the Young Leaders Program.

forge its own path for forming leaders, many of its structural components came out of the Young Leaders Program playbook, including:

- The participants were recruited, referred, and selected rather than self-applying;
- The process was funded by scholarships rather than fee-based;
- The cohort met over the course of a year;
- The extensive use of personality instruments;
- The use of key readings and homework to provide some of the "glue" that holds together content from the in-person gatherings;
- The focus on systems-thinking and understanding dynamics of power within systems;
- The gaining of practical wisdom from key practitioner leaders; and
- The formation of a strong peer network of relationships.

I participated in the Young Leaders Program in 1995, while still a pastor at Effort Baptist Church, and even today count it as a seminal point in my development as a leader. It instilled personal confidence and clarity and taught key leadership competencies as I led a growing church. It also demonstrated many of the principles that became foundational for the formation of our first Uptick. I remain grateful to Bob Dale to this day for his friendship, mentorship, and pioneering work in the Young Leaders Program. Uptick, in key ways, stands on the shoulders of what he started.

FROM YOUNG LEADERS PROGRAM TO UPTICK

During a time of organizational transition in the BGAV, and as he moved closer to retirement, Bob Dale served as the first, quarter-time director of the newly formed Spence Network. For years, the Young Leaders Program and other initiatives in the Center for Creative Leadership had been funded by interest income from a small endowment given in the 1980s, which typically provided about $25,000 of operating revenue annually. As I came aboard in 2007, as the first full-time leader of the network, this income now became available for new initiatives, including Uptick. The rest of the funding for programming we would have to raise. Little did we anticipate the economic crash of 2008, and the disappearance of this specific funding stream for nearly five years. But, for the first year, it at least provided some "Kingdom venture capital" to launch Uptick.

Uptick represented a departure from the Young Leaders Program process in some key ways. Most significantly, we aimed at leaders aged twenty-three to thirty-two, post-college but "pre-nuclear family nesting" stage. Whereas Bob preferred to invest in leaders who had been leading "long enough to have a few dents in their fenders" and thus teachable, Uptick tilted toward younger leaders at launch stage. Our reasoning was that we were simply losing too many leaders even before they reached their thirties, and that those dents in the fenders were too often disabling crashes. (This is what John Upton was highlighting in his alarming statements about a leadership pipeline crisis.)

We also moved from a model based inside of headquarters, and predominantly led by a capable teaching expert, to a traveling model that featured many nationally and internationally known practitioners and thinkers. It was more expensive to do so, but irreplaceably important. We believed that if Uptick was to be a pioneering initiative, it could not be housed inside of denominational headquarters, but had to explore the frontier of mission in the nation and engage directly with some of the scouts who were doing so. Bob had been a seminary professor and was an excellent teacher, but Uptick was not primarily designed to be a "teacher/ student" environment. My fivefold "missional intelligence" is apostolic, and so Uptick took on this flavor of engagement with the frontier.[24]

I could go on in great detail about how Uptick borrowed, and yet was different, from the Young Leaders Program. Suffice to say, the connection should demonstrate that any Uptick-like initiative within a denomination, congregation, or other organization will share these marks:

- Fits within the larger core metanarrative or "founding missionary story" of the parent organization;
- Can borrow some key ideas and leverage relational assets from previous iterations that are parallel to the Uptick goals; and
- Significantly benefits from any financial jump-start funding to help with launch—but also benefits from having to raise its own financial support.

---

24 Fivefold is another name for the APEST (apostle, prophet, evangelist, shepherd, teacher) mentioned in Ephesians 4:11.

AVOIDING THE UNNECESSARY "TAXES"

One of the frameworks we frequently use in Uptick is Bob Buford's life continuum:[25]

Struggle—Success—Significance—Surrender

These stages are certainly not linear—we often take two steps forward and one step back. But they describe an overall trajectory of the stages of maturity. The best way to move into the next stage of a ministry or business is to live as if you were inhabiting *two stages beyond* your current station. In other words, if you are in the middle of "struggle," then the way to progress toward "success" is to inhabit the realm of "significance." Ask yourself, "What is the meaning of the ministry I'm involved in or my business? Why does it matter? What is it trying to accomplish in the fullest sense?"

In the same way, after a decade of struggle (lots) and success (some), I find myself as an Uptick leader inhabiting the world of "significance." This is, in part, because of my age and stage of life. Becoming a grandfather is a world-reframing event! You begin thinking about the last third of your life, and the remainder of your workplace expression of vocation as a part of that. Americans in middle and upper-class socio-economic brackets are often free at this point from some of the most pointed financial struggles of earlier years, and have the opportunity and luxury to contemplate and act on what they determine matters most. Their "finish lines" come more clearly in sight, and they have renewed energy to focus on the last leg(s) of the race.

In that construct, finding myself asking questions about the significance of Uptick, and praying about how it might outlive me as a Kingdom tool, I have come to believe that the path forward is to practice "surrender." Surrender means several things to me. One, it is a reaffirmation to invest myself, like a spiritual grandfather, in key leaders who I have helped to form, and who will carry the work of Uptick far beyond me. Two, it is to release and empower successors and to increase the volume of their shaping voices as I decrease my own. And finally (and probably most importantly), it is to be as generous as I know how

---

25 Bob Buford, *Finishing Well: The Adventure of Life Beyond Halftime* (Tennessee: Integrity Publishers, 2004).

to be in terms of sharing the Uptick model with "people of peace."[26] In other words, if there are individuals, denominations, or other networks that wish to contextualize the Uptick path for their own setting, I want to be as open handed and helpful as possible to capture our struggles and learning for the benefit of others.

So, the purpose of this book is to consolidate and capture some of the gains of a decade-plus of experiences in launching and leading Uptick networks, and to reinvest those dividends so that the model can be used as widely and as well as possible beyond our specific contexts.

Dallas Willard noted that a rocket burns most of its fuel leaving the launch pad.[27] In the same way, Uptick required significant investment in fuel up front, and later became self-perpetuating. We spent plenty of time, energy, and resources in the "struggle" stage. You'll have to do some of that if you want to launch an Uptick network. Some of the struggle, suffering, and hard work simply comes with the territory of pioneering ministry.

However, as I mentioned earlier, I am no fan of meaningless suffering, and there are plenty of things you can learn on our nickel. There is no need for you to experience unnecessary hardship. My friend, an accountant, says that his job is to help you *avoid* taxes, not *evade* taxes! The same holds true here. My deepest prayer for this book is that it helps you *avoid* unnecessary "taxes." My hope is that we can demonstrate how one group (the BGAV) launched Uptick as an example of how you can launch one in your own context—and do so more efficiently and effectively.

---

26 In the Octagon LifeShape, a "person of peace" is someone who is receptive to your Kingdom message and perhaps to following your model of a discipleship life. (LifeShapes are eight word-pictures which focus on the core competencies of what it means to follow Jesus as his disciples. LifeShapes will be explained more fully throughout the book.)

27 Personal conversation with Willard, 1993.

The Journey I Hope You'll Take

As you begin to think about how you might start and lead an Uptick network, here are five vantage points that should help you clarify how to begin. (Later, I will refer to these as the "five capitals.")

SPIRITUAL

Beginning an Uptick network is first and foremost about hearing and responding to God. The first work in launching an Uptick network is spiritual work. No matter their vocational setting, people have started Uptick networks when they come to believe that God has called them to do so. The foundational competency for a disciple of Jesus is captured in the ability to know what God is saying to you and resolving what you are going to do about it. It perhaps sounds a bit clichéd, but if you are sensing that you should perhaps start an Uptick, the first thing to do is pray about it. Spend enough time listening to God—through prayer, immersion in Scripture, holy conversation—until you receive the clarity on which you can act.

RELATIONAL

I hope you will talk with others about what you are sensing from God and learning about as you read this book. If possible, find others who have been a part of Uptick and pick their brains. Look for people around you who have been "Kingdom multipliers" and bounce ideas off of them. Find some of your own mentors and get their input and wisdom. Look for peers who have a similar calling but have other leadership capacities and discuss whether there are ways you might be able to help each other. Build a denser network of your own "Vital Friends" (more on this later)—you may be surprised that some of them are quite eager to walk with you on your journey to lead an Uptick.

PHYSICAL

Most (but not all) people who end up leading an Uptick network have physically experienced being part of an Uptick network, either as a participant or as a mentor/teacher/presenter. Because of this, they have tangibly experienced the ethos of the Uptick experience, which is very hard to otherwise comprehend. Find out if there are ways you might do the same. If you can't participate directly in another Uptick network, then double down on the relational capital, and look to connect with others who have. They will be able to give you a wealth of knowledge and wisdom from their own experience and can serve to coach and direct you.

INTELLECTUAL

This is where reading the book can sharpen your thinking in light of the other three capitals above. Learn the shared vocabulary and vehicles (e.g., huddle) that work across all Uptick networks. This will help you connect relationally with others who can guide and mentor you as you lead. There are other books that can help as well, particularly Mike Breen and Steve Cockram's *Building a Discipling Culture*. (See the section, *For Further Reading* for other suggestions.)

FINANCIAL

Don't expect the funding for your Uptick network to appear by magic. Securing funding is actually a critical step in sharpening your focus, so that it makes for a compelling "ask" to individuals and organizations. Make sure that you are investing enough of your own "skin in the game," so that you are not asking others to do what you yourself are not willing to do. Any donor worth her or his salt will want to know that you have a personal and financial stake in this and that it is not merely a lark or experiment for you.

Section 1

UPTICK HALLMARKS AND PRINCIPLES

In this opening section, I will try to demonstrate some of the *hallmarks* or *principles* that characterize *how* an Uptick network is formed. These hallmarks include both *ethos* (akin to a "spirit") and *pedagogy* (a specific philosophy of discipleship formation). I'll try to demonstrate ways of enacting these principles, and because they are principles, rather than methods, they can be applied whatever context you find yourself in.

1
Uptick Ethos

Remember, not everyone was part of the 12 with Jesus. Don't think for a second the 72 didn't want to be part of the 12 or that the 120 didn't want to be part of the 72. But Jesus realized a truth that we need to grab onto: We have a limited amount of time and energy, and so we need to spend it as wisely as possible.

Recruit people who have the ability to lead groups of at least 50 people. A high percentage of people simply aren't able to lead at least 50 people. So, we must be strategic in whom we recruit.[1]

MIKE BREEN

There are essential differences between an institution and a movement: The one is conservative, the other progressive; the one is more or less passive yielding to influences from the outside, the other is active in influencing rather than being influenced; the one looks to the past, the other to the future. In addition, the one is anxious, the other is prepared to take risks; the one guards boundaries, the other crosses them.[2]

H. R. NIEBUHR

---

1 Mike Breen, *Multiplying Missional Leaders: From half-hearted volunteers to a mobilized Kingdom force* (1st ed.) (South Carolina: 3DM Publishing, 2012), Kindle edition, Kindle locations, 1680–83, 86–88.
2 Quoted in Hirsch, *The Forgotten Ways*, 190.

Ethos
/ˈĒTHÄS/
noun

the characteristic spirit of a culture, era, or community as manifested in its
beliefs and aspirations.

If you are going to start an Uptick network, the first thing you must
get right is its *ethos*. There is something, irreducible and elemental,
that makes an "Uptick" network an "Uptick" network. That sounds
straightforward. However, what makes this slippery is that ethos is a
matter of the "feel" of a thing. It is more akin to the culture of a group
than its organizational charts, personnel manuals, and official vision
statements (though such artifacts can provide valuable clues about an
organization's ethos). Ethos is about climate, atmosphere, ecosystem.
It can be described by excavating deeply held (though sometimes
unspoken) VABEs: Values, Attitudes, Beliefs, and Expectations.

When asked about how to start an Uptick network, I have often
replied that if you can get the ethos right, then you have lots of flexibility
in shaping its content to the needs of your candidates, context, and
particular goals.

I am a product of my North Carolina upbringing, and grew up in an
oral culture and family system where shared truth was often transmitted
in short sayings, proverbs, axioms, idioms, word pictures, shorthand
signals, and what today could be called "memes." Accordingly, here are
some key memetic slogans or mottos that paint a picture of the culture
or ethos of any Uptick network. They carry deep symbolic importance
in telling the Uptick story and transmitting its VABEs or ethos.

"BUILD ON ISLANDS OF HEALTH AND STRENGTH"

Uptick always looks to make a disproportionate investment in the few
for the sake of the many. It does not believe in an egalitarian principle
that asserts the best way to effect transformation is through equal
investment to everyone in the system. Remember that while Jesus spent
time in public ministry with crowds, his most significant investment was
with the twelve disciples who followed most closely.

Mary and I tried to raise our sons, Preston and Roland not equally
but equitably. We love them both fiercely. But we never agreed to treat

them equally at any given point in time. Rather, we sought to treat them adequately or equitably over the long haul. Just because one got a gift or attention one day didn't mean the other got the same/equal treatment that same day. Over the long haul, our parental investment in them will end up around fifty-fifty. But at any given moment, it won't be divided fifty-fifty. Our belief is that you attend adequately to the one who needs attention, and that attention ebbs and flows. Sometimes Preston got 70 percent and Roland 30 percent; then it would shift to forty-sixty, and so on.

The point of the parenting example is that sometimes, for the sake of the whole family, it is good and right to devote more attention to some members of the family than others. You go to the one where attention is needed at that moment for the good of the whole family.

This sounds reasonable and harmless enough, but in my particular Baptist system, this is a challenge to the prevailing ethos of "fairness" that insists on treating everyone absolutely equally at all times and in every moment. To be sure, Uptick is not trying to create unfair systems of exclusion. Over the years, we have at times had to respond to accusations that Uptick is "elitist."

The larger point we try to make is that it is more strategic and utilitarian for the overall mission if we find the capable and willing potential leaders and double down on them. Just as Jesus loved everyone equally but invested in people differently, so also we invest (unequally) in the few for the sake of the many. If you want to get the wagon train to the frontier, you don't feed every horse the same; you feed your fastest and strongest horses who can ensure that the whole caravan will get there.

Or to use another metaphor, it is easier to hold things together solidly with a few nails driven deeply, than with a multitude of thumbtacks pushed in lightly. It is better to pay for a year-long investment with twelve high-ceiling Uptick leaders (Jesus himself did something like this!) than to spend the same amount of capital on a one-day conference with one thousand undifferentiated leaders. There will be more harvest from twelve well-planted trees than a thousand seeds dropped randomly from a moving truck. Investing in the rising leaders who can become "islands of health and strength" within wider systems is a sound strategy and part of the Uptick ethos. You may have to fight for this value—we certainly have!

"THINK 'KINGDOM VENTURE CAPITAL'"

Venture Capital
/ˈvenCHər ˌkapədl/
noun
capital invested in a project in which there is a substantial element of risk,
typically a new or expanding business.

Think of Uptick as an infusion of "venture capital" in the life and leadership of high-potential leaders as they launch into adulthood and Kingdom of God-oriented work. Disproportionate investment now can lead to disproportionate return on investment over the long haul. Uptick may seem expensive and lavish early on, when candidates are generally in entry-level roles. But you are looking to catch lightning in a bottle. And you are playing the long game with return on investment.

Financial advice company The Motley Fool taught investors to look for "Rule Breakers"—"first movers" in emerging industries. In the 1990s, I took their advice by investing in six stocks they predicted would become Rule Breakers. Four of those companies went belly-up and are no longer in business. I completely lost my investment on those four. However, a quarter century later, two of the six are doing okay: Amazon and Starbucks. (Today, it's hard to imagine a world and life before those two companies!) I more than made up for my losses on the investment whiffs. My overall gains far outstripped ordinary expectations, simply because catching a Rule Breaker early on means earning explosive market gains at the most critical moments. If even a quarter of your Uptick candidates become high-impact leaders over the course of thirty years, what you spent on the entire cohort will in retrospect look like a bargain. While the Uptick investment (money, time, and effort) is disproportionately costly at the beginning, the payoff can also be disproportionately high.

With Uptick, we have always found this to be true. We look for high-potential, high-capacity young leaders. And because such leaders are not yet fully formed and thus volatile, it is not a fail-safe process. Certainly, we have had a few "swings and misses," where, despite Uptick investment, we have not seen demonstrable Kingdom benefits as envisioned.[3] However, we have seen many Uptick young leaders

---

3 Of course, there may be fruit we don't see or hasn't yet happened, so please don't put too fine a theological point on this or deem it as overly judgmental.

grow explosively and begin to impact their settings (and beyond) in exponential ways. Occasionally, we find a true Rule Breaker who rockets to high impact early on.

"Diffusion of Innovations" theory describes systems as composed of innovators, early adopters, middle adopters, late adopters, and never adopters.[4] Most estimate that innovators make up about 2 percent of any system and early adopters about 14 percent. However, if you can influence and guide these two groups, you can begin to "tip" entire systems toward innovation.

When looking for Uptickers, we have often used the phrase, "look for the 16 percent." Again, this is sometimes an unpopular approach in democratic contexts. It feels unfair, exclusionary, and elitist. But if your framework is "maximum growth of Kingdom venture capital," then you will look to invest in significant Kingdom gains for three to four decades to come. You want to equip such leaders to reach their best "influence platforms" as quickly as possible and help them bring return on investment over the long haul.

Think "venture capital, disproportional investment, rule breakers, the 16 percent!"

"RELEASE THE 'APES'"

Uptick uses the "fivefold" language of Ephesians 4:11–12:

> The gifts he gave were that some would be apostles, some prophets, some evangelists, some pastors and teachers, to equip the saints for the work of ministry, for building up the body of Christ[5]

We will discuss the fivefold in more detail later. For now, it is enough to say that in our BGAV system, approximately 80 percent of our leaders had shepherd (pastor) or teacher competencies. These are valuable and irreplaceable. But our lack of leaders in the system who have apostolic, prophetic, and evangelistic intelligences was crippling our mission and system. Uptick needed and needs to focus on finding apostles (A), prophets (P), and evangelists (E). Not entirely joking, we said that our

---

4 Everett Rogers, *Diffusion of Innovations* (New York: Simon and Schuster, 2003).
5 We commonly change the word "pastor" to the word "shepherd" in the North American context to avoid confusion between the missional role of shepherding and the culturally understood congregational role or office of pastoring. For more, see Alan Hirsch, *5Q: Reactivating the Original Intelligence and Capacity of the Body of Christ* (Georgia: 100 Movements Publishing, 2017).

mission was to "Release the APEs!" Apostles, prophets, and evangelists are not intrinsically more valuable than shepherds and teachers. As Mike Breen has said, "Without pioneers (APEs), no new land is taken; without developers (shepherds/teachers), none of it is farmed." The specific goal has been to make sure that all five missional voices are singing in the musical. Our original Uptick cohorts partially launched because the BGAV zoo lacked APEs!

Alan Hirsch says, "Quite simply, a missional church needs missional leadership, and it is going to take more than the traditional pastor-teacher mode of leadership to pull this off."[6] Perhaps your context doesn't have such a strong imbalance of the APEs; if so, you can adjust this dimension of Uptick ethos accordingly. But I suspect that, more often than not, when scouting for Uptickers, you'll be looking for lots of APEs.

"UNDERSTAND THAT 'LIKE RECOGNIZES LIKE'"

This is a more adult way of phrasing the childhood sayings, "It takes one to know one!" and "What you say is what you are!" What these sayings capture is that our powers of recognition are far stronger than our powers of recall. (This is why we do better on multiple-choice exams than fill-in-the-blank exams; when we look at the choices, sometimes one jogs our memories and we recognize it to be correct.)

In terms of leadership, what this principle means is that the best way to find a high-potential leader is to ask someone who has personally made the journey from "high-potential leader" to "established leader." Such folk have a set of "lenses" that help them recognize someone else who has the capacity, character, and potential to make that same kind of journey. Given multiple choices into whom they might invest, they have an experience-based, sometimes intuitively powered ability to "recognize" the best answer. This instinct is not infallible; but it is right more often than not.

When recruiting potential Uptick candidates, there are two common wrong turns. One is to ask non-leaders for leadership recommendations. This is common, for instance, in denominational systems that are driven by concerns other than unearthing the hidden gems of premium, untapped young leaders. Is your primary concern to have leaders that

6 Hirsch, *The Forgotten Ways*, 152.

represent different regions of your area? Or would you pick the top ten leaders even if they were all from one city? There is a correct answer here! But when you ask for recommendations from non-leaders, you'll get candidates that reflect the source of the referral. Fundamentally, we see what we are. Be careful when selecting folk to send Uptick candidates your way. You want referrers whose leadership embodies the mature qualities and abilities into which you hope your Uptick candidates will grow.

The other common mistake in recruiting candidates is to invite people to apply to participate in an Uptick rather than recruiting them. Over the years, I have received scores of recommendations for participation in an Uptick network. Some have said, "Uptick will be a great experience for this person." While we certainly hope Uptick would be a great experience for whomever participates, one person having a great experience is not nearly a high enough bar to warrant such a disproportionate investment. We want the candidates we recruit to have the potential to produce "a hundredfold harvest" (Mark 4:1–20). Thank heaven that, by divine grace, the Sower God can and does throw seed on path, sand, thicket, and good soil. However, when we are recruiting Uptickers, we must look to plant seeds for maximum harvest.

A concise way to say this is that Uptick works by referral and recruitment, not by application or volunteering. A person does not get to enter an Uptick track simply because they are sincere or willing. They need a referral. They need the assessment of someone else who leads well and can recognize the stuff of leadership and discipleship in them.

This feels far-removed from American democracy, in which one person's vote is as good as anyone else's. But I strongly encourage you to hold the line here. Look for the leaders you most admire. Get referrals from them. Ask other strong leaders to "see" people you cannot see. Let most of your candidate pool be built this way. As Jim Collins would say, first, "get the right people on the bus."[7] The success of any Uptick track directly depends on the quality of candidates participating in it.

---

7 Jim Collins, *Good to Great: Why Some Companies Make the Leap... and Others Don't* (New York: HarperBusiness, 2001), 13.

"SMALL, DENSE NETWORKS WILL CHANGE THE WORLD"[8]

Uptick is, fundamentally, an intensive process of mentoring and formation over the course of roughly one year. The arc of involvement in an Uptick network can vary by context, but must be long enough to form a strong, trusting, relationally dense network. It must also be time-limited enough to bring the kind of intensity and intentionality to relational capital that can only be forged in settings bounded by a finite beginning and ending. Great bridges in spiritual capital happen through building great bonds of relational capital.

Herein lies one of the advantages I have experienced in working with millennials: they are often better at forming strong relational bonds more quickly than boomers like me. Time will tell if they are as good at forming *durable* relational networks. But in the short-term, millennials are "microwaves" to my "convection oven!" Part of this is the incredible hunger today's emerging adults have for living in meaningful community. Often this is driven by a sense of displacement or isolation. Sometimes it arises from brokenness in family background or dysfunction in work environments. Other Uptickers are pining for the loss of deep fellowship they once experienced in college, at a workplace, within a city/neighborhood, on sports teams or military units, or in other environments where they once enjoyed a ready-made pool of potential peers and friends. Dislocated from those ready-made sources for friendship, they often find themselves surprised, adrift, and bewildered about how to build relationships that feed their souls. Ironically, many are adept at building community among others, even while living in personal relationship deserts. Here's how 2018 Upticker Matt Boschen puts it:

"

> *If Uptick has shown me anything, it's how lonely I was. I have friends and family in my area; however, many aren't following Jesus very closely. Our conversations never touched on how anyone was doing spiritually. My spiritual capital was struggling because no one was keeping me accountable and I wasn't being challenged in my faith. This was happening in the midst of my parents' divorce, the infancy stage of parenthood, a new job, my*

---

8 Used repeatedly in James Davison Hunter, *To Change the World: The Irony, Tragedy, and Possibility of Christianity in the Late Modern World* (1st ed.) (Oxford: Oxford University Press, 2010).

grandfather's failing health, and my mother's addiction issues. I was drowning and didn't realize it. Instead of bringing my issues to the foot of the cross, I was zoning out and avoiding them. There was no one to pull that to my attention on a regular basis. I have realized the deep need to create a community with accountability for my relational capital, but also for my spiritual capital too.[9]

99

Whatever the drivers, by the time some Uptickers arrive for the beginning of a year together, they are absolutely starved of friendship. And I have often told them, "If this year together is successful, then you will finish the year with some people who can be your friends for a long, long time." Therefore, one of the metrics for success in an Uptick year is whether people in the group have begun to form significant friendship bonds. Why is this so important? Because these friends or peers become some of the key people who keep you in the game. They are the ones who talk you out of quitting or giving up in discouragement. Again, Boschen says,

66

Uptick has shown me that bringing people together in an intentional way is super-important, because what is missing in my life and ministry is connection. Often in the church, we don't connect through prayer, and we don't connect through Scripture. We talk about the Bible together, but we dance along the surface. Uptick allowed us to dive in through intentional time together. That investment has taught me how to invest in others in the same way.[10]

99

In the long term, the wider system benefits from containing relationally rich pockets of friendships such as those formed through the Uptick experience. When the ecosystem of a larger system (such as the BGAV) becomes relationally denser, all kinds of unanticipated benefits begin to accrue. You find that the overall talent quotient is extended, and team depth grows. Candidate pools for strategic job openings become wider. Informal coaching happens across friendship lines, often functioning as preventive maintenance or crisis management. It is impossible to

9 Upticker Matt Boschen, Mechanicsville, Virginia.
10 Ibid.

capture comprehensively the benefits of a better relationship ecosphere for a system.

Uptick functions as a hothouse to help relationships grow quickly. It is a magnified environment that can grow a community of trust quickly, in almost laboratory-like fashion. Dallas Willard said, "The guidance system takes over once the rocket leaves the launch pad" and "the power steering works once the vehicle is in motion."[11] Conversations within trusting friendship spheres accelerate the growth. Many of the formation benefits of Uptick happen simply because participants tend to take moderate risks in vulnerability early in the process. This builds friendship bonds, a community of trust, and environments where much of the teaching is "side-to-side," that is, peer-to-peer. When Uptickers are learning from one another rather than simply from an individual teacher, opportunities for learning and growth multiply. Augmenting teacher input with "side-to-side" learning builds deep group trust and opens doors more widely for all kinds of spiritual formation. In this way, forming a small, dense network makes many things possible.

Finally, to develop world-changing, small, dense networks, Uptick attempts to address some of the pressing issues immediately affecting the participants' generation, stage of life, and world.[12] We speak of how to build networks of Vital Friends. We talk about how to network for key relationships. We try to deal with derailers common to this stage of life: rhythms of work and rest, navigating singleness/dating/marriage, culture clashes, workplace issues, making decisions about transitioning ministries and churches. When there is exchange on these deeply-pertinent issues, covenantal conversation tends to flow quite freely. That is a key ingredient in the recipe for friendship-building.

Indeed, small, dense networks will change the world.

"CREATE A 'PAY IT FORWARD' CULTURE"

Generally, Uptick candidates are poor in some things—money, leadership experience, a long track record of wise decisions, and strategic relational networks. However, they are rich in other things—promise, ability, a leadership horizon of many decades, native ability within emerging generations, optimism, new ways of thinking—among many

11 Uptick gathering, Chevy Chase, Maryland, February 2013.
12 We have found Meg Jay, *The Defining Decade: Why Your Twenties Matter—And How to Make the Most of Them Now* (New York: Twelve, 2013) to be incredibly helpful in addressing the issues commonly faced by Uptickers.

other things. When our network invests the capitals we have (money, experience, wisdom, and networks) in Uptick candidates, the candidates tend to "pay it forward", both in their current leadership contexts, and also by reinvesting dividends in the Uptick for its expansion. It is no accident that most of our donors are churches directly connected with the Uptick experience. They have seen first hand the value added by Uptick and want to "pay it forward." Uptick graduates are challenged to honor their scholarship by recreating the Uptick process in their own leadership contexts, and to be generous to the wider Uptick movement in both the present and the future.

Peter Drucker recounts the story of a university executive who arranged $10,000 grants from the school to its most promising entrepreneurial graduates:

> In the 1920s, the president of Pomona College [...] realized that Southern California and its college population would grow fast and that he would need a great deal of money for the college. He started by actually founding local new businesses and running them for a couple of years until they broke even. Then he called in a top-flight new graduate, literally gave him the business and $10,000 to boot (which was a great deal of money in those days), and said, "It's yours. You build it. But if it is successful don't repay us. Remember us." That's why Pomona and the whole Claremont group are so well endowed today. He built an enormous constituency – long term. The fruits didn't come in for twenty years, but they came in a thousand-fold. I'm not saying that this is the way everyone should do it. But it is one example of building up a long-term constituency, people who remember, who are not giving simply because someone rings a doorbell. They see the support of the institution as self-fulfillment. That is the ultimate goal of fund development.[13]

Turning down the repayment of the $10,000 gift, the university later benefited from a multimillion-dollar legacy gift from that same initial recipient. It was used to build an endowment which exponentially multiplied the school's ability to grant similar future gifts.

From the beginning, it has been an Uptick principle to grant scholarships to participants. When we can provide financial capital to help Uptickers participate, we reduce what is often a chronic source of

13 Peter F. Drucker, *Managing the Non-profit Organization: Principles and Practices* (New York: HarperBusiness, 2006).

stress in their lives. Countless Uptickers have shared stories of crippling debt from school loans, low salaries, unexpected illness, and churches unwilling to provide budget for professional and personal growth. A scholarship takes those worries off the table.

Furthermore, it creates a culture of buy-in, full presence, and appreciation. Canadian Upticker Rebecca Machacek says, "You treat people like gold, and it motivates me to ask how I can treat people around me in the same way."[14]

Frankly, participants are often stunned that someone else has paid for their Uptick experience. When they hear stories of anonymous people who have paid for their cost of participating, they become connected with and accountable to a larger family, and a bigger story. "It's one thing to have someone say that they believe in you," says Upticker James Warren. "It's something else to see them *invest* in you."[15]

To be thankful for someone else footing the bill for you is a form of "honoring your father and your mother" spiritually. Furthermore, it creates a sense of responsibility to become spiritual fathers and mothers who invest in others who come behind them. It can seem financially risky to scholarship an Uptick group, not unlike the gulp that comes with buying expensive seed. But the harvest at the end means we always forget about the initial outlay. Giving an Upticker a scholarship has the power to change their participation from the realm of the transactional into the realm of the transformational; from the contractual to the covenantal.

So, when Uptickers, out of gratitude ask how they can repay us for the experience of Uptick, we always say, "Don't pay it back; pay it *forward*." Many do so, both in the realm of their own leadership context, and often by giving to the larger Uptick and BGAV movement that once invested in them.

A similar dynamic occurs in 2 Timothy 2:1–2, when the mentor Paul encourages his protégé with these words: "You then, my child, be strong in the grace that is in Christ Jesus; and what you have heard from me through many witnesses entrust to faithful people who will be able to teach others as well." Paul wants to see Timothy thrive for the sake of the gospel mission. Such flourishing includes the replication and reproduction of leadership beyond their individual relationship and into a wider ripple and multiple generations.

14 Upticker Rebecca Machacek, Lacombe, Alberta, Canada.
15 Upticker James Warren, Virginia Beach, Virginia.

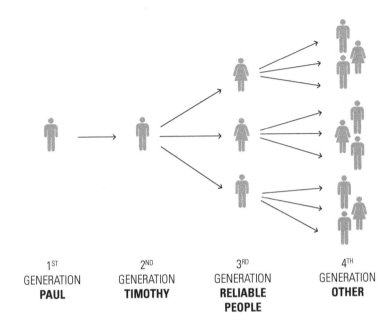

1ST	2ND	3RD	4TH
GENERATION	GENERATION	GENERATION	GENERATION
PAUL	TIMOTHY	RELIABLE PEOPLE	OTHER

16

As Uptick began to gain momentum within the BGAV, one of the ways our Uptick board set goals for system influence was to use the idea of adding enough "innovators" and "early adopters" to a denominational system. Using the wisdom of Everett Rogers' *The Diffusion of Innovation*, (and, honestly, some rather loose math!), we posited that if we were to introduce 222 new leaders to a system of 1,400 churches, we might have a chance to "tip" the larger BGAV system toward movemental disciple making and reproduction. For the Uptick board, our biblical basis for aiming for this benchmark of 222 new leaders was 2 Timothy 2:2. We wanted to find those "faithful people" we could entrust to "teach others as well." The movement is from Paul to Timothy, Timothy to his congregation, the disciples of his congregation to their social and relational spheres, and into the wider world.

It sounds a bit corny, but for our Uptick board it was a *"Kairos moment"*[17] of insight that helped us to focus strategically on how to multiply Uptick networks movementally. It is a different way of utilizing your board's function when you aim to fuel a movement.

16 Taken from *The Church as Movement* by JR Woodward and Dan White Jr. Copyright ©2016 by JR Woodward and Dan White Jr. Used by permission of InterVarsity Press, P.O. Box 1400, Downers Grove, IL 60515, USA. www.ivpress.com .
17 A *"Kairos* moment" is a breakthrough moment when the Holy Spirit gives revelation, wisdom, and truth to a disciple.

2
Uptick Pedagogy

*Experimental groups seeking to engage the Christian faith
in a postmodern context will often lack the resources,
profile or success record of the Boomer congregations.
By definition they are new, untried, and relatively
disorganized and fearful of self-promotion. They reject
the corporate model of their Boomer forbears, and thus
do not appear, according to existing paradigms, to be
significant. But don't be fooled. Somewhere in the genesis
and genius of these diverse groups is hidden the future of
Western Christianity. To dismiss them is to throw away
the seeds of our survival.[1]*

GERARD KELLY

In the 1990s, Henry Blackaby jolted the imagination of many North American Christians when he said that the key to knowing and doing the will of God was to "watch where God was at work and join him there."[2] God is clearly at work in the lives of many promising young adult leaders; the question is, how do we join God in what God is doing in their lives? Uptick is an attempt to join God in this way. If we are to do this successfully, it will involve evaluating what has gone before, recognizing that the Christendom expression of faith founded in the Builder and Boomer eras were not *the* perfect reproductions of biblical Christianity.

---

1 Gerard Kelly, *Retrofuture: Rediscovering Our Roots, Recharting Our Routes* (Illinois: InterVarsity, 1999), as quoted in Hirsch, *The Forgotten Ways*, 69.
2 Henry Blackaby, *Experiencing God: Knowing and Doing the Will of God* (Nashville: Lifeway Christian Resources; Workbook edition, 1990).

PEDAGOGY: A WAY OF FORMATION

Pedagogy
/ˈpedəˌgäjē/
noun
the method and practice of teaching.[3]

True pedagogy transcends merely imparting *information* and instead aims for *formation*. Uptick's intent is the formation of leaders using the lens of discipleship. Its pedagogy is, by definition, a way of formation in the Kingdom of God, as demonstrated by Jesus Christ. This is not a matter of simply adding leadership-specific competencies; it is a larger matter of shaping young adults who happen to lead as robust disciples.

There are volumes devoted to a theologically robust and precise definition of discipleship. Without entering the intramural fray, it is enough to say that, for our purposes, a disciple is a follower of Jesus. "Follower" means more than "learner" or "believer." It is someone who actively listens to the Lord through the Holy Spirit and commits to action by responding rhythmically and spontaneously to God. A disciple will learn to live in such a way that this pattern of hearing and responding is possible, normal, and life-altering. The disciple will obediently follow Jesus into his practices by imitating Jesus' life. (More about this in chapter three.)

Because of this, our emphasis on formation is not on accruing knowledge but on growing in the character and competency of Jesus. We want to form Kingdom-oriented disciples who can then repeat that sort of discipleship formation across numerous contexts.

I always hesitate to call Uptick a "program," though that is the only mental framework some people have and use when trying to describe Uptick. I think words like "track" or "process" better describe the Uptick pedagogy. A program adds competencies; a pedagogy deals with that, but only alongside attending to character. A pedagogy is more broadly concerned with *all* aspects of human and spiritual formation. And a "track" or process indicates that this work is lifelong.

---

3 "Since in Greek *agogos* means "leader", a *paidagogos* was a slave who led boys to school and back, but also taught them manners and tutored them after school. In time, pedagogue came to mean simply "teacher;" today the word has an old-fashioned ring to it, so it often means a stuffy, boring teacher. The word pedagogy, though, is still widely used, and often means simply "teaching". And pedagogic training is what everyone majoring in education receives," https://www.merriam-webster.com/dictionary/pedagogy .

The central point here is that Uptick is a pedagogy toward replicating networks of disciples. New iterations of Uptick networks are like different "species" which belong to the larger "genus" of disciple making.

Another helpful metaphor comes from Steve Cockram, who refers to "DNA," "Skeleton," and "Skin." This is helpful imagery for determining:

- What stays the same across every Uptick network (its discipleship **DNA** and ethos, as described in the previous chapter);
- What looks roughly the same but with contextual and generational adaptations (its **skeletal** pedagogy, generally similar across all Uptick networks); and
- What will always look unique from one network to another (some of the **skin** particulars of participants, schedules, and proprietary conversations based on the context of the network).[4]

Thus, we want to lay out the pedagogy, or process, or philosophy of formation. We wouldn't want ethos or pedagogy to depart philosophically from one iteration to the next, even while expressions or "skins" of that philosophy vary in outer appearance. An "Uptick Worship Leader" network may focus on some competencies unique to that craft, and an "Uptick Entrepreneur" network may devote extraordinary time to how we deal with money and success. Their "skin" or appearance differs in that way. But their DNA of discipleship remains the same beneath appearances.

Put another way, pedagogy is like the "key" in which the song is written. Or, pedagogy is like the "family resemblance." Not everyone in a biological family looks exactly alike, but there are traits, characteristics, stories, sayings, and mannerisms that cause grandparents to be reflected in their grandchildren. If there were one thousand expressions of Uptick that are five generations deep, pedagogy should carry the "key" or "family lineage" all the way through.

---

4 https://giantworldwide.com/ . Alan Hirsch refers to it as "Apostolic Genius," "mDNA" or "missional DNA" composed of six interrelating elements: Jesus is Lord, Disciple Making, Missional-Incarnational Impulse, Liminality and *Communitas*, APEST Culture, and Organic Systems. Hirsch, *The Forgotten Ways*, 83.

TEN MARKS OF UPTICK PEDAGOGY

Here, then, are ten marks, the "skeleton" of the Uptick pedagogy or process of formation:

1. Leadership through the lens of discipleship
2. Language creates culture
3. Rhythm of "character" and "competency"
4. Multiple-voiced leadership
5. Information, Imitation, Innovation
6. "Bonding" and "bridging" capital
7. "The next 20 percent" and "intelligent, but not academic"
8. The journey: self-awareness → self-regulation → social awareness → social regulation[5]
9. Honor the experience
10. Future Story

1. LEADERSHIP THROUGH THE LENS OF DISCIPLESHIP

Let's start with a fundamental axiom: "to live the 'listening life' is not easy." When recruiting Uptick candidates, one of the first things you need to establish is whether candidates are fundamentally interested in listening, both to others and to God. That doesn't mean they already have to know how to listen well. But we want to assess very early on if it is something the person even *desires*. Personally, I am by nature a rather "selective listener." This is not something I'm proud of, but it is a reality of my mind and temperament. However, I work very hard at being a better listener, and I want deeply to become a better listener. I devote time to building my "listening muscles" every day.

The desire to listen is indispensable when assessing whether someone is a good candidate for Uptick. Are they hungry to learn? Teachable? Eager to be in the company of peers, mentors, coaches, and teachers who have something new for them? Or, are they primarily interested in demonstrating their current skill or expertise, giving their own "takes" on whatever conversation is at hand? John Upton once told me that many see themselves as "experts" and fewer as "learners"—and that he always wanted to be counted among those who view themselves as learners, bringing a "beginner's mind" to every conversation.

---

5 Elizabeth Jeffries, *What Exceptional Executives Need to Know: Your Step-by-Step Coaching Guide to Busting Communication Barriers, Keeping Top Talent & Growing Your Emerging Leaders!* (North Carolina: Spark Publications, 2018), 191–92. I cannot emphasize enough my indebtedness and gratitude to Elizabeth for this framework and her extensive work with Uptickers over the years to help with this journey.

According to Upticker James Wilson,

❝

This Uptick experience has been phenomenal for me. The question we started with was, 'What is God saying to me, and how will I respond?' And the reality is, I haven't been listening to God as much as I should be. This process has helped me to listen more for God and begin responding.[6]

❞

Focusing on "followership" skills is foundational. In the next chapter, we will explore in detail some key tools we use to help Uptickers grow in hearing and obeying what God is saying to them.

Introducing tools to help willing learners become better listeners can initially be met with resistance, but these tools soon prove to be transformative in the lives of those who utilize them. Vehicles such as huddle, coaching, Future Stories, learning to use LifeShapes[7] to encounter Scripture, and the prophetic words of trusted peers and leaders can open people to new levels of discipleship:

❝

At the beginning of this year, I was working in a church, feeling good about it, and living a pretty good life. But Uptick has interrupted me in a way I didn't expect. I feel like I am hearing God's voice and hearing the place that I am supposed to be, solidly, for the first time as an adult. The people I've been exposed to, and the relationships I've built have made it possible and given permission for me to do some things I never thought would be a reality.

God has been busting my 'Plan A' and I am really good at planning. But how wonderful to know the desolation and consolation of my plan is not working. I had to get my own voice out of the way in order to get God's voice in the center.[8]

❞

---

6 Upticker James Wilson, Hampton, Virginia.
7 Mike Breen speaks of LifeShapes as the "language of leadership" or "vocabulary which creates a language which in turn creates a culture." See Mike Breen "Lifeshapes: an insider's look," February 25, 2010, https://mikebreen.wordpress.com/2010/02/25/lifeshapes-an-insiders-look/ .
8 Upticker Carlisle Davidhizar, Newport News, Virginia. Listening to God for Carlisle resulted in a move to another state for seminary, starting a family, and a commitment to ordained ministry.

Over the course of the Uptick year, we teach and practice listening skills. Much of this involves the spiritual discipline of submission: the willingness to place oneself in a posture of humility and honesty under the authority of God, Scripture, and the wider community of believers. The vehicles used in Uptick iterations vary widely—from times of prophetic prayer, to exercises in processing labyrinth walks, to the use of art as a vehicle for community discernment. The vehicles are a means to an end: to help disciples-in-formation learn, practice, and develop some habits that will build their capacity to listen to and follow the Spirit of God.

In summary, the pedagogy for *leadership through the lens of discipleship* is:

- The best leaders are the best followers.
- The best followers are the best listeners.
- The best listeners are able to live in such a way that they can hear from God.
- Those who hear from God gain the ability to respond to God as part of the daily rhythm of their lives.

2. LANGUAGE CREATES CULTURE

If "discipleship" is the key lens or "eye" within the Uptick pedagogy, then "shared language" is the "mouth" through which this pedagogy finds its voice. Shared language is critical on an elemental level. For an individual, a useful language "grammar" creates a kind of scaffolding onto which s/he can articulate, interpret, and process otherwise amorphous experiences. Within a group, the common language enables shared experiences that build group cohesion, trust, and interaction. Across Uptick groups, we have found that sharing a common vocabulary creates unanticipated benefits and even movemental momentum.

> A common language is often the most obvious outward sign that people share a common culture [...]. For this reason, groups seeking to mobilize their members often insist on their own distinct language [...] and according to some linguists, languages not only symbolize our culture but also help create a framework in which culture develops, arguing that grammar, structures, and categories

embodied in each language influence how its speakers see reality. For example, because Hopi grammar does not have past, present, and future grammatical tenses, Hopi speakers think differently about time than do English speakers.[9]

Shared language frames identity, and identity frames mission. For instance, new football coaches coming to work for underperforming teams often speak of their first work as "changing the culture" of the team or program. A big part of changing the culture is creating a team-specific playbook, play calls, and team slogans—that is, creating new and shared language.

People are more capable of doing this than you might first estimate. When I walk into any Starbucks and hope to receive the drink I prefer, I must first use the particular words, "skinny venti espresso Frappuccino light extra ice double blended with half whip." A twelve-year-old can do that. If at Starbucks I order a large frozen coffee with whipped cream, I will get (at least) a strange look, and perhaps not the drink I hoped for. In the same way, we can teach language that creates new discipleship frameworks for interpreting our experience as we walk with Jesus in the world.

From time to time, some have questioned why Uptick uses the 3DM "LifeShapes" as our foundational language of discipleship. My typical response is that LifeShapes is not the only grammar of discipleship, and perhaps not even the best one (though I think it's pretty darn good). But these eight shapes give vocabulary and framework to eight undoubtedly key competencies that mark followers of Jesus Christ. The use of shapes helps people who learn visually, and I have found that it also crosses some intellectual, socio-economic, and cultural barriers. For example when I have practiced the Triangle[10] with young adults in Argentina and Austria, they are able to enter very quickly into the heart of the conversation about living Up toward God, In toward community, and Out toward the world. As we will discuss in chapter three, the ease of access into the heart of discipleship through the portal of LifeShapes is at times breathtaking.

9 Mike Breen and Steve Cockram, *Building a Discipling Culture: How to Release a Missional Movement by Discipling People like Jesus Did* (South Carolina: 3DM Publishing, 2011), 55, quoting David B. Brinkerhoff, Lynn K. White, Suzanne T. Ortega, *Essentials on Sociology* (Boston: Cenage Publishing, 2013).
10 The Triangle is one of the eight LifeShapes. It connotes living well in three foundational relationships: An "Upward" relationship with God; an "Inward" relationship with core community; and an "Outward" relationship with the world. This Up/In/Out picture becomes a lens through which we can evaluate whether we are living in a "flat" or two-dimensional relational world, or a robust, three-dimensional world. The organizational name "3DM" comes from this idea of living "three-dimensionally."

So, an Uptick group *always* starts with LifeShapes language. Each cohort may supplement LifeShapes with alternative and additional vocabulary, and various iterations of Uptick networks will do that differently. But an Uptick group always starts with learning language together, and those first language lessons are the LifeShapes. They are akin to grammar—the verbs, nouns, adjectives, etc., upon which we construct a larger shared construal of reality. We insist on learning and practicing LifeShapes in the same way a high school language teacher insists on students practicing verb conjugations.

The shared language of LifeShapes is sometimes striking to Uptickers because it is both *familiar* and *foreign*. Fred Craddock often spoke of good preaching as bringing about in the hearer both the "nod of recognition" (connection with the familiar) and the "shock of recognition" (connection with the foreign).[11] In the same way, most Uptick young leaders immediately recognize just how pivotal it is to be able to "hear and respond to God" (the nod of recognition). They just haven't seen that process worked out so clearly as it is in the picture and language of the Circle[12] (thus the shock of recognition). Mike Breen argues that the church has created a "religious" culture through developing a language particular to the church that some might call "Christianese." He contends that this language needs to be excavated and refreshed toward creating discipleship language.[13] This is what LifeShapes attempts to do.

When it comes to learning and using a new language, the older you get, the harder it becomes. This is yet another reason why it's important Uptick works specifically with young adults. Small children can learn multiple languages while in the home. My son Roland added Portuguese and Spanish to his repertoire as a young adult. Because he and my older son, Preston, were Spanish majors in college, I have been inspired to learn Spanish as well. Unfortunately, I have realized it is far more difficult in my fifties than it would have been had I been immersed in the language from childhood or learned it with the agile mind of a young adult.

---

11 Fred B. Craddock, *Craddock on the Craft of Preaching* (Missouri: Chalice Press, 2011), chapters twelve and thirteen.
12 The Circle is the first and foundational LifeShape. It describes the process of "repent and believe" spoken by Jesus in Mark 1:15. When God gets our attention, a disciple will turn or "repent" (observe, reflect, and discuss this encounter) and "believe" (plan, account for, and act on the new and God-directed path).
13 Breen and Cockram, *Building a Discipling Culture*, 66.

It is a great benefit for Uptickers to learn, practice, and then share LifeShapes language. Most young adults are still trying to determine how to tell their stories. They are, at this point, linguistically pliable and conceptually impressionable. Given these language tools, they are then able to interpret previous and subsequent experiences and are able to pass on the same tools as they multiply disciples. In fact, many are eager to experiment with sharing LifeShapes language as a tool for mission.

> To become disciples, we really need a common language, something we can all understand and reference (Spanish 101, 102, and 201 for example). You go to Barcelona and have a lot more fun if you know the basics of the language, but you become fluent once you are in Barcelona. We become fluent when we are on a mission. [...] Disciples are those who have a new framework of truth, enabling them to build biblical principles into their lives and grow together in authentic community. This is the whole point of the shapes. We can make disciples who, because they have an easily understood language that is making them more like Jesus, can make disciples themselves, thus building a community (the church) in the process.[14]

To summarize, the pedagogy of *language creates culture* is:

- For individuals: agreed-upon discipleship vocabulary accelerates learning and formation.
- Within a single Uptick group: shared language is an on-ramp for elevating conversations that lead to spiritual breakthrough. It helps build cohort identity and closeness. The common language also gives good inroads for continuing interaction with group peers, years after their initial Uptick experience.
- From one Uptick participant to another Upticker outside of her/his cohort: common vocabulary accelerates networking, collaboration, depth of interaction, and other serendipitous and movemental benefits.
- For individual Uptickers after they finish Uptick: those who master LifeShapes language then have a very portable tool to use within their own context of multiplying disciples.

14 Ibid., 226.

3. RHYTHM OF "CHARACTER" AND "COMPETENCY"

C. S. Lewis rightly understood that the purpose of the church was to draw people to Christ and to make them like Christ. He said that the church exists for no other purpose. "If the church is not doing this, then all the cathedrals, clergy, missions, sermons, even the Bible, are a waste of time." [15]

—WILL VAUS AND DOUGLAS GRESHEM

Whereas mere leadership can be solely a matter of competency, leadership through the lens of discipleship must combine *competency* (what you do) with *character* (who you are). We believe that *soul* work must always accompany *skill* work. A despot can rally crowds to action, a surgeon can operate successfully while having an affair, and a pilot might land the plane safely even while drunk. But only a person of character can be a disciple who makes disciples. Uptick counters the U.S. overreliance on technical mastery of leadership skills by focusing on the health and maturity of one's covenant relationship with God, as well as growing in the skills required to partner with him in Kingdom mission.

Jesus mastered the rhythm of attending to his interior world (relationship with God) and his external ministry (his given responsibility from God). In the same way, Uptick focuses on helping us find this rhythm through calibrating *being with* God and *doing* things for God. Being, without doing, can become self-absorbed; doing, without being, can become stressful, exhausting, and frustrating. But when we calibrate *soul* work with *skill* work, we can follow Jesus into his practices.

This work always begins in character formation. The first discipleship huddle of the Uptick year always focuses on the story of Jesus' temptations in Luke 4:1–13—namely, temptations to succumb to our appetites, to ambition, and to the approval of others. "We need to look at the issue of identity, because it is the main battlefield when it comes to character. It is where the Devil attacked Jesus, and where he attacks us, and, if not addressed, can sideswipe a missional leader." [16]

---

15 Will Vaus and Douglas Greshem, *Mere Theology: A Guide to the Thought of C. S. Lewis* (Illinois: InterVarsity Press, 2004), 167.
16 See Breen, *Multiplying Missional Leaders*, chapter 3.

Uptickers may come into the year expecting tips, hacks, tactics, and strategies for leading. But we always reset the conversation toward character formation first. The destination of discipleship is to have the character of Christ (which is then expressed through competencies). If you get the destination wrong, it doesn't matter how far, high, or fast you fly; you will still end up in Seattle instead of San Diego.

Of course, mastering the rhythm or calibration of character and competency is not a one-and-done job, but is the ongoing work of our life on this earth. How to grapple this calibration is perhaps the most frequent topic of conversation throughout the Uptick year, in large part because we live in a day that overemphasizes the importance of competency at the expense of character.

Here are some of the early and common *character* formation conversations in Uptick:

- What it means to have the perspective of joining God's work rather than building my own empire;
- Skills for "winning the first battle of the day"—learning to listen to God each day before engaging with technology and activity;
- Creating daily, weekly, and seasonal rhythms of life that create the conditions for hearing God speak to me; and
- Growing in humility, having a mentor/apprentice mindset, and putting myself in a posture of being a continuous learner and listener.

By the same token, we want to help Uptick leaders grow in their competencies, skills, and practices. While specific skill-training may vary from one Uptick group and context to the next, here are some of the early and common *competency* formation conversations across Uptick:

- Learning from the best of the best—how do I grow from having access to some of the sharpest thinkers in the world who have come to teach and train at Uptick?
- Skills in self-awareness and self-reflection, combined with appropriate but vulnerable sharing in community;
- Learning concrete pathways for networking and building a portfolio of life-sustaining friendship/community; and

- Training in how to present myself in social and public leadership situations.

By way of example, in one particular network—"Uptick Voice," which is a network for women who are leading, or will lead, significant networks across the Baptist movement in the United States and Canada—we focus on the following:

- In terms of *character*, the huddles throughout the year are designed to help participants identify the step into the truest and best use of their God-given "voice." This is deep soul work on identity and calling.
- In terms of *competency*, we help them grow in how they use their physical voices, especially in public settings. We give expert-led training in how to interact with the media; how to speak when on stage, on camera, or in the pulpit; and how to overcome bad habits and vocal tics that detract from the message they are trying to communicate.[17]

In short, the pedagogy of calibrating a *rhythm of character and competency* means Uptick wants to:

- Start with forming character, soul, and identity formation as fundamental.
- Teach and model calibration and rhythm skills.
- Give top-quality competencies training that is contextually appropriate.

In all of this, we want to form discipleship leaders who, like Jesus, know that *who they are* comes before *what they do*, and that all doing flows out of being. Competency gets you in the room, but character keeps you there.

---

17 The powerful, soulful technical work of Kate Burke from the University of Virginia has been pivotal here. Thank you, Kate!

4. MULTIPLE-VOICED LEADERSHIP

It's been said that Christianity started out in Palestine as a community, moved to Greece and became a philosophy, went to Rome and became an institution, and went to Europe and became a government. Finally, it came to America and became an enterprise. What might it take for us to return to community? One way it can return to community is by the fellowship of church leaders sharing leadership under the direction of our head, Jesus. [...] We need to create leadership structures that model the kind of mutual community we're seeking to form.[18]

—JR WOODWARD AND DAN WHITE JR.

Uptick always embodies the Ephesians 4 impulse that leadership has five missional voices: apostle, prophet, evangelist, shepherd, and teacher. More on that later; for now, it is enough to say that Uptick pedagogy is indelibly marked by multiple-voiced leadership. In stark contrast to the celebrity-oriented, charisma-fueled, expertise-certified, "sage on the stage" model of leadership widely embraced in Western culture, the Uptick path to formation assumes that it takes many voices to shape a group in a healthy way. Uptick's pedagogy tries to model this by ensuring many voices rotate into the leadership role. When asked about his role as cultural architect of the congregation he leads, Erwin McManus says,

> (It) is to equip the pastors rather than to serve as "The Pastor." To equip the pastors, to equip the teachers, to equip the evangelists, and to equip every believer in what they're uniquely called by God to do. I'm just not gifted enough to lead this congregation! I really believe that the gifts that are necessary to do what God wants here are encompassed in no one human being.[19]

Here are some key ways Uptick embeds multiple-voiced leadership:

---

18 JR Woodward and Dan White Jr., *The Church as Movement: Starting and Sustaining Missional-Incarnational Communities* (Illinois: InterVarsity Press , 2016), 53. See the entire chapter, "Polycentric Leadership," 53–69.
19 Erwin McManus, quoted in Chandler, *Courageous Church Leadership*, 91.

Side-to-Side Formation

Of course, every group has an initiating leader, and one of the key roles of someone who wants to start an Uptick network is to function as a *convening* leader. A convener initiates, recruits, gathers, prepares environments, and manages group and time dynamics. But to be a convener is not the same as being a "boss, dominator, top expert, or sole authority." In an Uptick environment, we assume that every participant has the capacity to hear from God and respond, and that there is great value in hearing many voices with different intelligences. Formation is not simply expert-to-novice, leader-to-learner, master-to-apprentice. Rather, it is often peer-to-peer, side-to-side, and profoundly democratic.

One advantage of this approach is that it opens up particular space for prophetic voices at the table. We have discovered that, without intentionality, we rarely hear from those who are introverted, quiet-by-nature, or whose voices often go unheard societally because of age, gender, race, socio-economic status, temperament, etc. There have been times of revelatory encounter with God when we have created side-to-side space into which prophetic voices can speak. One such prophetic leader spoke this to her Uptick group:

66

> *I must realize that leaning into being an introverted prophet will allow the people around me to grow in their Kingdom identities [...] There is a famous quote that states, 'It takes a village to raise a child.' I believe this wholeheartedly because a village of Trinidadians and Puerto Ricans raised me. But I do believe that a mother does not allow everyone in the process of her child's upbringing; she is discerning and intentional about her tribe. I have to build a tribe of people, who will ask the hard questions, hold me accountable to the plans I make, and nurture this life [...] Uptick has been a change of legacy for me. It has uprooted some old wounds and taught me how to restructure my entire life. Because of this, I claim my calling as a prophet, and I know where I am going.*[20]

99

Without embracing side-to-side formation, we would never have heard from this prophetic and important voice.

---

20 Upticker Shanice Alexander, Norfolk, Virginia.

Intentional and Mutual Apprenticing

Akin to side-to-side formation in the group is the idea that the Uptick leader should always recruit an apprentice to co-lead. There are several reasons for this:

- The co-leader will see and say things that the leader can't (or won't) see and say.
- Having an apprentice is an opportunity for investment in the confidence and competence of that emerging leader.
- Having two sets of eyes and ears on the group provides a better read on how the cohort is doing and what it needs.
- A good apprentice always sharpens, enriches, and teaches the convening leader. Over the years, I have gained much wisdom from Uptick co-leaders.[21] I am no longer surprised when they take the helm in an Uptick group and lead conversations in ways that I would have never envisioned nor would have been able to facilitate alone.
- Finally, it is always vital to engage in the work of multiplying leadership; leading alongside another helps with this.

Exposure to a Diverse Range of Leader and Participant Voices

This is a lesson I learned the hard way. Early on in Uptick, I selected an entire cohort of participants who were evangelist-leaders. That group was a lot of fun and had a ton of energy, but it was hard for them to focus at critical junctures. Another year, I selected a cohort where most of the participants fell within the same theological bandwidth. Their chemistry was almost instant … but they struggled to learn from other leaders who were from different places on the theological or stylistic spectrum. Finally, it has been an uphill struggle to put together cohorts with significant breadth in racial, economic, educational, and social diversity. But when we do, those groups have tended to grow the most and go the furthest.

From this, we have come to believe that it is vital to create cohorts with a broad range of experiences. And we believe it is important to expose Uptickers to a wide array of Kingdom leadership voices: men

---

21 There are many, but Laura McDaniel, Carey Sims, Ruby Fulbright, and Katie McKown have been central here. I am so grateful!

and women, North American *and* global, conservative *and* progressive, cerebral *and* free-expression, young *and* old, thought-leader *and* practitioner ... the list could go on. Bear in mind, we do believe that the range has its limits within the centered-set of confessing "Jesus is Lord," and more broadly within the range of a centrist posture and orthodox faith. But there is a lot of space within the range of those parameters, and we are intentional about helping Uptickers become healthier, more curious, and well-rounded "free-range leaders."

Broader exposure to multiple voices of leadership often has the effect of helping Uptickers become more versatile, conversant, inquisitive, appreciative, and collaborative. One participant commented, "Uptick, for me, was a reminder of the great cloud of witnesses that surrounds me. I forget about that often, and Uptick was a reminder to me of it at the right time."[22]

To model multi-voiced leadership, we often invite "trip mentors" to sit in on individual Uptick meetings. These could be local leaders, board members, or people who themselves are interested in starting an Uptick cohort. Having them in the room adds another new voice and is also a good way to help the cohort not become too settled and prematurely cozy in its perspectives.

In short, the pedagogy of *multiple-voiced leadership* means Uptick wants to:

- Champion side-to-side peer learning.
- Always co-lead—and look for opportunities for mutual enrichment in the process.
- Diversify the portfolio of leadership voices, both within the group and addressing the group.

5. INFORMATION, IMITATION, INNOVATION

We suggest that if you want to be a disciple, and if you want the people you disciple to be able to disciple others who then disciple others, you will need to follow the path of Information to Imitation to Innovation. Information is incredibly important; but having it right in our heads

---

22 Upticker Kristen Peyton, Williamsburg, Virginia.

isn't enough. We need to see how that Information becomes knowledge and is incarnated in the everyday life of another person. We then apprentice ourselves to that person, learning not only the Information but also how to do what he or she does. And finally, after becoming confident in knowledge and practice, we have the capacity to innovate new ways of discipleship and mission.[23]

—MIKE BREEN AND STEVE COCKRAM

Uptick gives people information about discipleship and leadership. But it also gives participants examples of leaders whom they can imitate as a springboard for innovating through their own leadership. Just as Paul exhorted followers to "Be imitators of me, as I am of Christ" (1 Corinthians 11:1), an Uptick candidate will frequently say to a mentor, "I want your life!" This is more than imitating a mentor in the generic sense; this becomes a mimicking of how Jesus himself reproduced disciples. Such is not an "unnatural reproduction (clone) of Christ" but the "transposing of Christ into the stuff of his daily existence."[24] This is the rich backdrop of "imitation" upon which discipleship and spiritual formation can occur.

Uptick forms candidates through regular intervals of disciple-making interactions. The combination of in-person and online platforms ensures ongoing formation for innovation. In agreement with Mike Breen, we believe that a fundamental fallacy of Western education today is the idea that better information alone can lead to innovation. Rather, transformation occurs when one has access not only to better information, but to imitation—to other people who have so absorbed this information that they are living transformed lives. These peers and mentors are people whom those in formation can imitate. Growing leaders need more than "what you know." They need access to people demonstrating "how you live."

Here's the visual depiction:

---

23 Breen and Cockram, *Building a Discipling Culture*, 50; see also chapters three and four.
24 Romano Guardini, *The Lord* (London: Longmans, 1956), 452.

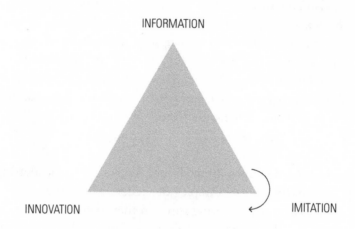

I have often used the example of learning to ride a bicycle to illustrate this in action. A child sees someone ride a bike and wants to learn how they might move so effortlessly and joyfully through the neighborhood. Reading the owner's manual for a bike (perhaps) gives certain useful information. But the only way to learn is to get on the bike and try to ride. First, they watch. Then, someone walks alongside as they wobble unsteadily. They guide the child until s/he gains momentum and confidence, and then the helper lets go. The steering becomes easier as the child learns to pedal more rapidly. And having learned to ride, s/he is able to take a bike to new and innovative places.[25]

So also, in Uptick pedagogy, participants don't simply need new information from their leaders. They need access to our lives.

> To get to transformation, one must first go through a process of imitation. We need models, mentors, demonstrations, living examples. We need people who can, step-by-step, show us how a word from God became part of their life. For this reason, Paul repeatedly said to his young churches, "Imitate me, just as I also imitate Christ" (1 Corinthians 11:1). The Incarnation demonstrates that we need knowledge embodied, modeled, and lived out before it can become part of our way of being and doing. Only then does knowledge become wisdom and revelation.[26]

25 See John P. Chandler, *Praying New Beginnings: Mining the Torah for Daily Leadership Guidance* (Virginia: Uptick Imprint, 2013), 4.
26 Breen and Cockram, *Building a Discipling Culture*, 15.

Disciples-in-formation need to probe how their mentors live, how disciples make daily decisions about things as ordinary as schedule, budgets, and fitness. They need proximity and someone who will take their calls. They need to be able to approach us with how to handle conflict, how to make marital decisions, whether to stay in a certain ministry setting. They need access to conversation and guidance at key junctures of life as part of increasing their own confidence and competence as family members, decision-makers, and discipleship reproducers. One Upticker recently called to discuss whether to take a tempting but risky job offer within a month of getting married. Eventually, he will grow the discipleship "muscles" to make those kind of decisions for himself, as well as to counsel others. But in this stage of his life, he needed (in his own words) "to update you on a current job/ life situation and ask for your wisdom and advice."

This is the logic of why medical doctors in formation pass through a process of medical school, internship, residence, fellowship, and only then independent practice. Likewise, three decades of research at The Center for Creative Leadership in Greensboro, North Carolina reinforces this "information – imitation – innovation" process, which it christens, the "70-20-10 Model." This model suggests that leaders learn from:

- Dedicating time for leadership application (70 percent—*innovation*);
- Intentional mentoring and processing of that application (20 percent—*imitation*); and
- Instruction (some on the front end of the process, some on the back end) (10 percent—*information*).[27]

This process best happens when leaders are given tough assignments and the ability to unpack and be coached in those assignments with a seasoned leader.[28] Unfortunately, the same research shows that most organizations do the opposite of "70-20-10."

The takeaway: Uptick pedagogy insists on an *information, imitation, and innovation*-based process of formation. This means ensuring that

27 Bob Eichinger and Mike Lombardo, "*The 70-20-10 Rule for Leadership Development*," Center for Creative Leadership, https://www.ccl.org/articles/leading-effectively-articles/70-20-10-rule/ .
28 Cindy McCauley, "*Putting Experience at the Center of Talent Management*," Center for Creative Leadership, https://www.ccl.org/articles/white-papers/putting-experience-center-talent-management/ .

Uptickers will:

- Learn from leaders' lives, not simply their ideas.
- See ways of living modeled, rather than simply being handed abstract theological or conceptual frameworks.
- Have access to the actual lives of leaders as part of how they are being formed as disciples.

6. "BONDING" AND "BRIDGING" CAPITAL

Later, we will share about "five capitals" an Uptick network seeks to encourage in the lives of its individual participants. However, in addition to increasing those individual capitals, Uptick is also trying to build something communal, social, environmental, and societal—something relationally rich.

In 2001, Harvard's Robert Putnam sounded the alarm for the decline of social capital in *Bowling Alone: The Collapse and Revival of American Community*.[29] He noted that in the past three decades, the number of Americans attending club meetings declined 58 percent; Americans enjoying family dinners declined 43 percent; and those who regularly entertained friends declined 35 percent. Putnam's forecast that the decline of social capital would only accelerate proved correct—since 2001, those figures have continued to spiral down. He also pointed out the high societal costs of the declining social capital reflected in those statistics.

Putnam's remedy to this situation was to suggest that societies increase both "bridging" and "bonding" capital. "Bonding" capital is the "super glue" strength of the relationships between the members of a group of people—a family, an affinity group, ethnic group, club or church. "Bridging" capital is the "WD-40" or "lubrication" that facilitates interface among diverse segments of society. Healthy systems and societies work strategically to create space for intentional incubators of bonding and bridging capital development. For example, universities in the United States often facilitate the development of intramural sports teams, residence hall networks, and a Greek system of fraternities and sororities. Likewise, the New Testament speaks

---

29 Robert D. Putnam, *Bowling Alone: The Collapse and Revival of American Community* (1st ed.) (New York: Touchstone Books by Simon & Schuster, 2001).

repeatedly of intentional community or *oikos*, the "church in your house," to which many of the biblical epistles are addressed, as vehicles for building bonding and bridging social capital.

Applied to Uptick, our aim is to not only "build *on* islands of health and strength" (in the sense of investing in high-potential leaders), but also to "*build* islands of health and strength" (in the sense of creating cohorts that are relationally rich). We want each Uptick cohort to become an "island" within a larger system which enriches the landscape within that system. To do this, we make sure to build both *bonding* and *bridging* capital into the fabric of the Uptick experience—and to model for the participants how to replicate that in their own contexts.

Building **Bonding** Capital

During the course of the year, we try to create environments in which Uptickers can bond in trusting friendships. Here are some of the ways we work toward that "super-glue":

- Before the Uptick year even starts, we give repeated and varied introductions to upcoming participants. Beyond information sharing, this facilitates their connection on social media, and often leads to their making individual connections before the year starts.
- A month or so before our first in-person gathering, we host a videoconference in which participants can see each other face-to-face, make introductions, and share a few of their hopes for the Uptick year. Because of this preliminary introduction, the first in-person face-to-face meeting starts at a deeper relational level.
- From the first whole-group gathering, Uptick asks for the conversations to be confidential and covenantal, meaning that personal information is not to be shared outside of the room, other than with spouses (if the group contracts for that). This signals that individuals can share beyond a superficial level—and many do.
- Early in the first gathering, we often schedule an evening of "play with a purpose." Plato allegedly said that we can learn more about a person in an hour of play than in a year of conversation;

we have seen the truth of that statement repeatedly! We usually play a game, and generally there will be a prize (such as an iTunes gift card), so that everyone eagerly engages. The game will often take the form of self-revelation. For instance, in one game, we ask people to write a sentence about themselves on a slip of paper, detailing something that would surprise everyone. Of course, many share light-hearted quirks, but others will reveal something more serious or deep. We then see who in the group can match the statement with an individual. This builds a great deal of group cohesion.

- We intentionally vary roommates over the course of the year so that each participant has a chance to share a room with every one of the other participants. While Uptick is not a full-time residential immersion, it involves steady interpersonal engagement through the course of a year. These times together build a platform for side-to-side learning, intimacy in sharing, and trust-building in relationships. Sometimes the most pivotal conversations toward future collaboration take place over early morning exercise or late-night laughter.

- Around mid-year, we engage the entire group in a physical challenge. These activities have included rappelling (supervised and safe, but terrifying for a first-timer); a challenging hike; and a ropes and obstacle course facilitated by someone who helps process the experience for leadership lessons.

- We spend time on how to build a more robust network of Vital Friends (more on this later), giving handles on how to invest intentionally in life-sustaining bonds of friendship.

Building **Bridging** Capital

In addition to creating bonding capital for *friendships*, we also try to add bridging capital toward building *networks*. Here are some of the ways we work toward "WD-40":

- Most of our presenters in Uptick believe deeply in its mission and very openly give access to participants, including their cell numbers. Some Uptickers have capitalized on this opportunity and some have acquired jobs, entry into degree programs, or received world-class coaching or advice through these relationships.

- As mentioned earlier, we often invite "trip mentors" to sit in on Uptick sessions. These practitioners can become additional network resources, and sometimes future employers.

- Frequently, we conduct a session on intentional event networking skills. For instance, did you know that the best place to stand at a networking event when you know very few people is near the food and drink table? (That's where most people will circulate and where people will stand if they are not already locked in another conversation.) There are "best practices" one can learn for networking—from how to write a thank you note, to how to act at a business dinner. Some of these practices are both revelatory and incredibly helpful to Uptickers in building networks.

- During and after the Uptick year, we coach participants who are looking to advance into new vocational opportunities. This can be simple résumé coaching or can be opening relational doors of introduction and résumé sharing. The right "insider recommendation" has often made the difference in Uptickers receiving valuable and hard-to-access opportunities.

- Over time, we have been able to build a "talent pool," for churches and organizations looking for competent and Christlike leaders. Many hold the view that Uptick serves rather like an "imprimatur" or "Good Housekeeping Seal of Approval," validating a high caliber of leadership.

Again, the hope is to build more relationally rich environments, systems, and networks. The best path toward this common good is what University of Virginia sociologist James Davison Hunter calls a "new city common"— a society of high bonding and bridging capital in which intentional networks enable human flourishing in every sphere of life.

In *To Change the World,* Hunter argues that Christians particularly could exercise a "faithful presence" leading toward this common good by their posture within culture.[30] Hunter believes the intentional creation of "small dense networks" of people exercising such faithful presence to be the pathway for changing the world. As memorialized on the Berlin Wall at its fall are the words, "Many small people in many small places, who take many small steps, can change the face of the world."

30 Hunter, *To Change the World.*

Ultimately, each Uptick cohort represents one small, dense network that is attempting to contribute to a larger ecosystem of relational richness.

To summarize, the pedagogy of building *"bonding" and "bridging" capital* means that Uptick seeks to:

- *"Tighten the net"* through friendship-building exercises and environments that facilitate trust, vulnerability, and deeper in-group bonding; and
- *"Widen the net"* by helping Uptickers build bridges of relational networks with other capable leaders who may be helpful during and beyond the Uptick year.

7. "THE NEXT 20 PERCENT" AND "INTELLIGENT, BUT NOT ACADEMIC"

Theological education was created for a world that didn't have Google. Why memorize Hebrew parsing when there are programs that do it better? We have doubled down on knowledge (a technical skill) when wisdom is more valuable.[31]

—TOD BOLSINGER

Eric Hoffer said, "In times of great change, learners inherit the earth, while the learned find themselves beautifully equipped for a world which no longer exists."[32] We have mentioned how critical it is to recruit Uptick candidates who are hungry, humble, teachable, and eager to be listeners. This goes hand in hand with a posture that communicates, "I have yet more to learn than what I already know," and propels disciples not to rest on their laurels, but to pursue growth.

Bob Dale, former seminary professor of leadership, and founder of the Young Leaders Program, once told me that the best seminary experience possible gave pastors only about 20 percent of what it would take to lead effectively in a local church. "Seminary," he often said, "means seedbed. And even the best of seminary experiences only gets you out of the ground and on a path to growing."

---

31 Tod Bolsinger conversation with Uptick, November 2018, Richmond, Virginia.
32 Eric Hoffer, *The True Believer: Thoughts on the Nature of Mass Movements* (New York: Harper & Brothers, 1951).

Through both personal experience and widespread observation, I have found this insight to be very wise. My seminary experiences were excellent. They gave me the ability to interpret the Scripture and a theological framework for understanding faith. As I've already mentioned, they did very little to help me in some concrete matters of personal spiritual habits, ministry and family, dealing with difficult people, and how to preach about money.

This is not a broadside against seminary and the first 20 percent gained through it. It is simply to say that academic formation may be necessary but certainly is not sufficient for discipleship. The problem is well-stated by Alan Hirsch:

> Perhaps the single most significant source of the malaise of leadership in our day comes from the way, and the context, in which we form leaders. For the most part, the would-be leader is withdrawn from the context of ordinary life and ministry in order to study in a somewhat cloistered environment, for up to seven years in some cases. During that period, they are subjected to an immense amount of complex information relating to the biblical disciplines, theology, ethics, church history, pastoral theology, etc. And while the vast majority of this information is useful and correct, what is dangerous to discipleship in that setting is the actual *socialization* process that the student undergoes along the way. In effect, he or she is socialized out of ordinary life and develops a kind of language and thinking that is seldom understood and expressed outside of the seminary. It's as if in order to learn about ministry and theology, we leave our places of habitation and take a flight into the wonderful abstracted world of abstraction, we fly around there for a long period of time, and then wonder why we have trouble landing again [...]. I simply do not believe we can continue to try to *think* our way into a new way of acting, but rather, we need to *act* our way into a new way of thinking.[33]

In short, academic settings tend to form academic leaders (in the mold of professors); practitioner settings socialize one into the practices of

---

33 Hirsch, *The Forgotten Ways*, 121–22. Erwin McManus has often noted that a Christendom old pattern was *Believe*, (then you can) *Belong* (to church), then *Become* (a disciple). The new post-Christendom pattern is that you *Belong* (to a people) which helps shape you to *Become* (a changed person) which enables you to *Believe* (new things). See Eric Bryant, "Belonging Before Believing in the Scriptures," June 23, 2009, https://www.ericbryant.org/2009/06/23/belonging-before-believing-in-the-scriptures/ .

leading. The setting embeds and embodies the formation. The result of successful academic leadership is accreditation and tenure. The result of successful practitioner leadership is risk-laden growth and cultural creation/impact. Bolsinger notes the irony of "people who go into libraries that are climate-controlled, beautiful spaces, where people are shushed into quiet so they can create world-changing books." On the other hand, he says that in Google X (the future technology development wing of Google), "If you want to be a leader, run to the hardest part of the problem. And then try to break your project. The first person who does this gets an award and paid vacation." Ministry leadership programs fail, Bolsinger says, when they are:

- Too sheltered: disconnection of learning from context;
- Too safe: disconnection of learning from actual work;
- Too heady: disconnection from character formation; and
- Too rote: disconnection of learning from reflection.[34]

All to say, the idea that academic or seminary formation gives individuals about 20 percent of what they need to lead seems about right. And if seminary gives the first 20 percent, then Uptick hopes in like manner to give the next 20 percent. It is decidedly not academic, but is hopefully thoughtful, integrated, rigorous, and intelligent. Most critically, the Uptick process takes place while participants are in practitioner contexts. It is designed to invite reflection within the context of active leadership.

Leith Anderson has spoken in Uptick conversations about discipleship being somewhat like the process of manufacturing paper.[35] From timber to a single sheet of paper, there are about seventeen steps in paper processing. These stages include planting the forest and harvesting the timber; logging and pulping; bleaching and inking; packaging and shipping. Disciple making, Anderson said, is a lot like that. Rarely do you get the opportunity to walk with someone along all seventeen steps. More likely, you are given a chance to help in the process for a few steps at most before the person moves out of your purview.

The Engel Scale[36] has been a useful tool for describing the incremental

34 Bolsinger, Uptick conversation, November 2018, Richmond, Virginia.
35 Uptick gathering, Hampton Virginia, November 2017.
36 See "Engel Scale," *Wikipedia,* https://en.wikipedia.org/wiki/Engel_scale .

steps one takes in the journey before becoming a Christian. The below modification attempts to elaborate on growth beyond the point of conversion (step 10):

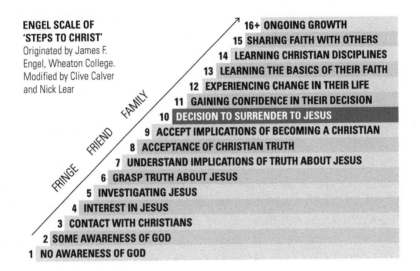

While I applaud that this model has added *some* additional material beyond conversion, ideally, there should be a scale with steps 17–32+. While we've thought well about stages leading up to conversion, we haven't done as well with naming post-conversion steps of discipleship. In this picture, Uptick would give expanded attention to *Learning Christian disciplines*, *Sharing faith with others*, and *Ongoing growth*. (Notice that at the top, there's a "16+"; the scale lacks any description of the future in discipleship beyond!) In short, Uptick generally starts around step 14, and tries to help people progress far beyond 16. This is part of adding the "next 20 percent" to their discipleship formation.

We attend to "ongoing growth" by pivoting from a seminary-like focus on developing intellectual rigor in the knowledge of faith, toward learning and practicing some of the spiritual and relational habits that enable one to listen and respond to God for the rest of life on earth. In this way, Uptick aspires to be "intelligent, but not academic." Its goal is not to transmit proprietary information which creates an elitist class of experts. Rather, the goal is to deploy sturdy, dependable tools for the work of discipleship. Some of these simple tools in "the next 20 percent" include:

- Specific habits and practices that enable individuals to listen to God as a way of life;
- Rhythms of daily, weekly, and seasonal life that create sustainable joy and fruitfulness;
- Creating relationally rich spheres of communion and community;
- Forming growing disciples and networks; and
- Understanding and operating out of calling.

Rather than a class of the academically learned, we are trying to create a class of leaders who are adaptive learners. We want to leverage our few steps to help form lifelong disciples who will name, practice, and transmit the next sixteen steps of that Engel Scale.

To summarize, Uptick pedagogy is not against the work of the academy; it simply doesn't wish to replicate its work. It is neither opposed to nor interested in formal credentialing. Its "20 percent" belongs to the realm of forming new spiritual and relational habits.

In short, the pedagogy of growing "*the next 20 percent*" in ways that are "*intelligent, but not academic*" means Uptick wants to:

- Augment what has been learned in academic contexts with leadership and discipleship skills shaped by engagement with a broader social context.
- Offer a highly helpful toolbox of practices for context-appropriate leadership outside of university or seminary settings.
- Create and encourage a posture of expecting that Uptickers will be lifelong learners.

8. THE JOURNEY: SELF-AWARENESS → SELF-REGULATION → SOCIAL AWARENESS → SOCIAL REGULATION[37]

A huge part of "the next 20 percent" Uptick hopes to impart would fall under categories such as "soft relational skills," "emotional intelligence," "social graces," or "the stuff you have to know, or you'll get fired." We will discuss some of the specific ways we learn and practice developing these skills in chapter nine. For now, it is enough to say that

---

37 Originally taken from Daniel Goleman, *Emotional Intelligence: Why It Can Matter More Than IQ* (10th Anniversary edition) (New York: Bantam Books, 2005). For the most masterful application of the emotional intelligence knowledge base to Uptick pedagogy, see Jeffries, *What Exceptional Executives Need to Know*, 191–92.

we want every Upticker to begin a lifelong journey from *self-awareness* (understanding your own internal world) to *self-regulation* (tempering behavioral reactivity to your internal world) which can lead to *social awareness* (understanding the dynamics at work in others around you) and *social regulation* (responding properly in group situations because of strong understanding of yourself vis-à-vis others). Learning one step opens the door to work on the next step(s). No one masters the entire journey in a single year, but we aim to launch Uptickers on a lifelong path in this direction. Self-awareness brings proper confidence based out of accurate self-assessment. Self-regulation can give us qualities of adaptability and filtering. Such self-awareness and self-regulation can augment social awareness (which builds our capacities for empathy), and social regulation (which helps us manage relationships and conflict, motivate others or build teamwork, and become a catalyst for organizational change).

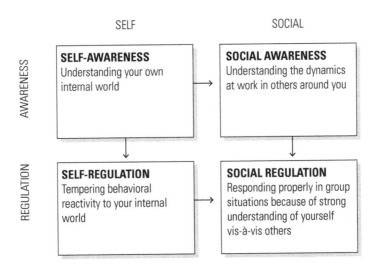

It is hard to overestimate how vital these skills in building relational capital can be. Many Uptickers are new in their vocational environment and quite unprepared for the interpersonal dynamics they find there.

For instance, it can be particularly distressing for those who begin work in a church for the first time, if their only prior experience with church has been as a congregant. There often exist political environments, longstanding grudges, and complicated relational webs that can be surprising, disconcerting, and disorienting. Moreover, working in these arenas can exacerbate all kinds of reactive responses.

> In a survey published in Your Church magazine, the following were revealed as reasons ministers leave the ministry or are pressured to resign: 46 percent left the ministry because of a conflict in vision between themselves and their church. 38 percent left because of personality conflicts with board members. 32 percent because of the unrealistic expectations placed on them. 24 percent because of a lack of clear expectations. 22 percent because of theological differences [...] Good men and women with a calling for the Lord's work become exhausted, then defeated, and finally leave the ministry. It is our observation that the average minister is highly committed, confused by the unrealistic expectations of others, and overwhelmed and frightened by incomprehensible conflict. What goes wrong for pastors everywhere, over and over again? Faulty expectations that lead to intense personal conflict.[38]

Obviously, there are plenty of workplace conditions that lead to this turbulence. But the internal world of the young leader placed in the context is just as much, if not more, of a factor in the distress.

> Here's an interesting paradox. The more pastors care, the more they are set up to fail. The reason they fail is because they tend to make perhaps the most serious error a leader can make. They attempt to meet all of the expectations of their congregation. This attempt has two consequences: 1. Leaders run themselves ragged and destroy their own lives and the lives of their family members. 2. Leaders send the wrong message to their congregations, and especially to those needy individuals who have a great deal of woundedness from the past. This message is, "Yes, I can do it all. I can heal those wounds. I'm the right person for you." But sending this message is a recipe for disaster because leaders invariably are unable to meet all of their congregants' expectations [...]. Life, and certainly church life, has this annoying way of serving up problems that don't lend themselves to easy answers. Even so, people look to those in authority to deliver solutions. Unfortunately, pastors all too often are more than willing to assume these expectations. Instead of solving the problems, the

---

38 James P. Osterhaus, Joseph M. Jurkowski and Todd A. Hahn, *Thriving through Ministry Conflict: A Parable on How Resistance Can be Your Ally* (Michigan: Zondervan, 2010), Kindle edition, Kindle locations 1564–72, 91–98.

pastor becomes the one upon whom the congregation can dump all of its ambivalence, anxiety, and anger."[39]

It is also fair, reciprocally, to say that young leaders also can dump all their ambivalence, anxiety, and anger onto their workplace settings (as well as at home, in family systems, friendships, and social networks). Therefore, to help participants better understand themselves, the pedagogy of Uptick makes liberal use of personality assessment, inventories, and surveys. Some of the most useful have included the Keirsey-Bates MBTI, DISC, APEST, Enneagram, Discipleship Dynamics Assessment, Emotional Intelligence, StrengthsFinder, etc.

However, Uptick doesn't test for these simply for the benefit of the individual to understand his or her own style (self-awareness); we use assessments to help leaders make adjustments (self-regulation), particularly toward how they present and are received in social situations by others (social awareness and regulation). The assessments help us see ourselves as we are, which is the first step toward understanding how we see and respond to how others are.

Tod Bolsinger suggests that growth in emotional intelligence is inextricably connected to spiritual practices for self-transformation, including:

- Practices for **Learning**— staying a lifelong learner (try to engage in activities that make you feel stupid or a novice, e.g., learning Spanish, cooking, art, etc.);
- Practices for **Listening**—to God and to others (learning to keep contemplative spiritual disciplines such as solitude, silence, and confession); and
- Practices for Facing **Loss**—learning to lament as a leadership practice (such as writing laments out, creating lament playlists for listening, reading literature by non-culturally-dominant writers).

Over the course of a year, this training helps Uptickers grow emotional intelligence. The cohort itself provides a safe place to receive honest input in contexts where your job is not on the line. The various personality assessments are typically devoured by participants, who are hungry for the insights. And group processing around them is usually

---

39 Ibid., Kindle locations 98–105, 1952–55.

filled with energy, laughter, and "aha" moments as they begin to grasp how helpful the insights will be. The Uptick cohort functions as a kind of laboratory in this sense. Not every assessment is a source of insight for every Upticker. But there is typically at least one during the year which is the source of significant revelation for each individual.

This journey enables leaders to grow in their capacity to learn to live in the cool "Blue Zone" of *reflective* response rather than the hot "Red Zone" of *reactive* response:

> Conflict is necessary and beneficial, if it is focused properly (i.e., in the Blue Zone). As conflict strays away from issues and accesses personal stories (i.e., in the Red Zone), conflict becomes unmanageable and destructive. The Red Zone is where the atmosphere is characterized by a lack of professionalism and by emotional heat, which can burn those who get too close.[40]

The takeaway: Uptick pedagogy aims to build emotional and relational intelligence, taking them on the journey of: **self-awareness** → **self-regulation** → **social awareness** → **social regulation**. Uptick does this through:

- Helping participants understand and practice self-awareness and self-control; and
- Building relational capital by teaching and practicing skills that lead to social awareness and regulation.

9. HONOR THE EXPERIENCE

Long ago, Lyle Schaller contrasted "voluntary association" churches with "high expectation" churches.[41] Members of voluntary association congregations come and go as they please, give whatever and whenever they feel, and generally interact with their church however they please. On the other hand, those who are part of high expectation congregations tend to understand that becoming part of such a community means they will meet church-defined standards about attendance, giving, service, and training—or they don't (or can't!) join in the first place.

Counter-intuitively, high expectation churches tend to grow at a much faster rate than voluntary association churches. This calls to mind Groucho Marx's famous quip "I'd never belong to an organization that would have me as a member."

40 Ibid., Kindle locations 1636–40.
41 Lyle E. Schaller, *Activating the Passive Church: Diagnosis & Treatment* (Tennessee: Abingdon, 1981), 149–53.

In the same way, Uptick is designed to be a "high expectation" experience. As mentioned earlier, Uptick is a disproportionate and significant investment of time and resources into a select group of people. With that level of investment, it must demand seriously upgraded expectations of how those leaders engage with the process. It must also deliver a far-above-average process, whose quality shows through in the details—from how we meet to what we eat. The Uptick pedagogy is to *honor the experience*, which means that it both delivers to a high standard and also expects high commitment from participants.

For an example of a covenant between what Uptick promises to deliver to, and what it expects from, its participants, see appendix four. This particular example was given during the recruiting of an Uptick Entrepreneur cohort. Candidates see up front what they would gain in the Uptick year—and what would be expected of them.

A candidate for Uptick must "pre-agree" to prioritize Uptick participation over ordinary and frequently interrupted/unpredictable daily schedule. Before agreeing to commit to the process, they must get the blessing from their boss and (if married) spouse. They must work out calendar conflicts in advance.

Through a friendship with a chaplain in the University of North Carolina athletic program, I learned of Jeff Janssen's work with coaching high-performance athletes. Janssen uses a visual aid called the "Commitment Continuum™,"[42] which features seven progressing levels (resistant, reluctant, existent, compliant, committed, compelled, and obsessed) that represent increased levels of commitment.

Every athlete in this high-accountability system is assessed by their coach and as a result has their current status placed above their locker, so that they (and everyone else) know exactly where they stand. Coaching therefore serves to help those who are motivated to move to the next, higher level. Team leaders are those who are at the highest level of commitment. These are the culture-makers of the team and program.

I think this system is brilliant! And while we don't use a system as well-defined and granular as this one, we make it clear to incoming Uptickers that we have high expectations of them. We are not looking for the resistant, reluctant, existent, or compliant. I have often said that

---

42 Jeff Janssen, "7 Steps to Move Someone up the Commitment Continuum™," Janssen Sports Leadership Center, http://www.janssensportsleadership.com/resources/janssen-blog/7-steps-to-move-someone-up-the-commitment-continuum/ . See also, Jeff Janssen, *The Athlete's Commitment Manual: The Complete Guide to Developing Committed and Compelled Athletes* (North Carolina: Winning the Mental Game, 2016).

I will not recruit candidates who I think are going to doubt and question everything we teach. (Challenge is welcome, but cynicism and obstinacy are not.) I am looking for the committed who have the potential to become compelled or even obsessed with Kingdom leadership.

So here is a snapshot of the high-expectation covenant that we set up to honor the experience and to gain maximum benefit:

What Uptick Expects from Candidates:

- I frequently tell Uptick recruits that Uptick is not a "dog ate my homework" kind of network. Don't justify missed expectations with lame excuses. In other words, don't make excuses mid-year about why you can't attend as scheduled, why you didn't show up on time or want to leave early. Don't tell me you need to visit Mrs. Smith before her gall bladder surgery, or your job is in its busy season, or you need to take the youth group on a mission trip. Either sign up for all of it—or don't sign up in the first place.
- When you're there, be *all* there. Be fully present. Amy Cuddy says, "Trust is the conduit for influence; it's the medium through which ideas travel."[43] Leave your phone behind. Show up on time, don't leave early. Honor each other through "SOLER" listening: square, open, leaning in, eye contact, relaxed.[44]

Frequent Uptick leader Bob Russell sets this tone very simply when he opens time together. First, he lays out a list of ways his team intends to serve the cohort lavishly. Then he says, "I have only two rules: 'Be on time, and no multitasking.'" In this way, he invites people to experience deep hospitality, and simultaneously lays down the law regarding full participation. It helps set ground rules for honoring the experience and getting the most out of it.

What a Candidate can Expect from Uptick:

- *A high-quality experience.* The places we stay, the food we eat, the books and resources we give—all of these will reflect the idea that this is a first-class gathering and is worthy of the interruption to normal routines of work, family etc. We are not

---

43 Amy Cuddy, *"Your Body Language May Shape Who You Are,"* https://www.youtube.com/watch?v=Ks-_Mh1QhMc, 2012. This is the second most-watched TED talk in history. See also Amy Cuddy, *Presence: Bringing Your Boldest Self to Your Biggest Challenges* (New York: Back Bay Books, 2018).
44 We will discuss this in more detail in chapter nine and the discussion on social/relational intelligence.

looking for the cheapest way to gather people; we are looking to create environments in which people can bring their best selves to the conversations.

- *A covenant group that models Kingdom community* and makes participants hunger for the time together. We want participants motivated by longing rather than duty, by attraction instead of promotion.[45] We will design gatherings that give Uptickers a chance to experience meaningful fellowship and form durable friendships.
- *Access to high-level discipleship*, leadership, and Kingdom conversations participants most likely couldn't access on their own.

An interesting by-product of "honoring the experience" is that it appeals to the most generous donors. Most seem to understand the value of giving toward something that is going to honor the experience of the participants. Donors seem to appreciate attentive cost-management, but none have ever expressed a wish for us to "take the low bid" on meals, housing, or experiences. Fundraising is an ongoing challenge for Uptick networks, but we don't try to meet that challenge by cutting quality corners. The Uptick pedagogy demonstrates that if leaders honor the experience by demanding much of participants *and* treating them very well, the process will both *set* and *meet* high expectations for growth.

To summarize, the pedagogy of *"honoring the experience"* means Uptick wants to:

- Model a high-expectation community that delivers a correspondingly highly rewarding group experience; and
- Signal the worth of the network by choosing high-caliber guest speakers, and creating environments that value quality, such as where we dine and lodge.

---

45 This phrase, taken from Alcoholics Anonymous, suggests that twelve-step programs work when people are internally motivated (and thus attracted to them) rather than externally encouraged (through promotion, being pushed, etc.).

10. FUTURE STORY

Alasdair MacIntyre taught us that humans are "story-telling animals." Our identity is derived from "stories that aspire to truth [...]. I can only answer the question, "What am I to do?" if I can answer the prior question, "Of what story or stories do I find myself a part?" [...] The story of my life is always embedded in the story of those communities from which I derive my identity. A Christian is a Christian in great part because of the stories that the Christian has heard. Much of the scripture is counternarrative to the stories that the dominant society imposes.[46]

—WILLIAM WILLIMON

The very name "Uptick" and its definition ("an asset that appreciates with investment") suggests a trajectory altered forward and upward. Part of the purpose of Uptick is to get talented young leaders to their peak capacity and maximum platform as quickly as possible, to influence systems and cultures as soon as possible. Another part of the Uptick purpose is to invest in the future of disciples who could be leading over the course of three or four decades—a span of wide and lasting impact.

Since some of the earliest uses of the word "Uptick" revolved around the financial sector, I always imagine it in terms of a graph something like this:

PERCENT

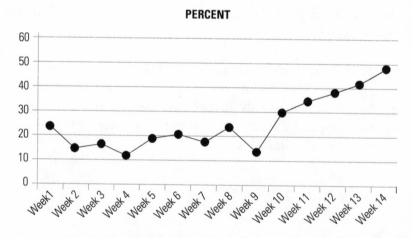

46 William H. Willimon, *Who Lynched Willie Earle?: Preaching to Confront Racism* (Tennessee: Abingdon Press, 2017), Kindle edition, Kindle location 115.

Somewhere around week 9 in this picture, there is an "uptick" from values in the teens-to-twentieth percentile. After the uptick, the "new normal" began in the thirtieth percentile and steadily climbed upward at an accelerated rate toward fifty. One imagines a continuing of this trajectory beyond week 15.

In the picture, the growth between weeks 9 and 10 represents what happens to an average young leader during the Uptick year. The year of high-invitation, high-challenge ethos and pedagogy creates a high growth, high-fruitfulness environment. Leaders speed forward at an accelerated pace and get a taste for life and leadership, flying at a higher altitude. Many Uptickers lament the end of the year together, fearing that the removal of the strong Uptick structure will leave them floundering. It rarely does. Such disciples have found a new normal and can (and do) continue growing beyond the Uptick year. They have learned how to build their own "upticks" in performance into their coming years.

To help with this, the Uptick pedagogy often uses what we call a "Future Story" exercise. In this, participants work with their coach through the course of the year to expand their imagination and sharpen their focus on what their ministry and life might look like in the future. At the end of the Uptick year, the participant writes the story. The exercise is open-ended. Some focus on what the metaphorical "weeks 10–14" might look like; others begin to envision "weeks 15 and beyond."

The point of the Future Story exercise is to help Uptickers choose (out of the multiplicity of possible stories) a powerful story of the trajectory of God's will being carried up, in, and out from their life. Once they name the story of God's faithful presence being carried out through their lives, Uptickers can develop eyes for what kinds of relationships, experiences, networks, wisdom, and ministries they need to accumulate in order to live into that story. Google teaches employees to: 1. Write the job they want in five years; then 2. Write the résumé they'll need to get that job (the experiences they'll need between now and then).

Some Uptickers need to build their résumé by adding Vital Friends. Some need to gain experience where they are. Others discern that it's time to move on from their current chapter of ministry. Some even write from the vantage point of the end of their career or life, looking back and sketching out a map of what many decades of discipleship looked like.

A Future Story may sometimes express uncertainty about next chapters of life and ministry, but with confidence and hope in the tools to address this state:

"

> *I'd like to say that the months after Uptick were filled with great spiritual revelations and prophecies fulfilled but, that's not what happened. I felt lost and lonely and retreated from most things that were related to my calling. I wanted to be near God but talking to him began to feel uncomfortable and I began to question all that I knew was true about gifts and purpose in the Kingdom. The beauty of God's love is that while I felt lost and confused, he continued to insert himself in my daily thoughts. And one day he reminded me of the promise that I made the final day of Uptick. During that final day, as I reflected on the story of Peter walking on the water, I identified with Peter who asked Jesus to show him how to walk on water yet grew afraid and lost focus once the waves began to roar, causing himself to sink. I stated that as Christ led me to walk on water, I knew the waves would begin to thrash, but I promised not to lose focus. I promised not to take my eyes off of Christ and I promised not to sink.*

> *I am not sure exactly what comes after Uptick. I know I want to be a well-known writer, speaker and event curator in the Kingdom, and I don't know how I'll get there, but I do know how to start. Entering this year, I am silencing the waters, strengthening my spiritual disciplines, picking back up the things that God has called me to do, and winning the first battles each and every day, as well as practicing self-care. I know that mastering these habits mean more to my soul and to my ministry than becoming a writer, speaker or event curator. Anyway, there's no way I'd accomplish the latter if I don't master operating in a healthy rhythm.*

> *I am excited about next year. In retrospect, I understand that this Uptick year was a pruning year. The biggest thing that has been stripped away is doubt. No matter what happens in the next twelve months, I am going to stay focused on God as I continue to walk.*[47]

"

Tools like Future Story, combined with the "pay it forward" mentality, help many Uptickers move quickly into investing in future Uptickers,

---

[47] Upticker Brittany Mingo, Philadelphia, PA, Uptick Voice 2018.

creating new networks of disciples in their own contexts, and even launching new Uptick cohorts that they lead.

In short, whatever the expression, Uptick aims to create a discipleship-focused leadership pipeline. The one-year experience is a laboratory for helping participants experience an "uptick" of growth during that period. It also helps them learn how to build in "upticks" of growth into their future as leaders. The trait of Future Story is all about teaching and embedding "acceleration of growth" into the ongoing development of leaders.

To summarize, the Uptick pedagogy around *"Future Story"* endeavors to:

- Teach concrete story-telling skills;
- Empower Uptickers with awareness of the power to *choose* which story to tell; and
- Help Uptickers begin to plot a leadership and vocational trajectory into the future.

To recount the ten marks of the Uptick pedagogy or process of formation (and the skills to grow within each):

1. Leadership through the lens of discipleship *(Value listening)*
2. Language creates culture *(Teach shared vocabulary)*
3. Rhythm of "character" and "competency" *(Attend to soul and skills)*
4. Multiple-voiced leadership *(Utilize all of the leaders)*
5. Information, Imitation, Innovation *(Model the way)*
6. "Bonding" and "bridging" capital *(Build friendships and networks)*
7. "The next 20 percent" and "intelligent, but not academic" *(Focus on spiritual habits and relational skills)*
8. The journey: self-awareness → self-regulation → social awareness → social regulation *(Live in the "Blue Zone")*
9. Honor the experience *(Expect a lot, make it desirable)*
10. Future Story *(Accelerate growth trajectories)*

Section 2

UPTICK CORE COMPETENCIES OF DISCIPLESHIP

Once again, Uptick is primarily a discipleship-formation and acceleration process. We noted earlier that a disciple is a follower of Jesus. "Follower" means more than "learner" or "believer;" it also means one who responds to and obeys what has been heard. In the words of the prophet, "The Lord God has given me the tongue of a teacher, that I may know how to sustain the weary with a word. Morning by morning he wakens—wakens my ear to listen as those who are taught" (Isaiah 50:4).

As a disciple of Jesus, daily listening and hearing lead to a response of speaking, serving, and living in ways that are life sustaining to the weary. Disciples actively listen to the Lord through the Holy Spirit and commit to action. This obedient response is both rhythmic and spontaneous. A disciple will become habituated to this recurring pattern of hearing and responding. In this section, we will describe what we call the "core competencies" of discipleship, and how we teach and apply them in the Uptick process.

3

Learning to Be a Disciple of Jesus

If you can't reproduce disciples, you can't reproduce
leaders. If you can't reproduce leaders, you can't
reproduce churches. If you can't reproduce churches, you
can't reproduce movements.[1]

NEIL COLE

There are no disciples without disciplines. Our first Uptick gatherings always begin with exercises in learning to hear and respond to God as the foundational competency of discipleship. This continues throughout the Uptick year, as we try to help participants "build muscles" of hearing and responding. The last command Jesus gave the church before he ascended to heaven was the Great Commission, the call for Christians to "make disciples of all nations" (Matthew 28:19). But according to philosopher Dallas Willard, Christians have responded by making *Christians*, not *disciples*. This has been the church's "Great Omission":

> The greatest issue facing the world today, with all its heartbreaking needs, is whether those who, by profession or culture, are identified as "Christians" will become disciples—students, apprentices, practitioners—of Jesus Christ, steadily learning from him how to live the life of the Kingdom of the Heavens into every corner of human existence.[2]

We need to be clear in our heads about what discipleship is. My definition: A disciple is a person who has decided that the most important thing in their life is to learn how to do what Jesus said to do. A disciple is not a person who has things under control or knows a

1 Neil Cole, quoted in Hirsch, *The Forgotten Ways*, 119.
2 Dallas Willard, *The Great Omission: Reclaiming Jesus's Essential Teachings on Discipleship* (Reprint edition) (California: HarperOne, 2014), xv.

lot of things. Disciples simply are people who are constantly revising their affairs to carry through on their decision to follow Jesus.[3]

Again, the best leaders are the best followers, and the best followers are both listeners and responders. The disciple is constantly asking *What is God saying? How is God getting my attention? What am I doing about it?* The best leaders are engaging with the core work of learning to listen to Jesus as Leader before trying to lead anyone else anywhere else. We build the muscle of leading by building our capacity as listeners to God through the Scripture.[4]

The workout for these muscles is based in what Willard calls spiritual disciplines of "abstinence" and "engagement."[5] In Willard's teaching, one must learn how to abstain from some things in order to detach from the world's claims on one's ear, mind, eye, and heart. This happens through practicing spiritual disciplines of abstinence such as silence, solitude, secrecy, and fasting. For instance, practicing silence helps us be free from controlling the world with our words; practicing solitude releases us from the need of constant input from others.

Having "cleared the lot" with disciplines of abstinence, one can then "build the house" through disciplines of engagement, such as study, fellowship, service, and worship. In these ways, Uptickers learn to listen—to God, to others, to themselves. A disciple learns to detach from the ways of the world in order to be free to attach to the ways of the Kingdom of heaven.

In many ways, this life of abstinence/engagement at first destabilizes and then re-stabilizes. Here are several metaphors that describe this journey:

- "Unfreezing" set patterns, then "re-freezing" into new molds.
- Military training that aims to strip cadets of their civilian identity (through shaving heads, issuing uniforms, calling them "cadet," and limiting their responses to "yes," "no," "I don't understand," "I don't know") in order to reform them with a military identity (based on rank, platoon, chain of command, commander intent, etc.).[6]

3 See Dallas Willard, "Rethinking Evangelism," http://www.dwillard.org/articles/individual/rethinking-evangelism .
4 Chandler, *Praying New Beginnings*, 12.
5 Dallas Willard, *The Spirit of the Disciplines: Understanding How God Changes Lives* (California: HarperOne, 1991).
6 See Larry Donnithorne, *The West Point Way of Leadership* (1st ed.) (New York: Currency Doubleday, 1993).

- Plato's journey from:
  1. *You don't know what you don't know,* to
  2. *You know what you don't know,* to
  3. *You don't know how much you know,* to
  4. *You know what you know.*[7]
- An engagement that progresses from:
  1. Stable but unsatisfying,
  2. Unstable and unsatisfying,
  3. Unstable and satisfying,
  4. Stable and satisfying.

In the last example, the practice of disciplines of abstinence can unlock and release us from unsatisfactory patterns or habit in our lives, for instance, being in a state of life that is "stable but unsatisfactory." The disciplines of engagement serve to move us toward what is truly satisfactory. Eventually the practice of both abstinence and engagement creates a stability in this way of life.

Over time, those on a discipleship journey begin to take on both the character of Jesus as well as many of his competencies to lead others. As usual, Mike Breen puts it well when articulating that character is always the "First Filter," the first criterion of discipleship. The questions of a person's capacity for leadership, chemistry as part of a team, and personal calling and confidence are "Second Filters." Here are his key questions for character and competency:

> **Character**: Are their lives characterized by grace? Peace? Love? Transformation? Patience? Humility? A deep relationship with the Father? A love of the Scriptures? Can they submit? Do they see the world through the eyes of the Kingdom and not the prevailing culture? **Competency**: Can they disciple people well who can then disciple others? Can they do mission well and see their everyday lives [...] as a mission field? Can they hear the voice of their Father and respond with action imbued with his authority and power? When they pray, do things happen as they did for Jesus? Can they read and teach Scripture well?[8]

7 In Mike Breen's "Square" LifeShape, this is represented as the progression from:
- unconscious incompetence
- conscious incompetence
- conscious competence
- unconscious competence
8 Breen, *Multiplying Missional Leaders*, Kindle edition, Kindle locations 506–12.

LIFESHAPES

Early in our history, Uptick began to adopt the discipleship language of LifeShapes, as taught by Mike Breen and Steve Cockram.[9] We found not only the eight LifeShapes but also other visual tools, pithy phrases (for instance, "invitation to relationship, challenge to responsibility"), and specific vocabulary to be very helpful. Soon, we began to use the shared language taught by Breen and Cockram within and across all Uptick groups.

Why LifeShapes? LifeShapes are lenses. They are a simple, agreed-upon grammar which reflects the key components of what it means to listen and respond to Jesus as one of his disciples. We have found them to be simple without being simplistic.

The fundamentals of basketball include very few components (such as defense, ball-handling, shooting, passing, rebounding). Good basketball teams execute these few fundamentals very well. In the same way, the LifeShapes represent eight core competencies of what it means to follow Jesus. If someone were to come to me and say, "Teach me to follow Jesus as his disciple," these eight LifeShapes would give me the lenses for a straightforward process in beginning that.

The first five LifeShapes are foundational,[10] with the Circle, Semicircle, and Triangle being embedded first. In a few words (more later!), here are the core competencies of discipleship they teach:

- How to listen to God and respond to God (Circle);
- How to live in a rhythm of life that makes such listening possible (Semicircle); and
- How to live in a relationally rich way—Up toward God, In toward community, and Out toward the world (Triangle).

In 3DM lingo, discipleship is "Simple but hard" (as opposed to "Complicated but easy"). Following Jesus is not a formula, but it does involve mastering some key fundamentals and repeatedly practicing

---

9 LifeShapes is a collection of eight geometric shapes, with each shape representing a foundational teaching of Jesus or principle from his life. The shapes are the Circle, Semicircle, Triangle, Square, Pentagon, Hexagon, Heptagon, and Octagon. See Breen and Cockram, *Building a Discipling Culture* for detailed explanations and applications of each.

10 The Hexagon, Heptagon, and Octagon are secondary, serving as "up-in-out" (Triangle) elaborations on:
- Passionate spirituality ("**Up**"—the Hexagon, using the Lord's Prayer);
- Radical community ("**In**"—the Heptagon, assessing the health of a community as an organic, living system); and
- Missionary zeal ("**Out**"—the Octagon, or relational evangelism through finding people of peace).

them until we become competent. In Uptick huddles and conversations throughout the year, we use a straightforward process of walking through foundational questions repeatedly, asking each time, "How is God getting your attention?" and "What are you going to do about it?"

Alan Hirsch has claimed that the Methodist movement lost its momentum the moment it created seminaries and divinity schools, and a credentialed clergy class. This separated preachers from people via a proprietary education and made "deeper life with Christ" extremely impractical for the masses. In short, a grassroots movement became elitist, with deeper discipleship belonging mostly to the credentialed.

LifeShapes, on the other hand, are simple lenses through which anyone can view the work of discipleship with clarity. How do I learn continually from the Lord? How do I pray transformationally? How do I live a listening life? How do I live well in relationship with God, community, and those who don't yet know the gospel? These matters are as elemental to discipleship as shooting, dribbling, and defending are to basketball.

At times, I have been questioned about whether LifeShapes is the most accurate and robust framework around which to base Uptick. My response is always that LifeShapes is not the *only* possible language for discipleship, and perhaps not the best. But it is clear, quickly grasped, elegant, portable and repeatable. It communicates across many cultures and socio-economic barriers. Because it arose out of Breen's dyslexia, it also bypasses many artificial academic (and elitist) barriers which would restrict it only to the literate and educated. I think it would be difficult to find better.

MEMETIC AND MOVEMENTAL

Shared language is necessary not only for single-cohort cohesion, but larger movemental potential and fluency.

In the past one hundred years, we have entered into an image-based culture, and we store large amounts of information, stories, and data by attaching them to images. Our brains are literally wired differently than they were a hundred years ago [...]. Because of this, the idea of attaching the teachings of Jesus and Scripture to a few basic images is perfectly in line with how our brains are already hardwired [...]. Now you are probably more than capable of taking these sociological principles and creating your own sticky, reproducible language for discipleship [...]. It is as if each LifeShape is a rabbit hole. You enter into it, and it seems small enough, easy to understand, but it takes you deeper and deeper into Scripture, the life of Jesus and the Gospel [... this is why] sociologists say that language creates culture.[11]

Jesus inhabited an oral culture, passing along guidance in proverbs, parables, and narrative. (This is why Uptick spends time building storytelling skills). He used subject matter from ordinary life and thus spoke both with clarity and profundity. The history of Christian art in the centuries to follow demonstrates that artists continued to follow this strategy:

The church sanctioned and encouraged the use of images both to instruct and to remind. St. Bonaventure (1221–74), the Minister General of the Franciscan Order, established a tripartite defense of religious art: that images were made for the uneducated, who may, through the images, understand that which they cannot read in scripture; that devotion is more likely to be aroused in those who see images of the deeds of Christ than in those who merely hear about them; and that those deeds are more likely to be remembered if they are seen than if they are only heard. It is this sort of thinking that stimulated the development of images [...]. St. Augustine on his mission to convert the English in 597 (and other missionaries) used illustrative narratives to explain the Gospel stories to those whom they wished to convert, many of whom would have been illiterate and so would have been unable to read the scriptures themselves. But narrative images were also, of course, used and enjoyed by those who were not necessarily using them as substitutes for written scripture, but in order to illuminate and illustrate scriptural texts that they may have known very well already.[12]

In this same tradition, LifeShapes provide Uptickers not only with lenses to view their own discipleship, but also tools to put in the hands of others. As natives to contemporary culture, Uptickers are accomplished

---

11 Breen and Cockram, *Building a Discipling Culture*, 59.
12 Beth Williamson, *Christian Art: A Very Short Introduction* (Oxford: Oxford University Press, 2004) Kindle edition, Kindle locations 1052–61, 1083–86.

in grasping and passing along memes. They are "fluent" in how ideas travel through images. The grammar of Uptick gives them a way to do this with the gospel. The memetic nature of LifeShapes unlocks possibilities for sharing faith widely and well.

THE CIRCLE

As mentioned in chapter two on the pedagogy of Uptick, the foundational competency of discipleship is the ability to live the "listening life." For that reason, the most important skills for Uptickers to gain are captured in the Circle LifeShape. The Circle demonstrates the ongoing process of hearing from God and responding to him. The fundamental question of the Circle is, "How is the Lord getting your attention, and what are you going to do about it?"[13] These are the questions of repenting and believing, responding to Jesus' pivotal words in Mark 1:15: "The time [Greek: "*Kairos*"[14]] is fulfilled, and the kingdom of God has come near; repent, and believe in the good news."

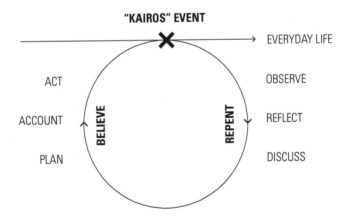

"Repent" simply means to turn, and the practices of *observe, reflect, discuss* are ways to stop going one direction and turn toward what God might be saying to us. These are lifelong practices, exercised individually and within community. Reflecting sometimes comes more naturally for

---

13 Breen and Cockram, *Building a Discipling Culture*, 60. Because this shape is well-described in Breen and Cockram's work, I will abbreviate discussion here.
14 The Greek word *Kairos* means "event or opportune time," as distinct from *Chronos* or sequential (chronological) time.

introverts whereas discussing often comes more easily for extroverts. The key is to be attuned to how God might be getting our attention and to become curious and open to that as the work of the Holy Spirit.

Tod Bolsinger is helpful when he says, "You don't learn by experiences; you learn by reflecting on experiences. Pay attention to what moves you, what disturbs you, what challenges you, what comforts you."[15]

We help Uptickers practice these "repentance" skills throughout the course of the year. Sometimes the "turning" is a gradual dawning for them; at other times, a jarring encounter. Mike Breen has a helpful framework of how *Kairos* comes by "eruption, erosion, earthquake, or excavation."[16] In whatever form it comes, *Kairos* leads to a habit of being "reframed" at a soul level, which becomes the source of leadership that helps other people reframe, repent, or turn:

"

> My greatest fear is that I will convince myself that the hope
> of the future of our church is contingent completely upon me.
> That somehow leadership for the church will be contingent upon
> my personality instead of creating an environment where my
> church can discern the voice of God and find out how their own
> discipleship will shape the future of our church and community
> at large [...]. If the next few steps of the journey are anything like
> the first, I will need to submit to the radically subversive Lordship
> of Jesus that challenges every presupposition and disrupts my
> tendency to see through the lens of binary options of how to
> participate in the world (choices between naïve hope and despair),
> and then ultimately I will take on the task of becoming a reframer
> [...]. My calling is to be a reframer, a traditioned innovator who
> helps ask some of the more difficult questions and participates in
> spurring on a new imagination. An imagination deeply engrossed
> in the story of God which changes the very way we see and
> participate in the world.[17]

"

Repentance then makes it possible for us to *believe*. Our modern English word "believe" derives from the old English "by live"; your "belief" is your "by-life." Believing isn't mere cognitive assent; it is redirecting and

---

15 Tod Bolsinger conversation with Uptick, November, 2018, Richmond, Virginia. Taken from his presentation, "Tempered: Forming Leaders for a Changing World."
16 Breen and the 3DM Team, *Leading Kingdom Movements,* chapter eleven, "Navigating the Spiritual Terrain."
17 Upticker Josh Hayden, Ashland, Virginia.

walking a new path. We "turn" upon the *Kairos* moment that God gets our attention. We resolve to turn and go a new way, and then we ask the community of faith around us to hold us accountable to carry through on our plans. When we *plan, account, and act* by moving in this new direction, we act in concert with the *Kairos* of the in-breaking Kingdom of God. This completes the reflection/action process, full circle.

Thus *Kairos* is both the beginning and end of the Circle process. At some point God gets our attention in a *Kairos* moment—through Scripture, life experience, the voice of another. We turn and reorient in a different direction, acting under the sway of this new path. This leads to spiritual progress or growth and makes it easier to listen subsequently for *Kairos* revelation. The process looks something like a slinky:

UNREALISTIC LEARNING PATTERN

MASTERY

INSTRUCTION

REALISTIC LEARNING PATTERN

LEARNING PROCESS

INSTRUCTION

MASTERY

Every time we complete the *Kairos* Circle, we build a muscle which makes it easier to respond to *Kairos* the next time. The journey of discipleship is never linear, but a life of ongoing *Kairos*, the cycle of repentance/belief, reflection/action, turning and acting in a new direction.

THE SEMICIRCLE

In the U.S., it is more acceptable to "work hard and play hard" than it is to "work hard and rest." We can confuse the empowering of the Holy Spirit with operating from adrenaline.[18]

—PAUL MACONOCHIE

In 1989, two years into my work as a pastor, I heard a phrase from Carl George at a conference that changed my life. Speaking about strategies for how one stays in ministry for the long haul, he spoke of the importance of learning to "divert daily, withdraw weekly, and abandon annually." How does a disciple/leader learn to make space in the course of a day, week, and season for listening to God, and hearing him speak to us our birthright in baptism: "This is my Son, the Beloved, with whom I am well pleased" (Matthew 3:17). I learned quickly that this is a lifelong work of discipleship and leadership formation.

This pivotal issue has been, without a doubt, the single most critical conversation in every Uptick cohort we have led: the issue of rhythm of life. How does a follower of Jesus/leader of people live with a rhythm more in tune with the Kingdom of God than the spirit of our age? In Dallas Willard's framing, how does one practice spiritual disciplines of detachment from the frenetic pace of Western life in order to be free to practice disciplines of engagement in a Kingdom not ruled by achievement, deadlines, haste, and the myth of "work-life balance"?

Early in every Uptick cohort, we introduce the Semicircle LifeShape as a simple tool describing how disciples follow the patterns of Jesus' own life. The Semicircle pictures an oscillation between our *covenant relationship* with God and our *Kingdom responsibility* from God.[19] Like a pendulum, swinging in constant movement, the Semicircle dynamically captures the complementary nature of covenant and Kingdom.

---

18 Paul Maconochie, conversation with Uptick, January 2018.
19 For a full theological treatment of the centrality of this framework, see Mike Breen, *Covenant and Kingdom: The DNA of the Bible* (South Carolina: 3DM Publishing, 2015).

COVENANT

- RELATIONSHIP
- ABIDING
- INVITATION
- REST
- PRUNING
- IDENTITY
- "COME UNTO ME"

KINGDOM

- RESPONSIBILITY
- BEARING FRUIT
- CHALLENGE
- WORK
- GROWING
- MISSION
- "GO THEREFORE"

JOHN 15:1-8

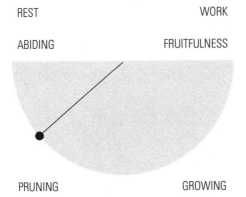

REST   WORK

ABIDING   FRUITFULNESS

PRUNING   GROWING

Almost without fail, this concept of rhythm of life resonates immediately with Uptickers. For most participants, the idea of a rhythmic life offers both a convicting challenge and an appealing invitation to a different way of living. Just as I did in the first stages of my ministry, young leaders often feel caught up in a tangle of internal and external expectations that are leading to a driven, unreflective, task-oriented, and exhausting life.

What happens when we push the pendulum and keep it toward work? Eventually, we crash. We don't rest; we recover. We don't vacation; we recuperate. It isn't an accident that our best ideas always come on vacation! We finally have enough space for our mind to breathe new ideas. And here's the thing; it is only in rest that we receive revelation – every child of God's birth right – the ability to hear God's voice, to be able to answer the question, "What is God saying to me?" [...] From this nourishing energy our work can flow, rather than pushing and pushing and pushing. By operating from rest, we work from the Lord's energy and not our own [...]. Not resting is a type of suicide, it's a stripping of humanity, and it's destroying the image we were made in.[20]

The only model many Uptickers have seen for what "success" might look like is an impossible and never-ending balancing act of the many facets of life:

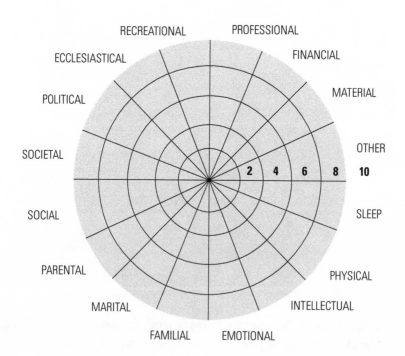

21

20 Breen and Cockram, *Building a Discipling Culture*, 244.
21 If you do a Google search on "balance of life wheel," you will find many iterations of this diagram.

This diagram represents the areas of our life in which we feel the need to succeed (moving from zero to ten); only if everything is at level ten does the wheel roll smoothly and we feel as if we are succeeding at life.

But this is impossible, and the Semicircle enacts a different way of being human. It pictures a different set of ideals (good rhythm) than an impossible-to-attain balance. Followers of Jesus are people on the move, people "of the Way," people who "live and move and have [their] being" in harmony with Kingdom rhythms (Acts 17:28).

Tod Bolsinger cites Bill Bowerman, legendary Oregon track coach and one of the founders of Nike, who revolutionized how runners train by utilizing the following equation:

"Training: Stress + Recovery = Improvement."

Rather than trying to improve runners simply by constantly adding miles, Bowerman said, "Take a primitive organism, any weak, pitiful organism. Make it lift or jump or run. Let it rest. What happens? A little miracle. It gets a little better. That's all training is: stress—recover—improve." Bolsinger likens this to the quenching work of water on hot iron, which serves to increase toughness while removing brittle hardness.[22] Discipleship training or formation involves both stress and recovery, work and rest, and is both task-oriented and relationship-oriented.

Uptickers often struggle with this rhythm. Generally high achievers, they tend to dwell largely in the realm of work or stress. To this, Breen and Cockram say:

> We can't – and shouldn't – try to avoid stress [...]. [But] why stand for this level of stress in our lives? We may proclaim, "Cast your cares on him, for he cares for you," but we don't live it ourselves. We quote from Matthew, "My yoke is easy, and my burden is light," but we continue to pack heavy burdens on our backs. Something has gone very wrong. God designed us to be productive. But we build our identities around our activities [...] We need a biblical framework for a rhythm of life that allows us to be fruitful (and) at rest.[23]

Foundational to Uptick formation is helping participants to develop "rhythm plans" for daily, weekly, and seasonal rhythms of life. We work on this throughout the year, and a couple of phrases connected with this conversation serve as shorthand for the accountability we give to one another in that training:

22 Bolsinger, Uptick conversation, November 2018. Also *"Tempered"* presentation, slide 69.
23 Breen and Cockram, *Building a Discipling Culture*, 100.

- *Are you winning the first battle of the day* (listening to God before engaging with technology)?
- *Are you working* out of *your rest or* resting from *your work (in exhaustion)?*

When Uptickers are able to progress in the rhythm of working from rest, the effect is palpable:

> ❝
>
> *The rhythm of rest and work has been one of the most revolutionary parts of my Uptick experience. By nature, I am a people-pleaser, and Uptick has taught me that, by saying no to things and really carving out time for rest, I can cultivate my gifts and Kingdom impact more. I am trying hard to say no to things I simply can do in favor of things I'm called to do. I'm healthier mentally and physically because of this.[24]*
>
> ❞

We have found the work of Steve Cockram and Jeremie Kubicek to be incredibly helpful in reframing this Semicircle picture into even more concrete terms.[25]

5 GEARS

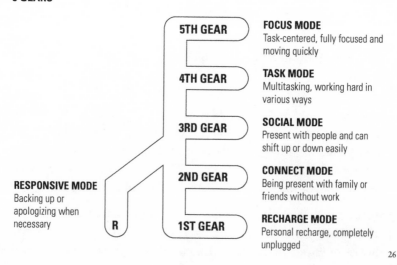

5TH GEAR	**FOCUS MODE** — Task-centered, fully focused and moving quickly
4TH GEAR	**TASK MODE** — Multitasking, working hard in various ways
3RD GEAR	**SOCIAL MODE** — Present with people and can shift up or down easily
2ND GEAR	**CONNECT MODE** — Being present with family or friends without work
1ST GEAR	**RECHARGE MODE** — Personal recharge, completely unplugged
R	**RESPONSIVE MODE** — Backing up or apologizing when necessary

[26]

24 Upticker Carlisle Davidhizar, Newport News, Virginia.
25 Jeremie Kubicek and Steve Cockram, 5 Gears: How to Be Present and Productive When There is Never Enough Time (1st ed.) (New Jersey: John Wiley & Sons, 2015).
26 Image used by permission of GiANT, with special thanks to Steve Cockram.

Using the metaphor of a manual auto stick shift, Cockram and Kubicek restate the core Semicircle language in ways that help Uptickers identify overreliance on "fourth gear" or "multitasking" as the core enemy of healthy rhythm. Most live in a state of "continuous partial attention"[27] and find the versatility of choosing other "gears" to be incredibly liberating and helpful. Cockram and Kubicek also provide all kinds of other tools to help Uptickers with rhythm questions, such as:

- Where do I get out of tempo and need to hit the "reset" on my daily, weekly, monthly, or yearly tempo?
- What activities should I remove from my weekly tempo?
- How do I reduce my blind spots? What is it like to be on the other side of me? (Ask your family, friends, co-workers.)
- How do I schedule and guard the things that are most important in my day, week, month, and year?[28]

Throughout the year, Uptick reviews these rhythm of life questions. It is such a critical matter of formation that we revisit it again and again, working out how to apply (and reapply) it in our lives. Breen and Cockram have said, "We often encourage leaders to break down the day into eight hours of sleep, eight hours of work, four hours engaging, four hours disengaging"[29] But those sixteen waking hours are a moving target, and it takes the course of a year together in Uptick to make headway in rhythm of life. When we do this work, however, the effect can be transformational.

"

There is a lot of work to be done on the inside of me. I am giving God open access to plant seeds of life in me, to prune the branches that are just dead weight, and allow that stream of living water to be the source of my growth. With the tools I have gained through my Uptick experience, I am finding my rhythm and seeing what works for me, even when I am uncomfortable. I am learning to work from rest, rather than rest from work.[30]

"

27 See "Continuous partial attention," *Wikipedia*, https://en.wikipedia.org/wiki/Continuous_partial_attention .
28 For even more fantastic resources, see https://giantworldwide.com/ and https://home.giant.tv/ .
29 Breen and Cockram, *Building a Discipling Culture*, 111.
30 Upticker Jenn Leneus, Uptick Voice, Newark, New Jersey.

We have seen Uptick participants reboot their schedules and routines, rediscover their sense of identity and calling, and reframe their ministry squarely within the framework of what God is doing within them to form them in the likeness of Christ. The Semicircle is a fierce weapon of holy formation.

THE TRIANGLE

Wherever Jesus went, he built community in three particular ways – UP with the Father, IN with the disciples, and OUT with the world. This forms the essential pattern for our life together if we want to truly live as a community of his followers.[31]

—BOB ROGNLIEN

The premise of the Triangle LifeShape is that the "listening life" is fundamentally a relational practice. The Triangle gives a simple framework of these three core communities (God, Church, and World) with which we can listen and respond.

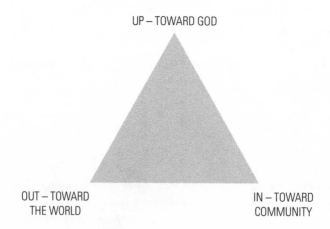

UP – TOWARD GOD

OUT – TOWARD
THE WORLD

IN – TOWARD
COMMUNITY

Essentially, the three points of the Triangle capture Jesus' Great Commandment (Matthew 22:36–40) and Great Commission (Matthew 28:19):

31 Bob Rognlien, *Empowering Missional Disciples: An Introduction to 3D Movements* (South Carolina: 3DM Publishing, 2016), Kindle edition, Kindle locations 669–70.

- **Up** *toward* **God:** "'You shall love the Lord your God with all your heart, and with all your soul, and with all your mind.' This is the greatest and first commandment" (Matthew 22:37–38).
- **In** *toward* **community:** "And a second is like it: 'You shall love your neighbor as yourself.' On these two commandments hang all the law and the prophets" (Matthew 22:39–40).
- **Out** *toward* the **world:** "Go therefore and make disciples of all nations" (Matthew 28:19).

This classic formulation of the spiritual life can be framed in any number of creative ways. One of my favorites is from JR Woodward and Dan White Jr., who see the Triangle as *communion* (Up), *community* (In), and *co-mission* (Out).[32] *Communion* with God includes our personal daily, weekly, and seasonal exercises of intentional listening to the Triune God. *Community* practices are the routine engagements with other believers in processing how God is getting our attention. *Co-mission* activities purposefully respond with what disciples have heard from God through engagement with the world God wants to redeem.

In Uptick, we utilize the Triangle as a lens, to be applied in two primary diagnostic ways:

1. For the *individual* spiritual journey, the Triangle helps us to assess which relational connection might be missing in our pursuit of imitating Jesus' life. This is about the growth and formation of our discipleship **character**.
2. For *leadership* settings, the Triangle helps us to diagnose groups we are discipling by assessing what relational connections are working and missing. The Triangle here is a lens that gives us **competencies** for disciple making.

USING THE TRIANGLE TO DISCIPLE INDIVIDUALS: **CHARACTER**

In his books *A Jesus Shaped Life* and *Empowering Missional Disciples*,[33] Bob Rognlien describes how Jesus chose to live three-dimensionally: Up toward God (John 5:19–20), In toward community (Luke 6:13–16), and Out toward the world (Luke 5:30–32). Rognlien's point is

---

32 Woodward and White, *The Church as Movement*, 152.
33 See Bob Rognlien, *A Jesus Shaped Life: Discipleship and Mission for Everyday People* (South Carolina: 3DM Publishing, 2016), Kindle edition, chapter two, and *Empowering Missional Disciples*, Kindle edition, chapter four.

straightforward: the "abundant life" (John 10:10) comes through letting the shape of Jesus' life mold our own lives. As we do this, our character begins to mimic the character of Jesus.

Thus, the Triangle becomes a clear lens for assessing the dimensionality or richness of my relational life as I seek to follow Jesus. Uptickers are asked to diagnose continually which of the three points of the Triangle is weak or missing in their lives. Following the practices of The Order of Mission,[34] Uptick uses questions from those classically used by John Wesley to assess the prompting of the Holy Spirit in the formation of the disciple's character:

---

34 https://www.missionorder.org/ .

CHARACTER UP

Do I make enough space for prayer?

Do I pursue intimacy with Jesus?

What is on my heart for intercession?

Am I living in the power of the Spirit?

Am I seeing personal revival?

Do I still feel pleasure?

Am I living in a state of peace?

Am I afraid or nervous?

Am I obedient to God's prompting?

CHARACTER IN

Do I love the flock?

Is time a blessing or a curse?

Am I resting enough?

How are my relationships with my friends?

Am I experiencing intimacy in relationships?

Do I keep my promises?

How easy is it for me to trust people?

Am I discipling others?

Is my family happy?

Am I sleeping/eating well?

Am I making myself vulnerable to others?

CHARACTER OUT

Do I have a heart for the lost?

How often do I share my faith?

Do I leave time for relationships with non-Christians?

Am I running the race with perseverance?

Do I have a vision?

Am I dying to success?

Am I proud of the gospel or ashamed?

Am I a servant?

Do I find it easy to recognise people of peace?

Can I take risks?

I never cease to be amazed at how these simple questions, filtered through the lens of the Triangle and asked prayerfully within a loving community, give voice to how the Spirit of God might be speaking at any particular moment to an Upticker. For instance, the question, "Am I sleeping well?" as an *In* question, often serves as a portal to a broken relationship with another disciple. In this example, an Upticker will sometimes realize with clarity that their insomnia arises from anxiety about unresolved conflict or brokenness in a key relationship. Brought into focus through discernment within the community, this has frequently led to actions of forgiveness and exercises toward contentment.

The Triangle can be used as a lens for assessing the individual's discipleship strengths and weaknesses. Uptickers practice this simple diagnostic to address their discipleship journey. Typically, they are flourishing in one or two of the three dimensions, but struggling in the third. They may be:

1. Strong in **Up and In**: an individual disciple may be too insulated from those outside of the church, cut off from the neighborhood, city, and world.
2. Strong in **Up and Out**: an individual disciple can be fervent in mission, but lose the rootedness and accountability that comes with being in intentional community.
3. Strong in **In and Out**: an individual disciple may be righteous in a generic sense but lack the supernatural power and sustainability that comes from intentional connection with the Spirit of God.

In this way, the Triangle can unlock areas for growth in character and imitation of Christ. This LifeShape is an elegant method for disciples to assess how they are growing. For instance, one Upticker who was strong in community-building (In) and missionally focused (Out), determined that he needed to grow in disciplines of prayer in order to connect with the divine source of relational and missional effectiveness:

"

What a beautiful design God has put into motion: 'Discipled to discipler.' I have a strength in relational influence, and my heart is to make disciples. I have been given the blessing to be able to connect with so many people, but if I don't recognize the purpose behind the blessing, it will be empty. So, I desire to become more disciplined in prayer. I recognize the humility and expectation that comes with prayer. However, it is a discipline for me, and it takes work—more work than I give to it sometimes. Not to just prepare a message, but to prepare my heart [...]. My dream is to build relationships with people and watch God do miracles as I get to witness an army of disciples that takes aim on the purpose that God has for their lives and for the purpose of his church.[35]

"

USING THE TRIANGLE TO DISCIPLE GROUPS: **COMPETENCIES**

At times, when leading a group, I have asked people to stand in a circle, and then posture themselves symbolically as being obedient to God. Nine times out of ten, the group spontaneously join hands, and face one another, to symbolize the fellowship captured by the **Inward** dimension of the Triangle. Rarely, some in the group will lift their hands toward heaven or bow or kneel in a posture of prayer. This captures the **Upward** dimension of connection with God through worship. I am still waiting for the day when the group will spontaneously join hands, look upward to heaven, and (with hands locked) turn and face **Outward** toward their community.

This is a simple example of how the Triangle can be used as a lens for assessing the discipleship strengths and weaknesses of a group. Uptickers practice this simple diagnostic to address the discipleship journey of the people they are leading. For instance, many churches do well on one or two of the three dimensions, but are missing the third dimension. They might look like one of these:

1. Strong in **Up and In:** Enthusiastic about worship and the gifts they receive from God, such churches also emphasize developing close community fellowship. But without the **Outward** posture, they may be functionally ignoring their neighbors, cities, or the world outside of their congregations. (This was an early temptation of the church at Jerusalem in the book of Acts.)
2. Strong in **Up and Out:** These churches tend to be evangelical, which stress a relationship with God and have evangelistic fervor to bring people outside of the church to faith. But without

35 Upticker Robbie Gaines, Bluefield, West Virginia.

the **Inward** dimension of community fellowship, they tend to be relationally thin, task-driven, and places where people experience friction, burn out, or drop out before long. (This was an early struggle addressed by the church at Antioch in the book of Acts.)

3. Strong in **In and Out:** These churches value relationship within the congregation. They are also intentional to love and serve the communities around them, often through social action and justice issues. But without the **Upward** dimension of a worship-centered life, they are virtually indistinguishable from the multitude of secular non-profits doing similar work, lacking the divine power to sustain them. (This was an early struggle overcome by the church at Ephesus in the book of Acts.)

The ideal, of course, is for the church to use the Triangle and to live three-dimensionally.

> The goal is not simply to get people into the church. This goal is not to get the church "correct." The goal is for the Kingdom of God to advance "on earth as it is in heaven." Growth and health are necessary but insufficient for the final work of the congregation. Gathering people into the church is but a prerequisite to forming them as disciples, which is but a prerequisite to scattering them as influencers in their families, relationships, communities, and the world. The final Kingdom work of the church is transformation of the cultures it is called to reach. The church, like salt and light, impacts the culture of which it is a part, changing it decisively.[36]

Mike Breen depicts such churches that model the full Triangle as living with Passionate Spirituality, Radical Community, and Missionary Zeal:

---

36 Chandler, *Courageous Church Leadership*, x.

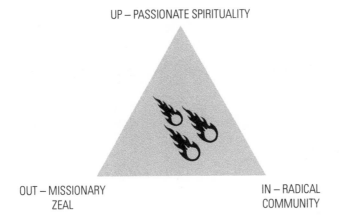

UP – PASSIONATE SPIRITUALITY

OUT – MISSIONARY ZEAL

IN – RADICAL COMMUNITY

"Red-hot sending centers" (where enough individual "torches" have melded into communal "bonfires") do all three. Jerusalem, Antioch, and Ephesus, the first disciple-sending cities in the book of Acts, ultimately learned to practice Up, In, and Out. "These three elements were present in each church. When we practice these things, they reflect the life of Jesus, and by practicing these expressions of his life consistently, we reveal that we are his disciples and welcome his presence among us."[37]

One practical way Uptickers learn to assess and address their contexts is through using adaptations of John Wesley's classic Up, In, and Out **competencies**[38] questions:

---

37 Breen and the 3DM Team, *Leading Kingdom Movements*, 194–196.
38 https://www.missionorder.org/ .

COMPETENCIES UP

Is the worship in my group dynamic and full of intimacy?

Do I find it easy to receive guidance for the next step in the life of my group?

How easy is it to talk to a whole group from "the front"?

Can I teach effectively from God's Word?

Does my group share the vision God has given me?

Do I feel relaxed about leading times of Holy Spirit ministry?

COMPETENCIES IN

Do members of my group feel cared for?

Am I effective at resolving conflict?

Do I take on the discipline of confrontation?

Is my group living as a community?

Have I defined my own boundaries well?

Am I flexible?

How are my weaknesses as a leader compensated for by others?

How do I cope with overly dependent people?

How do I cope with controlling group members?

Are there difficulties in my relationships with co-leaders/assistant leaders?

COMPETENCIES OUT

Is my group growing?

Am I too controlling as a leader?

How welcoming is my group to new people?

Can all group members identify at least one "person of peace"?

Am I using leaders in my group effectively?

Do I find it easy to multiply groups?

Are those I am discipling turning into effective leaders?

Is my group effective in regularly doing "out" activities?

Does my group have a single "people group" in mind?

Uptick leaders can troubleshoot problems and make adjustments to the overall trajectory of whatever groups they are leading by seeing how they themselves function—and what they omit—as leaders of those groups. Learning to do this helps them become more strategic in their leadership by monitoring via the metrics of the Triangle.

"

> *To ensure that movement is happening, and success is being achieved, it will be good for me to intentionally perform an annual audit. Taking several days, I can review what has been accomplished, look at all the responsibilities I've taken on, and set the course for the following year. This will help me celebrate breakthroughs, prune areas of waste, and grow in areas of weakness.*[39]

"

Any Upticker who learns to practice the Triangle will grow in both character as a disciple and competency as a disciple-maker.

THE PENTAGON

> *It's been said that Christianity started out in Palestine as a community, moved to Greece and became a philosophy, went to Rome and became an institution, and went to Europe and became a government. Finally, it came to America and became an enterprise. What might it take for us to return to community? [...] We need to create leadership structures that model the kind of mutual community we're seeking to form.*[40]

> —JR WOODWARD AND DAN WHITE JR.

> *We have reduced the church to a place and a gathering.*
> *We have reduced mission to evangelism.*
> *We have reduced worship to singing songs.*
> *We have reduced the gospel to bullet points.*
> *We have reduced Christology to the cross.*

39 Upticker Brandon Kelly, Findlay, Ohio.
40 Woodward and White, *The Church as Movement*, 53.

We have reduced discipleship to the transfer of information.
We have reduced the ministry callings/functions (Ephesians 4) to
shepherd and teacher.
We have reduced spirituality to withdrawal from the world.
We have reduced church planting to starting worship services.[41]
—BRAD BRISCO

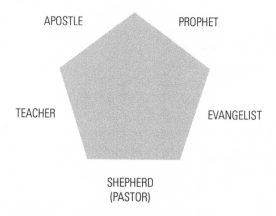

APOSTLE   PROPHET

TEACHER   EVANGELIST

SHEPHERD
(PASTOR)

The Pentagon LifeShape refers to the fivefold gifting, calling, missional intelligence, and functions of individual disciples. "The gifts he gave were that some would be apostles, some prophets, some evangelists, some pastors and teachers, to equip the saints for the work of ministry, for building up the body of Christ" (Ephesians 4:11–12).

Briefly, here are the functions of "missional intelligences" of each of the fivefold:

- **Apostles** help the community discern and implement new ways God is calling them to fulfill their unique mission or calling. Apostles help the church operate movementally.
- **Prophets** listen closely to what God is saying and share words and images of encouragement and challenge with the community toward repentance, health, and covenant faithfulness.
- **Evangelists** help the body of Christ connect with people of peace, in order to share the gospel effectively and increase its reach. (One

41 Brad Brisco, quoted in Alan Hirsch and Mark Nelson, *Reframation: Seeing God, People, and Mission Through Reenchanted Frames* (Georgia: 100 Movements Publishing, 2019), 53. See also https://www.facebook. com/bbrisco/posts/10155377813947006 .

does not have to be a "vocational evangelist" to help make the faith intelligible and transferrable for ordinary people.)

- **Shepherds** (sometimes called pastors) create relational depth and health. They pray for and comfort the hurting in the community.
- **Teachers** lead in explaining and discerning God's Word and how to apply it in our lives. Teachers bring depth and accuracy to individuals and groups, bringing health through valuing clarity, precision, and accuracy in matters of faith and practice.

Note that we change "pastor" to "shepherd" to avoid confusion between the congregational role of a pastor and the biblical function of shepherding or nurturing covenantal relationships (which doesn't require you to be on a church staff—we hope!).

We are quite blessed to be living in a time when the conversation around the fivefold ministry is more robust than ever. Particularly influential for Uptick has been the theological and missiological work of Alan Hirsch[42] in this realm, and the work of Steve Cockram and Jeremie Kubicek of GiANT Worldwide, who reframe and practically apply the Pentagon in wider organizational behavior contexts.[43] For the deeper, broader, and very worthwhile discussion of the exegesis, interpretation, and application of the fivefold, I point you to these unsurpassed resources.

When Uptick was beginning, our denomination estimated that four out of five of those who led BGAV congregations did so out of shepherd and teacher bases. We were a system that lacked apostle, prophet, and evangelist leaders, and Uptick was tasked to help find and develop some. (See point three in chapter one: "Release the APEs.")

According to Alan Hirsch, this pattern is typical across North America.

> The North American church is a precocious "T" (teacher) system, and thus the answer they give to every problem is that we need more "teaching!" But the answer is not more teaching alone, but teacher contributions alongside the contributions of the apostle, prophet, evangelist, and shepherd. It's an uphill climb. However, I have this hope: the seed of the future is in the womb of the present.[44]

42 See Hirsch, *The Forgotten Ways*, chapter 6; and 5Q
43 See especially Jeremie Kubicek and Steve Cockram, *5 Voices: How to Communicate Effectively with Everyone You Lead* (New Jersey: John Wiley & Sons, 2016) and https://giantworldwide.com , which contains a myriad of tools.
44 Alan Hirsch, conversation with Uptick, March 2018, Alexandria, Virginia.

By this, Hirsch means that apostles, prophets, and evangelists are "out there" and deployable for Kingdom leadership. They simply must be identified, equipped, and released.

There are countless ways to describe APEST, often quite creative and helpful. My colleague JR Woodward dubs APEST callings as "dream awakener (A), heart revealer (P), story teller (E), soul healer (S), and light giver (T)."[45] Hirsch surveys how these have been described as hero types, roles, archetypes, expressions of the character of God, and the marks of the church, for instance:[46]

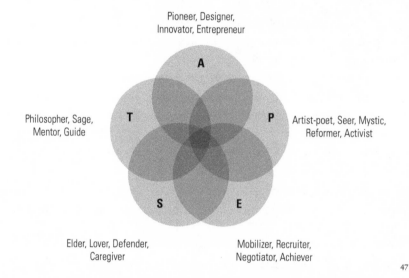

Pioneer, Designer, Innovator, Entrepreneur — A

Philosopher, Sage, Mentor, Guide — T

Artist-poet, Seer, Mystic, Reformer, Activist — P

Elder, Lover, Defender, Caregiver — S

Mobilizer, Recruiter, Negotiator, Achiever — E

[47]

For many Uptickers, the very idea of the Pentagon and the language around it is revelatory. It reframes their ministry identity around their fivefold functioning rather than their positional authority (or lack thereof). This liberates them to explore and serve in ways that are less connected to their role and more connected to their soul. One Upticker had previously held only a minor administrative role in the church. Upon discerning her fivefold gifting and exercising it in the congregation, her identity as a contributing leader grew exponentially:

45 JR Woodward, *Creating a Missional Culture: Equipping the Church for the Sake of the World* (Illinois: InterVarsity Press, 2012), 121.
46 Hirsch, *5Q*, 41, 44, 60, 79, 135.
47 Image from Hirsch, *5Q*, 41.

"

Giving myself permission to think of myself as someone who can be a leader has changed my life. I feel like I've spent a lot of time either sitting on my hands while trying to be a polite church lady or failing at that politeness and running off at the mouth! Uptick and learning about the fivefold gave me a way to think of myself as someone who has a voice and can use it in a way that's powerful and effective. I think that probably means that I have to leave my current church context to do that, and that thought makes me sad. But sometimes you must leave the safety of the family that raised you, so that you can pursue what God is asking of you. I'm excited to go to seminary and to say out loud that I want to be a youth pastor without worrying about who hears me. I think it's what God has been calling me to for a long time. Uptick showed me a way to think about it.[48]

"

Gaining clarity about one's own calling and gifting then opens a world of possibility for leading collaboratively. Each Upticker takes a simple (and very good) test at www.apest.org to discover their fivefold gifting. As Uptickers discover their primary and secondary missional intelligences, they are more likely to identify ways of serving that are fruitful to the mission and life-giving to them personally. They are also able to admit more freely where they have gaps.

"

Finding out my fivefold (apostle, teacher) was helpful, but also finding out where I am not gifted was equally helpful. I always thought of these as weaknesses but having my coach phrase them as 'things that tire me' was a weight off my shoulders. I know as an Enneagram 3 that I am weak at relating emotionally, so pastoral care is not a gift of mine. It was eye-opening to make these connections from my personality to my skill set.[49]

"

A positive, biblical framework, like the Pentagon, helps Uptickers to name strengths and weaknesses without shame. This makes it possible to discuss openly the common pitfalls or immature expressions of each form of leadership in the Pentagon. For instance:

48 Upticker Carlisle Davidhizar, Waco, Texas.
49 Upticker Vernon Gordon, Richmond, Virginia.

- **Apostle:** can lack focus, jumping into every new idea, leaving folk behind.
- **Prophet:** can assume they are *always* right, can neglect to give what they've sensed to the community for interpretation.
- **Evangelist:** can be reductionist (make the sale!), and "love 'em and leave 'em."
- **Shepherd:** can wallow in brokenness, failing to challenge people to redemption.
- **Teacher:** can wow people with intellect, while failing to get the point across that the purpose of the teaching is for life transformation in other people.

There are often sheepish confessions, nods of recognition, and even laughter as Uptickers identify their fivefold gifting, see each type's common pitfalls, and say, "That sounds just like me!" or, "I do that all the time!" This rigorous and refreshing honesty tends to move them to adopt a humble, listening posture as a leader. It also turns their eyes toward other leaders around them who have strengths where they have weaknesses.

"

I have learned again that shepherding is not my strength, but forward thinking is. So, I am going to gather folks around me who can shepherd and teach better than me, so I can be released to dream bigger. Allowing all of us to function better and more effectively will help build the Kingdom of God.[50]

"

Clarity around one's own fivefold is no excuse for avoiding growth in the other areas of the fivefold. Not all are apostles, but all disciples are sent on mission. Not everyone is a prophet, but each of us is responsible for listening to God. Every disciple is to share the gospel with others, not just evangelists. And we are all required to care for people and teach well, not just shepherds and teachers.

Everyone gets to grow as an apostle as we discern the new ways God is calling us to fulfill our unique missional calling. Everyone gets to grow as a prophet when we spend time listening for what God is saying and sharing with each other encouraging words and pictures. Everyone gets to grow as an evangelist when we go out and find ways to connect

50 Upticker Melissa Southall, Fredericksburg, Virginia.

with our people of peace. Everyone gets to grow as a shepherd when we pray for each other and comfort those who are hurting in our midst. Everyone gets to grow as a teacher when we discuss God's Word and how to put it into practice.[51]

So, we simultaneously seek to grow as well-rounded disciples in each of the fivefold and also major in our primary gifting, while supplementing our weaknesses with partners who have other fivefold strengths.

When the Pentagon "light comes on," we begin to see disciples looking around them to build leadership teams with various missional intelligences. This impacts how Uptickers attempt to equip and empower people around them, and how they match APEST with the work to be done and the team needed to do it. I will often hear, "I need to find an evangelist" or "We need a prophet in this chair." When this polycentric leadership[52] team begins to come together in ministry, the Uptickers are often taken aback at how powerful and effective this kind of shared leadership can be.

"

> [Fellow Uptickers] James, Shanice, Rachel, and I just got to lead seventy-one students together this weekend. We've gotten responses that I've never gotten from a retreat weekend at camp. Students weren't telling me that they loved tubing, or their favorite part was the obstacle course. I've got a sixth grader saying their favorite part was worship. A senior who is on the fringe of church life saying he enjoyed discussing his call with a leader during a prayer time. Another student asking for our worship set list. A ninth grader looking to join a discipleship program to love on other students. It is incredible; the Holy Spirit did some big things. So, I just wanted to say thanks for bringing us together in Uptick and APEST, because without that, this weekend wouldn't have happened, and I'm so happy it did.[53]

"

Once it becomes normal to think in terms of shared leadership, Uptickers first think of their own APEST contributions to the mission, and then strategize how to draw the right kinds of other leaders to the team. Some of the leadership breakthroughs that happen in their own setting occur once they activate folk who have been "hidden in plain sight"—gifted but heretofore untapped as leaders.

---

51 Rognlien, *A Jesus Shaped Life*, Kindle edition, Kindle locations 1352–56.
52 Woodward, *Creating a Missional Culture*, 209–23.
53 Upticker Matt Boschen, Mechanicsville, Virginia. This team was composed of leaders from each of the fivefold gifts/callings.

Steve Cockram, Jeremie Kubicek and the leaders at GiANT give particularly helpful instruction on the functions of APEST for the whole people of God (not just clergy), framing the fivefold as the "Five Voices," with APEST described in terms of:

- **Apostles as** Pioneers
- **Prophets as** Creatives
- **Evangelists as** Connectors
- **Shepherds as** Nurturers
- **Teachers as** Guardians[54]

It is a brilliant application of how individual leaders can find their "signal strength" on each voice, which paves the way to look for fellow leaders who get a better signal strength in places where their own might be weak.

THE FIVE VOICES

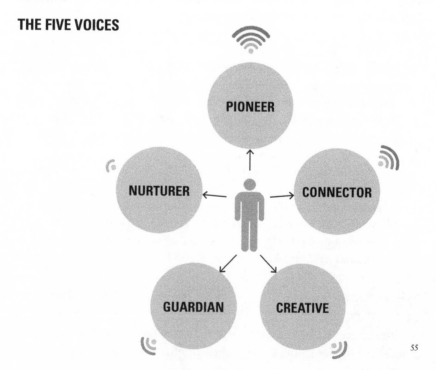

55

---

54 Kubicek and Cockram, 5 *Voices*, and https://giantworldwide.com . This excellent material from GiANT has been especially useful in our Uptick Entrepreneur cohorts.
55 Image used by permission of GiANT, with special thanks to Steve Cockram.

GROWING AS INDIVIDUALS, WORKING AS TEAMS

The liberating good news of APEST is the release from the loneliness, isolation, pressure, and friendlessness of trying to "go it alone" in leadership. Uptickers delight in discovering that they have unique contributions for the Kingdom cause, *and* that they have friends and fellow workers who had been waiting to be activated alongside them. They are sometimes shocked at how many people were sitting on the sidelines, available to get in the game, but who had never been asked to help in ways in which they were good at helping.

> Too often, in our typical church gatherings, only those with certain skills or knowledge get to take an active part in the spiritual life of a community. The singers sing, the readers read, the preachers preach, the prayers pray, and the announcers announce. Most of us are left on the sidelines watching. In contrast to this, Paul described the church as a human body and emphasized how every part is critical to the health of the whole. He specified five critical roles within the body that help us grow up into the fullness of Christ and strengthen his Body, the Church.[56]

The Pentagon unlocks a countercultural form of leadership and discipleship. The North American cultural milieu is one of radical individualism, where the "ideal leader" is a solitary hero. APEST is a path beyond that suffocating isolation in leadership. It gives relief from the idea that, "if it's going to be, it's up to me." It reminds us that there are many workers for the mission. And it gives an opportunity to walk and work alongside other fivefold leaders as an on-ramp to each leader's growth. As an apostle-evangelist, I often watch gifted shepherds lead fluidly in nurturing. It seems so difficult for me and so easy for them—and I thank God for them!

Ultimately, using the fivefold gifts enables disciples to create "environments" that contribute to the church's ability to move up, in, and out on mission to the world. Apostles create environments of *thriving;* prophets, of *liberating;* evangelists make sure we are *welcoming;* shepherds build atmospheres of *healing;* teachers develop communities of *learning.*[57]

Uptick teaches the Pentagon so that disciples will be able to develop ecosystems in which the mission of God thrives within communities of

---

56 Kubicek and Cockram, 5 *Voices*, Kindle locations 2794–801.
57 Woodward and White, *The Church as Movement*, 180–83.

practice. The integration of all five voices is key to the "unity of the faith and of the knowledge of the Son of God, to maturity, to the measure of the full stature of Christ" (Ephesians 4:13). When that happens, John Maxwell's famous chain reaction occurs:

> God has definite stages for Christian development to bring us from babies to Christian adulthood [...] to help stimulate their own personal growth and become an even more effective vessel for God:
>
> *Let God's Spirit Move In* [through the power of the fivefold]
> *Let the Pastor Move Over* [overcoming the cult of personality where only one person is successful for the mission]
> *Let the Laity Move Up* [activating the whole body of Christ for the work]
> *Let the Church Move Out* [releasing the church into the world with every sort of missional intelligence deployed].[58]

This illustrates the flow and growth of "the whole body, joined and knit together by every ligament with which it is equipped, as each part is working properly, promotes the body's growth in building itself up in love" (Ephesians 4:16).

Thus, what is true for individual growth is even more vital and true for the whole church. Pentagon/fivefold/APEST—these are harmonious tools for maturity and collaboration in the mission of God.

---

58 John Maxwell, quoted in https://www.sermoncentral.com/sermons/make-your-move-part-1-let-god-s-spirit-move-in-stephen-collins-sermon-on-servanthood-138028 .

4

Learning to Disciple Others: Multiplying Life

Ivan Illich was once asked what he thought was the most radical way to change society; was it through violent revolution or gradual reform? He gave a careful answer. Neither. Rather, he suggested that if one wanted to change society, then one must tell an alternative story. Illich is right; we need to reframe our understandings through a different lens, an alternative story, if we wish to move beyond the captivity of the predominantly institutional paradigm that clearly dominates our current approach to leadership and church.[1]

ALAN HIRSCH

Developing skills in storytelling is an integral part of discipleship formation in Uptick. Jesus was a masterful storyteller, and so if we are to imitate the way of Jesus, then learning to tell stories is a key competency Uptickers must develop. Jesus spoke in parables, which I envision as *parabolas*. A parabola is a mathematical term for a U-shaped curve, something that moves from point A to point B, not in a straight line, but in an arc, getting to its destination indirectly. So also, Jesus taught through telling stories that were more indirect than direct, and which landed with greater force because of that roundabout approach. As Dallas Willard often said, discipleship is not just cognitively accepting the ideas Jesus taught, but doing the things that Jesus did, following him into his practices. And as Jesus told lots of stories, maybe it's not a bad idea for us to do the same.

After all, the work of every disciple is to locate his or her own narrative within the metanarrative of the story of God captured in the gospel. We must know where the gospel story began, how it will end,

1 Hirsch, *The Forgotten Ways*, 53.

and where we are within its plot. We need to learn which "chapter" we are in and what chapter might be next.

In this way, skills in storytelling are related to the Square LifeShape (which is the process for multiplying disciples). Discipling other people is often an exercise in helping people to choose their story within the larger story of the Kingdom of God. When you are clear about your own story, you can help others become clear about their stories. Together, you can then walk further and further into the gospel story.

STORIES OF SELF, STORIES OF US

At the beginning of the Uptick year, we often find young leaders to be, at best, mediocre story tellers. Sometimes this is due to a lack of internal clarity, weak emotional intelligence, or even brokenness or dysfunction. (This is why surveys and instruments are so useful in helping Uptickers address their blind spots.)

In addition to lacking tools for clarifying their own individual stories, Uptickers often find challenges in the story within the context in which they are trying to lead. These congregational "systems stories" can either be virulently active or dangerously latent. It is one thing to learn skills in interpreting biblical texts; it is quite another to learn how to interpret the contexts in which we are leading. One of the tasks of Uptick is to help participants become aware of the implicit or explicit story within their own church, or other leadership setting, and what part they can play in bringing greater healing and wholeness into that narrative. Bill Easum comments on the systems story of many churches in the West and the impact that has on their missional capacity:

> Following Jesus into the mission field is either impossible or extremely difficult for the vast majority of congregations in the Western world because of one thing: They have a systems story that will not allow them to take the first step out of the institution into the mission field, even though the mission field is just outside the door of the congregation.[2]

A systems story may arise out of fear or out of past issues that defined the congregation at one point, but now no longer need to. For example, a BGAV congregation I know well has a latent "systems story" that the congregation is poor (when it is not) and therefore feels unable to spend

2 Bill Easum, *Unfreezing Moves: Following Jesus into the Mission Field* (Tennessee: Abingdon Press, 2001), 31.

money for new enterprises. Some long-time members recall having to shut down the congregation in the 1930s because of the Great Depression. But it eventually reopened and now thrives financially. However, the defining systems story is that "we may go under financially at any moment." The Upticker's challenge in this congregation is to transition the existing church story toward a better story—of how the congregation overcame a difficult chapter in the Depression. She needs to help the congregation see its story as "Overcomer" rather than as on the edge of "Bankrupt."

Sometimes there is a mismatch between the congregation's story (active or latent) and the Uptick leader's personal story. Other times the official or spoken congregational story doesn't match with the repressed or buried story. At times, the issue is that a congregation chooses a story that reflects its enveloping history or surrounding culture rather than one which reflects the story of the Kingdom of God.

When a congregation *is* able to retell its story, the mobilizing effect can be tangible. When I arrived at Effort Baptist, the congregational systems story was that the church was barely financially viable. It probably took five years before the church was able to tell itself a different story of being an "Overcomer." A critical moment in the church's history was what we called "Miracle Sunday," a single day in which we raised a one-time congregational gift nearly equaling our annual budget amount, for the purpose of relocating the church. Once the congregation experienced success beyond its highly-stretching goal, it began a journey of generosity that led from giving less than 1 percent of its income toward mission to giving over 17 percent of its annual budget for mission. Such story reframing takes place slowly and over time but can be crystalized in critical moments that change the trajectory of the congregation.

Thus, Uptick teaches storytelling skills as a way of helping leaders diagnose the core stories that drive them, and to identify the truest and best stories of those whom they lead.

> Storytelling describes the social and cultural activity of sharing stories, sometimes with improvisation, theatrics, or embellishment. Every culture has its own stories or narratives, which are shared as a means of entertainment, education, cultural preservation or instilling moral values.[3]

---

3 See "Storytelling," *Wikipedia*, https://en.wikipedia.org/wiki/Storytelling .

To that definition, I would also add that choosing the right stories grants the power to reshape people and lead groups to new places. In Uptick parlance, "Best story wins!" We want to help disciples think diagnostically and choose the best Kingdom story out of a multiplicity of alternative (and inferior) stories.

Tod Bolsinger often helps to uncover these defining stories in the lives of church leaders and congregations by asking questions like these:

Tell a story about your church's history:
- About a hero;
- About a cherished moment that is retold over and over again;
- One that says, "This was the moment when I was most proud of us";
- One that says, "This was when I knew I had found my people."[4]

These are pathways into understanding the "story of us" that the people you lead are either telling publicly, or perhaps are being driven by, unconsciously.

Learning how to excavate a "story of *us*" is an important leadership skill. But the pathway to doing that begins with being attentive and selective in telling the "story of *self*."

STORIES OF THEN, NOW, AND NEXT

Uptick storytelling pedagogy is indebted to Harvard lecturer and community organizer Marshall Ganz, who first taught the importance of the leader articulating their "story of self" and then a "story of us."[5]

Uptick teaches participants how to tell the story of self by asking them to select and recount a concise story of *then* (from their past), a story of *now* (the present), and, by the end of the year, a story of *next* (future). Each of these stories is shared with two or three fellow Uptickers, and perhaps later before the whole group. There are quite particular skills in these stories, the most important being that they are told in less than two minutes! (We time them, and it is surprisingly difficult for most.) The time limit is like a pressure cooker that forces storytellers to eliminate unnecessary details and get to the core drivers

---

4 Tod Bolsinger conversation with Uptick, November 14–15, 2019, Richmond, Virginia.
5 Marshall Ganz, "Why Stories Matter," March 2009, https://sites.middlebury.edu/organize/files/2014/08/Ganz_WhyStoriesMatter_2009.pdf .

embedded within the story. After a two-minute telling, there is three minutes of coaching from the group. Then, a second telling, followed by additional coaching.

The storytelling is given a basic structure:

> All stories have three parts: a plot, a protagonist, and a moral. What makes a plot a plot? What gets you interested? Tension. An anomaly. The unexpected. The uncertain and the unknown. A plot begins when the unknown intervenes. We all lean forward because we are familiar with the experience of having to confront the unknown and to make choices. Those moments are the moments in which we are most fully human, because those are the moments in which we have the most choice. While they are exhilarating moments, they are also scary moments because we might make the wrong choice. We are all infinitely curious in learning how to be agents of change, how to be people who make good choices under circumstances that are unexpected and unknown to us. In a story, a *challenge* presents itself to the protagonist who then has a *choice*, and an *outcome* occurs.[6]

Challenge, choice, outcome—this is what gives shape and movement to each story.

Often, Uptick storytellers find themselves overwhelmed with emotion as they unpack stories of *then* and *now*. It is as if they become fully aware of how pivotal these latent/active stories are in driving their values, attitudes, beliefs, and expectations. Similarly, fellow Uptickers are often deeply moved by the power of these shared stories.

Ultimately, practicing stories of *then* and *now* builds capacity for Uptickers to tell a story of *next*, or what we call a "Future Story." (Refer back to page 104 for more detail on that.) Sometimes, we will have Uptickers read *The Generosity Bet,* simply to accrue a variety of stories of generosity that help shape their own Future Story of generosity.[7] By making Uptick a story-dense environment, we are modeling how leaders can learn to select and then tell the best stories of *self* and *us,* and can choose to live into rich, profound, and impactful Future Stories.

---

6 Ibid.
7 William F. High and Ashley B. McCauley, *The Generosity Bet: Secrets of Risk, Reward, and Real Joy* (Pennsylvania: Destiny Image, 2014). This is an inspiring collection of stories from a variety of Christians who have strategically chosen to be extremely generous with their often substantial financial assets.

As my own leadership coach, Dan Elash, puts it:

We've all heard it said that we play starring roles in our life stories. But we are more than actors playing out someone else's script. We are also the authors of those yet unfinished novels. Sure, the story is about you; your choices, your struggles, and your triumphs. As long as we hold the view that we are merely actors playing a part in an unfinished script, we await what will be written with a variety of emotions ranging from anxiety, despair, joy, or anticipation. We are acted upon by forces beyond our control and our options are largely defined by what has been written before. What would change if we were to realize that we are also the author? For one thing, we would realize that we have the ability to develop our characters deliberately. We could change the story line. We could build on potentials, change our perspectives, and reinterpret the events from our pasts in ways that open new doors. My point is that you have an author's power over your story. By shifting perspectives, you can shift from reactor to creator [...]. Remember, the future is unwritten, the story is unfinished, and so, there is room for change and development.[8]

God is the author of the gospel metanarrative, and we need skills in hearing from and responding to God to shape our best responses to our place in that grand story. Elash reminds us that by "taking counsel in our regrets," "believing in our hopes," and "acting with the end in mind," we can be story shapers—holders of testimonies that have the power to set the trajectory of our lives and shape and share the power of the gospel with those around us.[9]

THE SQUARE: MULTIPLYING LIFE

Only 4 percent of Southern Baptist churches in America will plant a daughter church. Extrapolated across the denominations, that means that 96 percent of the conventional churches in America will never give birth. Many think this is fine. I have heard people say, "We have plenty of churches. There are churches all over the place

---

8 D. D. Elash, *"Rewriting Your Life Story,"* Leader Values, December, 2010, http://www.leader-values.com/Content/detail.asp?ContentDetailID=1461 .
9 Ibid.

that sit empty; why start new ones? We don't need more churches but better ones." Can you imagine making such a statement about people? "We have plenty of people. We don't need more people, just better ones. Why have more babies?" This is short-range thinking. No matter how inflated you think the world population is, we are only one generation away from extinction if we do not have babies [...] Imagine the headlines if suddenly it was discovered that 96% of the women in America were no longer fertile and could not have babies. We would instantly know two things: this is not natural so there is something wrong with their health. We would also know that our future is in serious jeopardy.[10]

—NEIL COLE

A church which pitches its tents without constantly looking out for new horizons, which does not continually strike camp, is being untrue to its calling [...] [We must] play down our longing for certainty, accept what is risky, and live by improvisation and experiment.[11]

—HANS KÜNG

Uptick is an investment in the Future Stories of the individuals who participate in the process. However, if individuals whose stories are being shaped by the Uptick process do not in turn multiply that same kind of shaping across their own contexts, then Uptick would turn out to be an expensive, non-movemental experience. We want to equip Uptickers to tell better stories so that they can integrate them in their own lives. They are then able to (re)shape the stories of many people so that their stories merge into the great story of Jesus.

For this reason, storytelling needs a simultaneous, rigorous pathway alongside it in order to become capable of multiplying discipleship. The Square LifeShape provides this process. Derived from Ken Blanchard's model of "situational leadership,"[12] Mike Breen designed the Square to picture the process by which Jesus formed disciples—and how we imitate

---

10 Neil Cole, *Organic Church: Growing Faith Where Life Happens* (1st ed.) (California: Jossey-Bass, 2005), 119.
11 Hans Küng, *The Church as the People of God*, quoted in Hirsch, *The Forgotten Ways*, 15.
12 See "Situational leadership theory," *Wikipedia*, https://en.wikipedia.org/wiki/Situational_leadership_theory .

Jesus in doing that. More robust than information-based onboarding, Jesus used an imitation-based process with twelve immediate followers (and many more at various degrees on the periphery). Jesus was able to spur a movement because he molded people in ways far beyond how we normally try to influence, persuade, and shape people around us. Breen says:

> I suggest that the problem for all of us is that most of our training is not comprehensive enough and that it is way too quick. The culture of the American church has largely borrowed from the corporate world in the way it builds its leadership pipeline. As a result, it's based on this leadership myth: Hire talent and fire people who fail. That is rubbish, and it's not even close to the New Testament model, which had a pipeline that reflected the way Jesus began the enterprise with his first disciples. The most important part of any missional leader is character, not talent. Second, failure is essential to becoming a missional leader. How else will someone learn? No one was born a great missional leader. You have to learn as you go, which is why the continued review and training is so important.[13]

Jesus did more than impart information; he also gave disciples access to his own life over a period of years. Later, the apostle Paul would mimic this, to the point where he could tell churches, "Be imitators of me, as I am of Christ" (1 Corinthians 11:1) and "Keep on doing the things that you have learned and received and heard and seen in me, and the God of peace will be with you" (Philippians 4:9). The Square describes both the clockwise work of the disciples in this process (D1 through D4), as well as the ever-evolving manner by which Jesus led them (L1 to L4).

---

13 Breen, *Multiplying Missional Leaders*, Kindle edition, Kindle locations 1662–63.

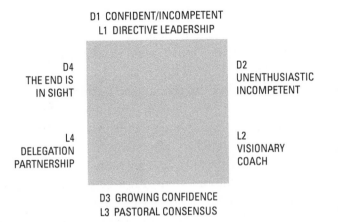

D1 CONFIDENT/INCOMPETENT
L1 DIRECTIVE LEADERSHIP

D4
THE END IS
IN SIGHT

D2
UNENTHUSIASTIC
INCOMPETENT

L4
DELEGATION
PARTNERSHIP

L2
VISIONARY
COACH

D3 GROWING CONFIDENCE
L3 PASTORAL CONSENSUS

14

The logic of the Square is simple:

- It describes the process by which Jesus formed disciples.
- Discipleship involves both *content* (Jesus' stories and teaching) and *process* (the manner by which he embedded others into his mission).
- We would do well to take our cues not only from Jesus' content but also his process—and replicate it.

Over the course of the Uptick year, we explicitly teach the Square, and work to model its process with participants. Thus, by immersive experience, Uptickers learn how to reproduce this discipleship pathway in their own context, creating a leadership pipeline where they lead.

IT ONLY WORKS WHEN YOU WORK IT

Remarkably, the Gospels record Jesus very quickly moving from calling disciples (Luke 5:1–11 and 6:12–16) to requiring that those disciples reproduce his work (Luke 9:1–6, 10:1–20). Of course, in between calling and sending, Jesus taught them. His teaching was full of stories (parables). But the disciples were sent out to practice what they had learned *long* before they felt competent to reproduce what they had seen Jesus do. The moral of the story is that you become a disciple not simply by sitting and soaking, but also by practicing and doing. Or, as

---

14 This process moves from the leader to the follower with these shifts:
1. Directive: "I do, and you watch." (Followers are confident, enthusiastic and incompetent.)
2. Coaching: "I do, and you help." (Low confidence and competence.)
3. Consensus: "You do, and I help." (Increasing enthusiasm, intermittent confidence, growing competence.)
4. Delegation/Replication: "You do and someone else watches." (Repeats process with high confidence and competence.)

highlighted in chapter two, **information**, filtered through the lens of **imitation**, is what leads to **innovation**.

Thus, very early in the Uptick year, we challenge participants to reproduce disciples in their own context. As soon as they learn the Circle and Semicircle, they are encouraged to find eager followers and lead them to practice it in a discipleship huddle. One doesn't need advanced training to do this, though there are usually howls of protest (or quiet terror) from Uptickers who think they are not yet ready to start. But we insist that they are actually more ready than they realize to transmit the life of discipleship to others around them. When an Upticker begins a huddle sooner than s/he thought or felt was possible, the report comes back similar to that of the disciples whom Jesus sent out to preach, teach, and heal: amazement that it worked (Luke 10:17)! Upticker Alan Miller, a pastor in small-town Orange, Virginia, began a discipleship huddle in a very traditional BGAV church, within several weeks of having started in Uptick. Upon using the Square with his leaders, he says:

"

Uptick has been an iteration of God's faithfulness to put a group together and shepherd it, in order to, quite literally, transform the lives of the participants, including me (and the leaders of the church in which I serve). It is giving us tools and relationships and the capitals that we need to flourish in ministry. For me, it is a beautiful picture of the blessing and sending of God's leaders into the future.

"

Alan launched out boldly into the process of disciple making, all the while feeling unsteady. He had questions (and maybe a little panic!) as he began. But in the words of Alcoholics Anonymous, "It only works when you work it." That is, just as sobriety depends on people actively participating in A.A. recovery meetings and the 12-Step process, so also becoming a disciple of Jesus is impossible without practicing the way of Jesus in making other disciples. It is a bit like teaching children to swim by throwing them in the water: they think they are going to drown, but the necessity of the situation draws out innate competencies in the students, supplemented by skilled instruction. Or, to change the simile, it is like teaching the baby bird to fly by pushing it out of the nest. Helping Uptickers to do this involves quite a bit of "just in time" training, as we challenge them to launch, all the while coaching them in the process. You learn the Square for yourself, in part, by challenging others around you to learn it from you.

KEY SQUARE VOCABULARY

As with the other LifeShapes, one of the key benefits of the Square is that it gives an Uptick cohort shared language and a framework to use and reproduce. Here are a few of the terms and phrases we commonly utilize, in conjunction with the Square, that have proven useful.

3/12/70/5,000

In chapter five, we will discuss Jesus' pattern of focusing his disciple-making efforts with the twelve disciples first. Within that, he had a special relationship with Peter, James, and John, with whom he shared his heart even more intimately. From there, he spent time in social settings, such as deploying the seventy for mission (Luke 10) and public settings in teaching, preaching, healing, and other forms of disciple making. The feeding of the five thousand (John 6:1–14) is one such example.

We use this pattern of Jesus' ministry in the Square to emphasize that disciple making occurs best when focusing on interactions in the *intimate* space (the 3) and the *personal* space (the 12) before the *social* (the 70) and the *public* (the 5,000). Discipleship works best from the inside-out. First, make sure that you yourself are on a discipleship journey. Then, look for a small group of highly motivated and (potentially) capable (even if raw) people around you in whom to invest. Finally, expand your scope of disciple making to social and public settings.

This process inverts how many ministers are taught. In my own experience, my seminary education instructed me that I could make maximum impact through one-to-many ministry (especially in preaching), and one-to-one ministry (such as counseling). There was little, if any, attention given to forming disciples through using small and social-sized groups and Vital Friends. Uptick intentionally reprioritizes in deference to Jesus' patterns of interaction, which emphasize personal and social space engagement.

Look Left/Look Right

When going clockwise around the Square, our instinct is to do so as a disciple (the D1 through D4 path), with Jesus in the role of leader (L1 through L4). However, at any given point, we function simultaneously as disciple *and* leader. There is always someone we are following on the discipleship journey—and there is always someone who is following us, whether or not we are conscious of it.

To raise awareness of this, we teach Uptickers to "look right" at the people who are ahead of them in the discipleship journey. Who are the mentors in the faith that can become vital resources in helping participants to move forward? Often, they are more plentiful and eager to help than we realize. Who is further around the Square (clockwise to the "right")? Seek out those people. In this work, Uptickers are traveling the D1 to D4 journey.

Simultaneously, "look left"—identify the apprentices (current and potential) who would consider the Upticker to be a spiritual leader. These followers are not as far around the Square as the Upticker and need the Upticker to teach, model, and lead them in the way of Christ. In this work, participants are traveling the L1 to L4 journey.

By concurrently looking "left and right," a disciple is always on a "followership" journey of becoming a disciple, and a "leadership" journey of making disciples. Doing both helps us to remain simultaneously teachable and humble, and (appropriately) bold, confident, and proactive in the mission.

Valley of the Shadow

By far, Jesus' disciples spent more time on the "D2" side of the Square than any other. The first disciples frequently misunderstood Jesus, misapplying his intent, and had to be redirected by him, gently or otherwise. For about three years, they generally seemed to take several steps forward and then a few backward as they followed him. Failure seems to be part of the core curriculum!

Jesus' response was to spend many waking hours with the Twelve. He would teach, ask questions, listen to faulty responses, teach again. He would demonstrate, ask even more questions, correct their answers, and work over the long haul to tilt their worldview toward the Kingdom. As a maker of disciples, Jesus may have spent more time doing this with his followers than any other activity. And more often than not, the Gospels record the Twelve as being confused, frustrated, petulant, angry, and exasperated. Many followers beyond the Twelve did in fact leave (John 6:66).

At some point in the journey, every disciple reaches a place of frustration borne out of sustained struggle, confusion, and lack of breakthrough. When in that place, it is common Uptick language to say, "I'm in D2 right now." Hearing this, other Uptickers will know exactly the experience an Upticker in D2 is referring to, and they can encourage and challenge each other to push through. When we don't recognize the patterns and when we don't have the language to express it, we are much more prone to just give up. In D2, discipleship has gotten difficult, and the temptations to back away from it are strong. We have gone from D1 "fandom" of Jesus, where we simply cheer about all of the awesome things Jesus does, to being asked to replicate his work—and that isn't quite as easy. Eventually, we reach the bottom of D2, which is the "Valley of the Shadow" (alluding to Psalm 23:4). At this point, we are very much aware of how little we know, conscious of our incompetence in following Jesus. There are then three choices:

1. Revert to D1, where there is far less challenge, and we admire Jesus more than follow him into his practices;
2. Drop out of following Jesus altogether; or
3. Persevere until we move to D3, and Jesus begins to show us that we are actually more capable than we realize.

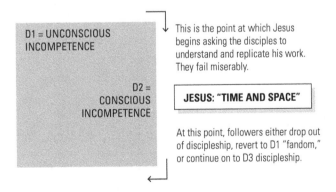

D1 = UNCONSCIOUS INCOMPETENCE

D2 = CONSCIOUS INCOMPETENCE

This is the point at which Jesus begins asking the disciples to understand and replicate his work. They fail miserably.

JESUS: "TIME AND SPACE"

At this point, followers either drop out of discipleship, revert to D1 "fandom," or continue on to D3 discipleship.

If disciples can make it to D3, it is because they have spent enough time and space in the presence of Jesus to have absorbed his manner of living, consciously and unconsciously. Their relationship to Jesus resembles something more like friendship than servanthood (John 15:15).

This evolution toward friendship and partnership of the disciples with Jesus would never be possible unless Jesus had first spent significant time with his followers and given significant access to his life. The creation of disciples takes time and space, and as a process, Uptick tries to give people these gifts. In Uptick, we frequently mention the Genesis 1 story of God creating out of chaos, fundamentally through the ordering of time and space. It is through the right ordering of time and space available to us that we can reorient our lives and "turn the corner" around the Valley of the Shadow, to begin to do what Jesus did—namely, to make disciples.

What marks this subtle but significant turn around the corner from D2 to D3? More than anything, it is a humility of spirit combined with a readiness to follow Jesus that overcomes even self-doubt. My wife, Mary, always had her seventh grade Sunday school class kids memorize Ephesians 5:10: "Try to find out what is pleasing to the Lord." When the hope of pleasing God outstrips the doubt that we know exactly how to do it, then a disciple is turning the corner to D3. This spirit is captured in the famous prayer of Thomas Merton:

> My Lord God, I have no idea where I am going. I do not see the road ahead of me. I cannot know for certain where it will end. Nor do I really know myself, and the fact that I think that I am following your will does not mean that I am actually doing so. But I believe that the desire to please you does in fact please you. And I hope I have that desire in all that I am doing. I hope that I will never do anything apart from that desire. And I know that if I do this, you will lead me by the right road, though I may know nothing about it. Therefore, I trust you always, though I may seem to be lost and in the shadow of death. I will not fear, for you are ever with me, and you will never leave me to face my perils alone.[15]

THE GOAL: MOVEMENTAL MULTIPLICATION

When any individual becomes a disciple of Jesus, it is a win for the Kingdom of God, and is to be celebrated. However, Uptick has its sights

---

15 Thomas Merton, quoted in Osterhaus, Jurkowski and Hahn, *Thriving through Ministry Conflict*, Kindle edition, Kindle locations 1550–56.

on more than incremental growth in discipleship. We aim for exponential or viral growth, where those who become disciples reproduce new disciples in their own contexts.

We often use the word "movemental" to describe this multiplicative effect of Uptick. Growth within a movement is not measured simply by flat numerical growth, but by more nuanced, comprehensive, robust, and healthy metrics. Speaking of church planting, JR Woodward and Dan White Jr. describe healthy movemental growth in this way:

DEEP	Movement is taking place when Spirit-filled discipleship and church planting goes three to four generations deep, with at least as many new births as transfer growth.
WIDE	Movements seek to expand into four spheres; from city, state and people groups to the ends of the earth, in a posture of listening, where we learn to be more like Jesus.
LONG	Movement can be long lasting and has the potential to become a permanent revolution with a commitment to shared leadership, faithfulness and sustainability.
HIGH	The cost of movement is high and takes faith-filled people who live risk-taking, intentional, sacrificial lives, finding our identity in God, not our image or reputation.

[16]

What is true of church planting movements is also true of discipleship movements: they grow *deep, wide, long,* and *high*. When we speak in Uptick of multiplying life, we are not simply referring to adding to the overall number of disciples. We are talking about the multifaceted growth of character that forms people in the image of Christ, and in the manner of the movement that Christ inaugurated.

CONCLUSION: FROM CONTENT TO ENVIRONMENT

LifeShapes language in Uptick provides the "scaffolding" of our disciple-making process. Imagine the Circle, Semicircle and these other shapes as akin to the framing, internal walls, and roof on the house. In

16 Taken from *The Church as Movement* by JR Woodward and Dan White Jr. Copyright ©2016 by JR Woodward and Dan White Jr. Used by permission of InterVarsity Press, P.O. Box 1400, Downers Grove, IL 60515, USA. www.ivpress.com .

the next chapter, we will talk more about how we "furnish" that house through creating environments that turn it into a home.

To use another metaphor: if LifeShapes provide the "grammar" of the Uptick process of formation, then we now turn to how Uptick tries to write *well*—not simply with correct "grammar," but through writing that is compelling. Again, this happens through careful attention to creating what we will call "environments" and "vehicles." To this we now turn.

Section 3

UPTICK TEXTURE AND STRUCTURE

In this section, we will discuss elements which give Uptick its distinctive texture, namely, by creating environments that:

- Set a movemental tone and expectation;
- Practice a posture of high invitation to relationship, combined with a high challenge to responsibility; and
- Strategically use the four spaces (intimate, personal, social, and public) in discipleship formation.

Then, we will in turn look at how to structure an Uptick network. This structure can be attained by field-tested Uptick vehicles including:

- Proper scheduling rhythms;
- The use of discipleship huddle;
- Leadership coaching; and
- Training in how to build networks of Vital Friendships.

The "environments" of chapter five will lead to healthy Uptick *texture*, while the "vehicles" of chapter six provide *structure* that ensures it is replicating the DNA of the Uptick way of disciple making.

5

Uptick Environments

*Guiding a denomination while being engaged on the
margins at the same time served to accentuate my
increasing conviction that the church in the West had to
change and adopt a missionary stance in relation to its
cultural contexts or face increasing decline and possible
extinction.[1]*

ALAN HIRSCH

*The task of leadership is to unleash, harness, and direct
distributed intelligence by creating environments where it
can manifest.[2]*

ALAN HIRSCH

In the previous two chapters, we discussed the core content covered
in any iteration of Uptick. Key LifeShapes (the Circle, Semicircle,
Triangle, and Pentagon) provide the essential vocabulary and conceptual
framework. Utilizing storytelling skills and the Square gives pathways
for more widely sharing the disciple-making process initiated through
practicing the key LifeShapes. All told using shared language creates a
common reality within a group (and also across groups, and beyond the
group). The content creates a common core that serves as the "framing"
which helps to build the Uptick house to specifications. LifeShapes give
basic structure to an Uptick network.

But just as a fully built house is more than the essentials of a slab,
framing, internal walls, windows, and roof, so Uptick is more than the sum
of its core LifeShapes content. A house is not simply its basic structure; it
is also completed by how it is furnished, inside and out. Will its siding be
brick or wood? Shingles or a slate roof? Painted or wallpaper? Hardwood
or linoleum floors? There is *framing*, and then there is *furnishing*. These
are the things that help a *house* begin to feel like a *home*.

1 Hirsch, *The Forgotten Ways*, 50.
2 Hirsch, *The Forgotten Ways*, 182–83.

In the same way, an Uptick experience is defined not only by its *content*, but also by its *tone*. There is an Uptick *environment* as well as Uptick *content*. To use a musical image, the particular chord on the score might be in the key of F#. But playing the F# note with a tone *forte* or *pianissimo* also matters. Well-played music is not just hitting all of the right notes, but with a kind of tonal "feel" that pays attention to volume, pace, time signature, etc.

In 3DM language, both *structure* and *texture* matter. We turn to Uptick *environments* to examine the furnishing of the house or tone of the music that works alongside the content to make an Uptick network function well. There are three components that help mark an Uptick environment:

1. Setting movemental tone and expectations;
2. Maintaining a posture of high invitation and high challenge; and
3. Strategically using proxemics.

1. MOVEMENTAL TONE AND EXPECTATIONS

Seen from a grand sky view at 30,000 feet, the work of Uptick is fundamentally (in the language of APEST) *prophetic* work. The aim of Uptick is to call people back to the core work of loving God (the Great Commandment, Matthew 22:37) and loving neighbors (the Great Commission, Matthew 28:18–20) by helping followers of Jesus become disciples who make disciples. This is always prophetic work because it calls people back to their relational covenant with God— the key function of the prophet. Out of our baptismal covenant identity as beloved daughters and sons of God (Luke 3:22), we are sent on a Kingdom mission into the world to love God and neighbor, to be disciples and to make disciples. Uptick accomplishes this through asking established entities to invest in and pay attention to emerging generations, especially to sacrifice financially for the sake of those on the front end of the leadership pipeline.[3]

A prophetic call thus demands that its listeners give themselves in loyalty to a calling far greater than their own individual aggrandizement and desires. For this reason, the first tone we aim to create within an Uptick environment is one of movemental expectations.

---

3 I also believe that the work of denominations is fundamentally prophetic. It asks its congregations to sacrifice for a cause greater than that of any individual congregation.

In short, we try to jolt Uptickers at the beginning of the experience by letting them know that Uptick is not simply to be a personal tune-up for their own individual gains in improved leadership. Rather, they are being invited and challenged by Uptick to participate in and spur nothing short of a movement of God in their vocational settings, their neighborhoods and cities, in the nation and the world. Prophetically, we ask them to envision the impact of the whole of their ministries and lives over the course of decades. We challenge them to consider things on a grand scale, like the (re)evangelization of the nation, or working toward a Third Great Awakening in the U.S. We want them to envision the thousands of people they will impact over the grand sweep of their lives. In this way, we are setting the tone and expectation that Uptick is not just about self-improvement, but *movement*.

How do you parse a movemental environment? What is the tone or texture of a movement that might show up in the lifelong work of an Upticker? Here are some of the "signature characteristics of movements," from the work of Howard Snyder:

- *A thirst for renewal*: A holy discontent with what exists precipitates a recovery of the vitality and patterns of the early church.
- *A new stress on the work of the Spirit*: The work of the Spirit is seen not only as important in the past but also as an experience in the present.
- *An institutional-charismatic tension*: In almost every case of renewal, tensions within existing structures will arise.
- *A concern for being a countercultural community*: Movements call the church to a more radical commitment and a more active tension with the world.
- *Non-traditional or non-ordained leadership*: Renewal movements are often led by people with no recognized formal leadership status in the church. Spiritual authority [rather than positional authority] is key. Furthermore, women are noticeably more active in movements.
- *Ministry to the poor*: Movements almost always involve people at the grassroots level. They actively involve the masses (the uneducated or socially outcast) and often start as mission on the edges and among the poor (St. Francis, the Wesleys [of Methodism], The Salvation Army, etc.)

- *Energy and dynamism*: New movements have the ability to excite and enlist others as leaders and participants.[4]

This is not an exhaustive list, but a helpful one. It helps ensure Uptick conversations not only address local contextual issues but do so with an eye toward participating in the larger work that God is doing in our day. One Upticker, Kristen Peyton, is a professional artist, whose work is ascending onto the national scene (not to mention the cover of this book!). She grasped that her painting was more than a way to make a living, or an expression of individual discipleship alone, but could be part of something far greater:

"

Since Uptick, I have begun creating more space to listen and watch for the movement of the Holy Spirit and his prompting. I am not in a typical ministry context and disciple making and Kingdom initiatives feel delicate. New language needs to be created to reach those culturally untouched or turned off from institutional Christianity. Uptick prompted me to create new language to better speak of God and mirror Jesus to my context that does not speak 'Christianese.' Esther had a unique position and power to speak on behalf of the Jews and advocate to the king for their salvation. She, however, had to speak the king's language and be in the king's sphere of influence. Although a Jew, she did not readily present as Jewish. I found great kinship with Esther and resonate with her story.[5] **"**

When an Upticker positions herself in the stream of the work of Esther and aspires to create new means of reaching people far from the faith of Jesus, then she has truly absorbed the movemental environment of Uptick.

---

4 Quoted in Hirsch, *The Forgotten Ways*, 193. See Howard A. Snyder *New Wineskins: Changing the Man-Made Structures of the Church* (London: Marshall, Morgan, and Scott, 1978) and *Signs of the Spirit: How God Reshapes the Church* (Wipf & Stock Pub, 1997). Hirsch concludes with this: "History is absolutely clear about this: most established institutions will resist a movement ethos. It's just too chaotic and uncontrollable for institutions to handle. That is why most movements are ejected from the host organization. This needn't be the case, but it does require a significant permission-giving at high levels of denominational or established organization leadership to ensure that they are not." Quoted from Michael Frost and Alan Hirsch, *The Shaping of Things to Come: Innovation and Mission for the 21st-Century Church* (Peabody, Massachusetts: Hendrickson, 2003), 206. For more distinctions between "Organic Missional Movement" and "Institutional Religion," see Hirsch, *The Forgotten Ways*, 196.
5 Upticker Kristen Peyton, Ashland, Virginia.

2. A POSTURE OF HIGH INVITATION AND HIGH CHALLENGE

Generally, commencement speeches are congratulatory. They pat people on the back for their skills and accomplishments and paint an overly-rosy picture of what they will soon achieve beyond graduation. We tend to dismiss these optimistic speeches very quickly. Why? Because they are too idealistic and fail to call attention to the hardships that soon await graduates.

Far better is a graduation speech that congratulates but also warns and exhorts. Here is an example:

> I wish for you to have the sorts of painful experiences that will make you better people. From time to time in the years to come, I hope you will be treated unfairly, so that you will come to know the value of justice. I hope that you will suffer betrayal, because that will teach you the importance of loyalty. Sorry to say, but I hope that you will be lonely from time to time, so that you don't take friends for granted. I wish you bad luck, again, from time to time, so that you will be conscious of the role of chance in life, and that you will understand that your success is not completely deserved, and that the failure of others is not completely deserved, either. And when you lose, as you will from time to time, I hope, every now and then, your opponent will gloat over your failure; it is a way for you to understand the importance of sportsmanship. I hope you'll be ignored, so you know the importance of listening to others. And I hope that you'll have just enough pain to learn compassion. Whether I wish these things or not, they're going to happen. And whether you benefit from them or not will depend upon your ability to see the message in your misfortunes.[6]

In 3DM lingo, this speech captures both *invitation* (affirmation of the success of graduating) but adds to that high *challenge* (to responsibility and growth). Uptick wants to capture an environment that is simultaneously high on invitation to covenant relationships (with God and each other) and high on Kingdom challenge or mission.

When practiced well, the Uptick cohort creates a discipleship culture

6 John Roberts, Chief Justice of the United States, speaking on antifragility and giving the commencement speech at his son's graduation from middle school. Quoted in Greg Lukianoff and Jonathan Haidt, *The Coddling of the American Mind: How Good Intentions and Bad Ideas are Setting Up a Generation for Failure* (New York: Penguin Press, 2018), 193.

by building dense communities of "high invitation" friendships. These Uptick groups are marked by deep personal support, confidential interaction, highly reinforced encouragement and prayer, and opportunity to build trustworthy and enduring relationships.

At the same time, the cohorts are forged by a high "challenge to responsibility." Participants are pushed and motivated to alter their rhythm of life, to learn top-performance leadership skills, to maintain rigorous accountability to their fellow Uptickers for practices of spiritual disciplines, and to make powerful behavioral commitments in many areas of life.

The art of leading Uptickers lies in the ability to calibrate when the individual or group needs invitation, and when they need challenge. The matrix below illustrates the environments that are created by the different combinations of high/low invitation and challenge, and is helpful in considering how to move people toward a discipling culture:

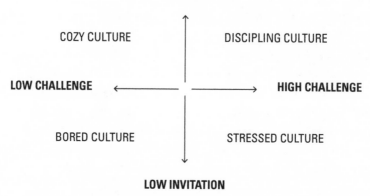

HIGH INVITATION

COZY CULTURE   DISCIPLING CULTURE

LOW CHALLENGE ⟵   ⟶ **HIGH CHALLENGE**

BORED CULTURE   STRESSED CULTURE

LOW INVITATION

On the journey toward a discipling culture, people often begin in the "cozy" quadrant, which is strong on invitation and weak on challenge. It is like the nursery—participants will feel warm and cuddled, but probably won't do any of the yard work. Other times, the path starts from or wanders through deserts of low invitation/low challenge— places of spiritual deadness. In either instance the path to discipleship often means calibrating with higher challenge, pushing the person or

7 Robert Neely, "How to calibrate invitation and challenge," *Wayfarer Blog*, April 10, 2012, https://wayfarerblog. wordpress.com/2012/04/10/how-to-calibrate-invitation-and-challenge/ .

group into the "stressed" quadrant. Then, once everyone understands and has experienced both invitation to relationship and challenge to responsibility, they have the potential to calibrate toward the "discipling" quadrant.

Over the years, some of the best Uptick leaders and presenters have discerned when the group called for invitation and when it needed challenge. I have seen presenters set aside plans in order to gather around, lay hands on, and pray for an Uptick individual who needed to know that he or she was not alone, and who needed a covenant community to surround them.

I also remember instances of hard challenge. One of the Uptick presenters, Jo Saxton, once discerned (correctly) that the tenor of the Uptick conversations had become too cozy. Masterfully, she used the "Out" corner of the Triangle to frame questions that very quickly challenged participants with responsibility for evangelism. The group discomfort and revelation that followed from her calibrating toward the challenge to responsibility was nothing short of the conviction of the Holy Spirit.

In another, similarly high-challenge instance, Tod Bolsinger warned Uptick pastors not to truncate the biblical model of shepherds as they led churches. "The biblical shepherd was a warrior-king," Bolsinger told participants. "They *lead* the sheep, not just care for and comfort them, but lead them to green pastures and still waters."[8] Yes, shepherds sit peacefully by still waters, but they also, like David, "killed both lions and bears" (1 Samuel 17:36), not to mention Goliath.

I was trained in seminary for a ministry model based on the Clinical Pastoral Education (CPE) movement.[9] It taught a helpful action-reflection model, not unlike the Circle. But it also framed ministry as high on invitation and low on challenge. In CPE, I was taught to sit with people at key passages of their lives (births, weddings) and crisis moments (illnesses, deaths). And my job was to listen and empathize, not instruct nor moralize. This is not a bad thing. However, it contributed, in my own faulty application, to creating a cozy, low-challenge culture among those with whom I ministered.

Coming into the beginning of their year together, most Uptick leaders have great capacity for empathy. They understand contexts that

8 Tod Bolsinger, conversation with Uptick, November 2018, Richmond, Virginia.
9 See "Clinical pastoral education," *Wikipedia*, https://en.wikipedia.org/wiki/Clinical_pastoral_education .

shape why broken people around them did what they did and do what they do. Often, we challenge them to respond to such people with not only empathy for their brokenness, but also to equip such people not to participate in the patterns that first led to that brokenness.

In a word, we are trying to create *resilience* in Uptickers so that they may in turn lead people in their contexts to develop greater resilience.

In this age of instant gratification and quick results, people often get uncomfortable when they have to work hard and solve problems. They reject negative feelings—but that's not going to make them any happier. However, it's healthy—almost necessary—to sometimes be unhappy in order to find lifelong well-being. While negative feelings clearly don't feel good, they are important tools for growth and learning. And while our environment affects our lives, it is entirely up to us to have the strength to overcome whatever's thrown at us. That vital trait—our ability to overcome and learn from our challenges, also known as resilience—is often neglected. We need to become more resilient to ultimately be happy.[10]

Resilience is not an inherited trait, but one we can all cultivate. Zelana Montminy says, "It's not entirely genetic. While some people have an easier time turning trauma into triumphs, resilience is a skill we can all develop. It is not a fixed state of being."[11]

Resilience forges a sense of identity that is foundational for carrying out one's mission. When people become resilient in response to challenge, it becomes a clarifying experience. It tends to bring greater focus onto doing what is essential.

Living with resilience is more than just "bouncing back"; it is about shifting our perceptions, changing our responses, and experiencing real growth. The only thing we have control over is the ability definitively and consciously to change how we respond to what life throws at us at any given moment. We all endure challenges, big and small, which are meaningful opportunities for learning and building strength. Highly resilient people seem to not only bounce back from hard times, but also grow and become stronger as a result— they experience posttraumatic growth. They found a way for their

10 Zelana Montminy, *21 Days to Resilience: How to Transcend the Daily Grind, Deal with the Tough Stuff, and Discover Your Strongest Self* (California: HarperOne, 2016), as quoted in http://www.danielplan.com/ , 2018.
11 Ibid.

struggle to redefine their life and fill it with new meaning. This type of growth is the cornerstone of resilience.[12]

3. STRATEGIC USE OF PROXEMICS

The third dynamic to be managed in creating an "Uptick environment" involves the strategic use of proxemics. Proxemics, the study of human "space," names four distinct spheres of human interaction: *intimate, personal, social,* and *public space*. Edward T. Hall, the father of proxemics studies, diagrams these spaces as follows:

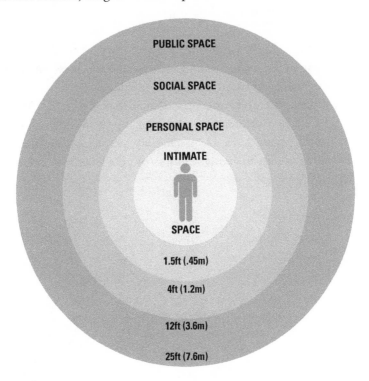

Uptick aims to form leaders through creating opportunities for growth in each of the four spaces. As we explored in chapter four, Jesus led in *intimate* space (for example, his relationships with Peter, James and John), *personal* space (the twelve disciples), *social* space (the synagogue, extended family, or the seventy commissioned in Luke 10), and *public*

12 Ibid.
13 Edward T. Hall, *Handbook for Proxemic Research* (New York: Anchor Books, 1974) [out of print].

space (his interaction with the crowds). So also, Uptick provides intimate space coaching, personal space discipleship huddle, and social and public space interaction in a variety of spheres.

We want an Upticker to function in transformational ways in all four spaces. It's the same process in which the apostles led the early church (Acts 2:42):

- Devotion to teaching (public space)
- Devotion to fellowship (social space)
- Devotion to the breaking of bread (personal space)
- Devotion to prayer (intimate space)

Breen notes that "Many people have written and taught sermons on the four legs of early Christianity found in Acts 2:42 and how, when we rely on them, they will keep us grounded and stable."[14]

To help Uptickers learn to operate well in all four spaces, the Uptick year models and teaches competencies in each space. JR Woodward and Dan White Jr. describe these skills as *vulnerability, accountability, availability,* and *visibility,* each with an average number of people we may interact with within the corresponding space.[15]

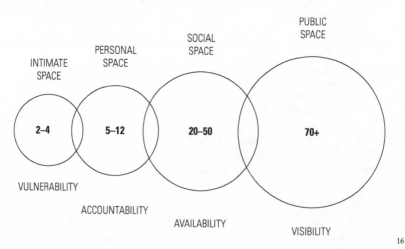

14 Breen and the 3DM Team, *Leading Kingdom Movements*, Kindle edition, Kindle locations 2313–15. This is a great scriptural example of the full use of the four spaces.
15 Woodward and White, *The Church as Movement*, 156.
16 Taken from *The Church as Movement* by JR Woodward and Dan White Jr. Copyright ©2016 by JR Woodward and Dan White Jr. Used by permission of InterVarsity Press, P.O. Box 1400, Downers Grove, IL 60515, USA. www.ivpress.com .

In my own experience and seminary formation for ministry, I received excellent training on how to preach and lead worship (a public space competency). To that end, I was taught "visibility" skills of how to engage and inspire.

As I noted earlier, I was also given tools for how to counsel the perplexed, pray for the distressed, marry the willing and bury the dead (primarily intimate space or "vulnerability" competencies). What I did not receive was any instruction on how to build a leadership pipeline or mobilize disciples. I learned nothing about leading a group or working with a leadership team. These are "accountability" and "availability" competencies, and they are where Uptick puts its primary focus.

I have shared with Uptickers that I have few regrets regarding how I learned and led pastoral ministry. But if I knew then what I know now, I would have invested much more time into personal and social space leadership than I did intimate and public space leadership. I believe they are largely the missing ingredients in helping our work become a discipleship movement. Carl George frequently quipped that disciples should never be "educated beyond the level of our obedience." By focusing on the obedience virtues of accountability and availability, found and utilized in personal and social spaces, we can move beyond mere education (understanding what Jesus required) and into obedience (actually doing it).

The wise use of proxemics can help diagnose what is missing, thus creating a continuum of opportunities to train people to lead well in each of the four spaces. Upticker Vernon Gordon understands this when he says:

"

I now know loud and clear that my people need me to lead them more than simply preach to them. I can't preach people into the changes they need to make. Preaching can serve, but I have to find other platforms to help lead people into the changes they need to make.[17]

"

From this, Vernon began to huddle leaders and staff, build a leadership pipeline, and attend to his relationship with God and his family by recalibrating his rhythm of life. It has exponentially multiplied his

17 Upticker Vernon Gordon, Richmond, Virginia.

effectiveness as a disciple-maker.

To recap, in Uptick, texture matters as much as structure, tone as much as hitting the right note. Curating Uptick environments is critical to building the resilience necessary for long-term Kingdom impact. We do this by setting movemental expectations, calibrating invitation and challenge, and building proxemics skill sets.

6

Uptick Vehicles

I'm not the typical guitar collector in the least. I've bought a lot of vintage pieces over the years, but I've destroyed quite a few of them. People might think, "How could you desecrate the Mona Lisa?" but I really don't care what something looks like. I'm more concerned with a guitar's functionality, sound, and playability. That's why I started building my own guitars. Other guitars wouldn't do what I needed them to do, so I made my own.[1]

EDDIE VAN HALEN

Environments are nebulous and hard to describe. You can measure whether an electric guitarist is playing in the proper key, or whether the guitar is in tune. You can measure whether a musician is playing the proper notes with the correct time signature. But a guitarist's *tone* is more elusive. For this reason, advanced guitarists spend limitless time discussing gear—types of guitars, amplifiers, strings, sound effects, etc. It is all in search of something that is vital but hard to pin down, namely tone. Yet, when tone is right, the music is magical. Van Halen, known among guitar aficionados as a "tone-seeker" calls his sought-after tone the "brown sound."

In a similar way, Uptick environments are elusive. If you have not experienced an Uptick environment, explanation is difficult; if you have, none is necessary! However, it is insufficient to leave environment to chance and hope it turns out for the best. How can we predictably and intentionally create conditions in which the right environments flourish? I believe the answer is through the use of proper Uptick *vehicles*.

Some guitar equipment is superior to others. A Les Paul will give a better tone than a pawn shop special. A quality Fender tube amp is better than a generic solid-state amp. New strings play better than old

1 Chris Gill, "Eddie Van Halen Shares the Guitars Behind His Quest for Tone," *GuitarPlayer*, May 22, 2019, https://www.guitarplayer.com/gear/eddie-van-halen-shares-the-guitars-behind-his-quest-for-tone .

ones. None of those guarantee great tone, but with a lousy guitar, amp, and strings, you will be hard-pressed to get the best sound.

Therefore, here are some quality Uptick vehicles that we have come to believe, through experimentation, testing, evaluation, and experience, will help create the right environments. This, in turn, will help the content of Uptick take root and grow in its ideal climate. The key vehicles are:

- *"Pearls on a string"*—scheduling that is conducive to enriching the spiritual and relational capitals of the group;
- *Huddle*—a series of personal space discipleship conversations within the Uptick year;
- *Coaching*—one-on-one guided conversations that help each Upticker integrate their experience with their context; and
- *Vital Friends*—the intentional work we do to help people experience deep community within their Uptick cohort, and to build a more strategic and relationally rich network for the rest of their lives.

These are four dependable, predictable, and repeatable vehicles that can greatly contribute toward creating the Uptick environments that can be so spiritually and relationally transforming. Again, they are not a silver bullet, but they are solid pathways to help anyone leading an Uptick network curate such an environment.

SPIRITUALLY AND RELATIONALLY DENSE: "PEARLS ON A STRING"

Our earliest outlines of the Uptick year were driven by very pragmatic concerns—our questions always dominated by, *what can we afford?*— more so than strategic or pedagogical ones. We introduced our first few Uptick groups into as many top-tier Kingdom conversation settings as we could manage. I leveraged some relationships with some very sharp people such as Bob Russell, Mike Breen, Tiffany Franks, Alan and Debra Hirsch, Jo Saxton, Doug Murren, and Alan Jamieson, convincing them to give an audience to a small but savvy group of young leaders. We often recruited speakers by asking them to come early or stay late to events for which they were already scheduled, thus splitting expenses with another hosting organization. In start-up days, we did what we had to do to provide quality experiences, even when that meant staying in homes instead of hotels and paying speakers what we could (which was less than they deserved). Because of the quality of the speakers, these gatherings tended to be stimulating and inspiring to the young Uptickers—we therefore began to think of these gatherings as "pearls."

But to make a necklace, something had to tie those pearls together. We determined from the beginning that the "string" that would hold together these experiences, and integrate them into a unified whole with a growth trajectory, would be *huddle* and *coaching*. (More on each of these in a moment.) Because of the work done in community (huddle) and individually (coaching), each Uptick "pearl" experience was not simply a one-off event, unrelated to anything that preceded or followed. Rather, Uptick could begin to have what I call a *trajectory*, so that it was moving in a forward direction, heading somewhere, pointing toward the future in a certain way. We learned early on that huddle was indispensable for this trajectory, while coaching also proved to be valuable.[2]

For our original Uptick networks, where everyone was driving to most gatherings, we aimed for about five or six gatherings, typically one to three days each. Once our trans-local reach involved air travel for participants, the schedule adjusted to about four to five gatherings of two to four days each. And with international travel, given its heightened transportation costs, we typically schedule three long (four to five day) gatherings.

In each of these models, the gatherings themselves are rich and intense times. But without the "strings" of huddle and (often) coaching to hold the pearls together, the cohort would lose momentum and continuity. It is of little lasting use to provide inspiring experiences that are ephemeral if they are not processed and incorporated as part of ongoing spiritual growth in a discipleship path. Without the "string," we would merely be providing three or four conferences a year.

On the other end of the continuum, some Uptick networks are hyper-local, located in a single city. For these, the schedule might look very different. For instance, one Uptick Entrepreneur group is based in Fredericksburg, Virginia. It currently meets ten times per year, but

2 The decision to include coaching with Uptick was and is often driven by budget considerations. Typically, it is a high cost-center. Our first Uptick coaches, Eric Howell and Kathryn McElveen, were very generous in providing coaching to Uptickers at a below-market-value price. And were it not for my BGAV colleague Ken Kessler and his coaching team at https://bgav.org/networks/empower/ , it would still be difficult to afford. They make it very doable—and for that, Uptick owes a huge debt of gratitude.

without any travel or overnight accommodations. Participants' spouses (if applicable) join the group for an evening dinner each meeting, and then the next day is a full day of Uptick for these young business leaders. The Uptickers then huddle mid-month between each of the ten meetings over a brown-bag lunch.

The point is that the rhythm of an Uptick year can vary widely, depending on the geographical makeup of the group.[3] In every instance, a cohort aims to become a spiritually and relationally dense network. Here are a few keys for jump-starting that:

FACILITATE BOTH ORGANIC AND ORGANIZED RELATIONSHIPS

Some Uptickers become fast friends (organically). Enjoy that serendipity! But also make sure that Uptickers get broad exposure and opportunity to become close with people they might not have first imagined as friends. Mix up the roommate list every gathering. Seat people intentionally at tables to encourage unstructured relationship building. Encourage people who live near each other to commute together. In these low-pressure ways, you can organize so as to build relational and spiritual density.

DON'T FEAR ONLINE COMMUNITY

Online community can be an effective tool for building spiritually and relationally dense networks. Most of our Uptick networks huddle at least five times a year using online rather than in-person platforms—and that number is growing. Excluding hyper-local (single-city) Uptick networks, online huddles equal or outweigh the number of in-person huddles. A growing body of research, such as that from Fuller Theological Seminary, suggests that hybrid models featuring patterns of in-person plus online community can be more effective (and certainly are more practical) in many ways than communities that meet only in person.[4]

SET A COVENANT COMMUNITY AND MODEL PERSONAL VULNERABILITY EARLY

We typically begin the year with an online introduction so that people aren't meeting each other for the first time when we gather in person. Some groups will send out short bios to everyone in the group, start

---

3 For more, refer to the Sample Schedules in Chapter 11, "*In*—How to Put Together the Uptick Cohort and Year."
4 See https://www.fuller.edu/wp-content/uploads/2018/09/Direct-and-Indirect-Evidence-in-Support-of-PLOs.pdf .

social media groups, etc. Then, once in person, the possibility of conversation moving beyond a "just-the-facts" depth is stronger. As mentioned in chapter two, we always ask a group to determine together whether they are willing to let conversations during Uptick remain strictly confidential (or at most permit them to be shared with one's spouse). Every Uptick group I have ever led quickly agreed to strong confidentiality. As a Boomer, I marvel at the courage of Millennial and Gen-Z leaders who are willing to "go deep, early" in sharing vulnerably with a new community. They are deeply hungry for the possibility of this kind of community. It is not unusual for Uptickers to share deep pain in the first gatherings—addiction to pornography, marital problems, unwanted singleness, infertility, or deep crisis within their vocational setting. I have seen the Holy Spirit move in these early conversations, bringing hope and healing.

JR Woodward, in creating rich communities to train church planters, employs a strategic use of proxemics to schedule gatherings that are "Intimate, Intensive and Intentional:"[5]

- First Quarter: **Personal**—Asks, *Do I have a life worth imitating? How is my soul?* (Focus on cultivating a life that values soul care, self-awareness and moving forward in vocational goals.)
- Second Quarter: **Relational**—Asks, *Do we have a community worth joining? How is our team?* (Develops fivefold APEST intelligence, team dynamics and understanding conflict transformation.)
- Third Quarter: **Incarnational**—Asks, *Do we have a mission worth dying for? What are the posture and practices of mission in the place we have been sent? How is our faithfulness?*
- Fourth Quarter: **Movemental**—Asks, *Is what we are multiplying reproducible? How are we reproducing disciples in light of the four spaces of belonging and systems thinking. How is our fruitfulness?*

In terms of scheduling meeting spaces that create community-building experiences across all four spaces, Woodward's training trajectory looks like this:

5 See http://thev3movement.org/.

- Intimate Space—Once a month—Breakfast, Lunch, Coffee
- Personal Space—Quarterly—Nice-Sized Living Room
- Social Space—Three Times a Year—Coffee Houses, Third Spaces
- Public Space—Once a Year—Creative Public Spaces[6]

We have discovered that when we give attention to *organizing* relationships strategically, then *organic* relationship-building tends to accelerate. This strategic organizing of relationships is the responsibility of the leader of Uptick, who often functions as a fairly directive convener. The convening work often consists of mundane but important things (scheduling, seating, types of meeting rooms, rhythm of the day, meal arrangements, rooming arrangements). If done well, it can ignite organically growing friendships that are the fuel for transformational change. Both are necessary to engender the spiritually and relationally rich environment in which Uptick does its best work.

Organic relationships left to their own devices, without organization, are too hit-and-miss—and you cannot afford that with the intensive investment of resources in these Uptick leaders. In the same way, organized relationships alone have proven inadequate. Speaking of this in regard to accomplishing the larger mission of the church, Alan Hirsch says:

> And what of structure? The organizational structures of Christendom are, in a real sense, worlds away from that of the early church—something like comparing the United Nations to Al Qaeda (one being a thoroughgoing institution with centralized structures, policies, protocols, and the other being a reticulated network operating around a simple structure with a focused cause.) [...] What I am saying is that because of drastically changed conditions, this configuration of church is literally outmoded. It will simply not be sufficient for the challenges of the twenty-first century.[7]

It is the responsibility of the Uptick leader to organize for the possibility of relationship success early, so that an organic momentum of relational and spiritual sharing may grow on its own from that platform. When it works—and it usually does—all sorts of things occur that the leader couldn't foresee. Participants begin to create social media groups for

6 JR Woodward, www.praxislocal.com , PowerPoint slides 6–11. Used with permission of JR Woodward.
7 Hirsch, *The Forgotten Ways*, 65.

encouragement and problem-solving. Uptickers who are local or regional to each other begin to build friendships that include their families. They begin to share work. Uptickers find affinity-based ways of collaborating on projects, such as student ministry. It is wondrous, because after the initial catalytic work, the Uptick leader doesn't have to run or maintain it. It is, in 3DM lingo, "lightweight and low maintenance," and therefore potentially movemental.[8]

We have much to learn about this when it comes to how we build Uptick schedules that are contextually appropriate but create "pearls-on-a-string" momentum. I believe there is much growth yet for us in learning how to leverage scheduled reunion opportunities beyond the Uptick year, which can also cross-pollinate one cohort with others. In the years to come, we hope to discern how better to schedule and curate similar rhythms of organized and organic Uptick connections across cohorts.

HUDDLE

Huddles are the vehicle that serves as the connective tissue that intentionally joins people together. Intentional discipling relationships are often the means by which God works the reforming process within a congregation. This makes sense given Jesus' model and his command for us to go make disciples.[9]

—MIKE BREEN

A huddle is a personal-space-sized vehicle (generally six to eight people) which replicates the model of Jesus as he interacted with his disciples toward their ongoing formation, through growing repentance and belief. A huddle has a prevailing ethos of discovering the word and will of God for one another's lives. Huddles model the "In" dimension on the Up/In/Out Triangle, creating radical community defined by attentiveness to the Kingdom of God and how the Holy Spirit is actively prompting us to move in that Kingdom.

---

8 See also Ori Brafman and Rod A. Beckstrom, *The Starfish and the Spider: The Unstoppable Power of Leaderless Organizations* (New York: Penguin, 2006).
9 Breen, *Multiplying Missional Leaders*, Kindle edition, Kindle locations 2442–44.

Because much has been written about huddle in other places,[10] here I will simply condense how the huddle discipleship vehicle is used in Uptick, using a "who, what, when, where, and how" format.

WHO

In Uptick, huddles typically consist of a huddle leader, often an apprentice or co-leader, and six to eight Uptickers. In a cohort of twelve Uptick leaders (the maximum for an Uptick group), we prefer to conduct two simultaneous huddles with six Uptickers in each. Having a co-leader or apprentice is helpful, not only for purposes of multiplication and training others in the art of leading huddle, but also to bring multiple APEST eyes and voices to leading the huddle. My fivefold gifting is apostle and leading alongside other APEST voices has often pivoted huddle conversations for the better in ways beyond my own apostolic lense.

Typically, simultaneous huddles are preceded by a short biblical teaching on the particular LifeShape we are using as a whole Uptick cohort, after which we break into two huddles of six people, each led by a single huddle leader. Groups any larger move from a "personal space" to a "social space" dynamic, which is not conducive for deep sharing. Jesus had twelve in his huddle of disciples, and Judas dropped out, so we don't suppose we could do better! Within the huddle, it will be natural for smaller subgroups to form for deeper sharing outside of huddle. Generally, this happens naturally and is beneficial to everyone.

Often when needing to split a larger Uptick cohort into two smaller huddles, these smaller huddles are segregated by gender. We have found that sharing within a gender-specific group provides a context in which Uptickers are more likely to share deeply, much earlier in the process. However, from time to time, we will have a woman lead a huddle of men, and vice versa. In Uptick, our interpretation of Scripture is that disciple making is a function of gifting rather than gender, and that it is important for disciples to learn from both women and men. Let your best disciple-makers be positioned to form the most disciples! To us, anything less would be a failure to obey rigorously the Great Commission. In Uptick, we normalize the idea that women and men can hear *Kairos* reflections from one another. I understand that some

---

10 See Rognlien, *Empowering Missional Disciples*, and Breen and Cockram, *Building a Discipling Culture*, among other www.3dmovements.com resources.

interpret Scripture differently on this point, but I do not understand how, in the battle to make disciples, we would dismiss half of the army before they could fire a shot.

WHAT

A huddle often contains a short scriptural teaching and presentation of the framework of a LifeShape as illustrated by that Scripture. Fundamentally, a huddle is a learning-action process, as taught in the Circle (repentance/belief) LifeShape. The two main questions of huddle are always Circle questions: *How is God getting my attention?* And *What am I going to do about it?* In that vein, an Uptick huddle largely resembles a Socratic process of asking many questions of participants, followed by flowing group dialogue to explore the application of those questions to the lives of each participant. The leader serves to focus and reign in extraneous conversation, keep the pace moving so that each person can learn and contribute, and to make larger process observations when appropriate.

Uptick huddles are not a top-down, teacher-to-learner process of downloading expertise, proprietary knowledge, and advice. Rather, huddle conversation is initiated and facilitated by the huddle leader, who is careful to tap the wisdom of the entire room, as individuals explore what is the *Kairos* for them. Truth does not reside in only one leader; that's how cults function. Uptick huddles are "side-to-side" processes, as disciples in formation learn not only from the huddle leader, but also from each other. We are confident that Peter not only learned from Jesus, but also from James and John, so we want Uptick huddles to do the same.

Therefore, you don't have to be a master teacher to lead a huddle. Rather, you simply keep the group conversation tightly focused on God, watch the time and pacing in order to maintain that focus, and be the initiator and terminator of the conversation. There is an art to doing it well, but also a very low barrier to entry for leading a huddle. After experiencing just a few huddles as a participant, one can (and should!) be ready to lead one.

An important word about time and duration: a huddle should last sixty to seventy-five minutes. I advise generally not to exceed that time, as conversations lose momentum and focus. Beyond that time slot, discussions generally turn into other types of sharing. I have seen huddles devolve into three-hour marathons. These may feel profound in the moment, but, in my observation, are typically more like a form of group therapy and advice-giving, than a discipleship huddle. Upticker TaNikka Sheppard said of those who habitually lead overly long-winded sessions, "Quit blaming the Holy Spirit for your own disorganization and rambling!"

Contract with the group for time and duration, and your participants will lock in. Let the process be open-ended, and you will find yourself scrambling to reel in all sorts of random conversations that tend not to be transformational. It may feel counter-intuitive and even rude to move conversations along at a good pace, but it is deeply respectful to group process and to the individuals if you respect the time and people by starting and ending as agreed. It will help in more ways than you can imagine. Honor the time by starting and ending punctually, and by setting and meeting expectations that Uptick participants will show up "dressed and ready to play ball." It creates ritual expectations that will become your friends in disciple making.

WHEN

In Uptick, huddle functions as the main "string" that holds the "pearls" of group gatherings and conversations together in a coherent trajectory. (As mentioned, Future Story and coaching can help with that as well.) In a typical Uptick year, there may be anywhere from eight to fifteen huddles. Eight is the minimum number, because you want to introduce the discipleship language of each of the eight LifeShapes as a framework for this group and future groups. Fifteen is not a hard maximum, but it is challenging to add more than this for most groups, on top of gatherings, which consume up to fifteen in-person days in a year.

In huddles based in a tight geographical area, it is possible to huddle frequently and always in person. However, to date, most of our Uptick networks have consisted of people in a broad geographical expanse (sometimes multi-state or even multinational). We have been driven by necessity to embrace video huddle alongside in-person huddles.[11] We have found, for the most part, these video huddles to be serviceable vehicles at worst (for example, when there are technological issues such as spotty Wi-Fi). Often video huddles are just as powerful as in-person huddles. We have seen many introverts who will share more freely online than in person.

11 We have used the https://zoom.us/ app for many years for video huddle and found it to be useful.

When the Uptick is locally based, we schedule a social event, including spouses. In this social setting, we ask participants to share basic information about who and where they are, followed by some sense of "why they said yes to Uptick." By introducing participants in this way, by the time we get to our first in-person "official" Uptick huddle, the conversation moves into deeper waters more quickly.

Then, during the Uptick year, we typically conduct one or two in-person huddles while gathered together, and one or two video huddles between in-person gatherings. This rhythm has proved useful in helping participants process their own *Kairos* reflection in conversations and in building group cohesion and trust.

Huddle is a cumulative vehicle in strengthening Vital Friendships and depth of sharing, and huddles often improve throughout the Uptick year. There is not a strict schedule of exact timing for when Uptick huddles should occur, as it depends somewhat on the length of time between in-person gatherings. Having said that, it is important not to allow a gap of more than about six weeks without a huddle during the Uptick year, or participants will lose continuity of conversation and momentum of discipleship formation.

Sometimes, we schedule a post-year video huddle, and/or "reunion" video huddles after the scheduled Uptick year. This can serve to build ongoing friendships beyond the structure of regular gatherings.

One last point: when an Upticker misses a huddle, the entire group process reboots to some extent and loses ground. It is key to commit to full participation in *all* huddles up front to avoid this. Other than the first prequel huddle and in-gathering huddles, we typically schedule subsequent video huddles while together in the gatherings. This allows people to calendar and commit well in advance, so that we only lose people out of video huddles due to emergencies. On the rare occasion that someone misses a video huddle, they will be encouraged by the leader to listen to the recorded video huddle as soon as possible (and certainly before the next scheduled huddle). This respects the group formation and its trajectory goals.

WHERE

The question of *where* the huddle should meet may be the least important consideration of all. So long as there is reliable Wi-Fi or cell reception, and the physical or online space permits non-distracted and sensitive conversation, it will do. It is not ideal for participants to be in multitasking (such as driving) or noisy (such as loud coffee shops or offices) situations for online huddles, but these can be stopgaps or rare exceptions. Better the Upticker in a pinch be able to participate in these ways than not at all.

HOW

Keep it simple! Start on time. Focus the conversation with a two-to-five-minute exposition on Scripture. Explain the LifeShape that gives focus to the huddle. Work the Circle process for each member vis-à-vis the LifeShape. If appropriate, ask for accountability on how individuals are doing with follow through and acting on *Kairos* from the previous huddle(s). Pace and manage the conversation so that each individual has time to share and benefit from the wisdom of the group. Don't let conversations devolve into simple advice-giving. Consider taking brief notes that you can send to the group in a threaded conversation to help focus individual accountability responses and how each person in the group can pray for the others. If appropriate, pair people up for between-huddle support and challenge conversations on specific issues surfaced. Close on time.

As LifeShapes language is irreducible to the Uptick process, so huddle is the "operating system" that forms disciples in Uptick. Huddles are lightweight, low maintenance, easily replicated, and reliable forums for the Holy Spirit to speak to people. In my opinion, any leader who wants to make disciples should begin huddling people immediately. And the only way to learn it is to practice. Believe me, once you are in it, you *will* ask God for help and wisdom, and you will experience divine guidance as you listen and respond to the Spirit.

COACHING

Coaching is so helpful because a coach helps you navigate your own mind and voice. Their wisdom is not simply to give you an answer, or to tell you what they think you should do, but rather help you to discern.[12]

—VERNON GORDON

---

12 Upticker Vernon Gordon, Richmond, Virginia.

In 2008, Kathryn McElveen and Eric Howell made a compelling case for including coaching as a core vehicle for Uptick formation, and became the first coaches of Uptick. Whereas huddle would serve to "string together the pearls" through a group process, coaching would do the same through working with individuals. Where huddle was a vehicle for communal discernment of the voice of the Holy Spirit and formation in discipleship, coaching could serve to give shape to the missional trajectory of an individual Upticker's life.

Through coaching, we have been able to help Uptickers form a Future Story and action plan into which they are able to live. This is rarely a rigid, step-by-step recipe or long-range plan for how their lives will unfold. But it is a purposeful set of guardrails and directional markers which sets the road on which they intend to travel.

McElveen defines coaching in this way:

> Put most simply, coaching is a way of partnering with people to help them get from where they are to where they want to be. Coaches understand that their clients are naturally creative, gifted, and capable of responding to the challenges and opportunities they face. Through focused listening, observation, and power questions, the coach acts as a thought partner to facilitate a learning and discernment process. Through this process, clients gain clarity to see "where they want to be" and build the bridge that will take them there.[13]

We clarify in Uptick what coaching is *not*. In contrast to other helping professions, it is not therapy. It is not a mechanism for offering expertise, advice, teaching, or telling you what to do. Your coach is neither a "paid friend" nor an organizational consultant. Coaches are typically not mentors (who guide primarily based out of wisdom gained from their own experience). Finally, the Uptick coach is not like your high-school basketball coach—directive and in charge of decisions as the boss or final authority.[14]

Rather, the Uptick coach generally assumes that individuals are capable of generating their own solutions. The coach's role is to provide disciplined and generous frameworks of invitation and challenge that lead Uptickers to discover these solutions. They do so by:

---

13 Kathryn McElveen, PCC, *"Introduction to the Uptick Leadership Coaching,"* paper edited by Ken Kessler, PCC.
14 See *"What is Coaching?"* on The International Coach Federation, www.coachfederation.org .

- Letting the Upticker set the agenda for personal goals and hopes and take responsibility for that agenda and those goals;
- Asking great questions through astute listening;
- Encouraging possibility thinking, thoughtful planning, and decision making;
- Challenging blind spots, fostering shifts of thinking that illumine new possibilities, and facilitating alternative scenario planning.[15]

Over the course of the year, Uptick coaching uses the vehicle of Future Story (see chapter two) to capture *Kairos* moments and help to frame them into a narrative that builds a bridge from the Upticker's present to their future. The process of envisioning personal trajectory then helps the Upticker to accumulate experiences, networks, and relationships that will be useful to living into that Future Story. Often, the practice of holding Uptickers accountable through persistent questioning around the Upticker's stated agenda is powerful:

"

My coach gave me concrete ways to grow, pointed questions, and directed conversation. He was incredible at getting me to step back, re-think goals, and to create tangible targets for the month. Just a great sounding board to vent to, be inspired by, and grow through.[16]

"

Tod Bolsinger points out that coaching can be a useful tool for navigating adaptive change through helping its recipients to conduct "safe, modest experiments." He likens it to a "crockpot" process in cooking, which regulates between the extremes of "nothing cooking" and "scorching." The heat is urgency, anxiety, conflict … and coaches can apply that heat steadily, rather than erratically. The resulting experiments can then help Uptickers to learn quickly what doesn't work, on the path to learning what *does*. Coaching may explore ideas that lead to actions that are:

- **Safe:** If it goes wrong, no one gets fired.
- **Modest:** The idea isn't unnecessarily costly and is repeatable. (Here one does not aim for a big win but focuses on "what can I learn?".)

15 McElveen, *"Introduction to the Uptick Leadership Coaching."*
16 Upticker Andrea Ackerman, Washington, D.C.

- **Willing to Experiment:** The outcome is either "I win, or I learn." (This is a posture of "fail fast in order to learn quickly.")[17]

Here, then, is a brief "who, what, when, where, and how" of Uptick coaching.

WHO

Uptick utilizes coaches certified by the International Coaching Federation.[18] We conduct an orientation at the beginning of Uptick to introduce the discipline of coaching. Coaching sessions are strictly confidential between coach and Upticker and are not shared with the Uptick leader(s) without stated permission. Uptick leaders match coaches with Uptickers at the beginning of the year, based on anticipated chemistry factors. In the very rare instance of a poor match, the Upticker can request a change of coach after two or three sessions.

WHAT

During the course of the year, the Upticker is given ten one-on-one coaching sessions, each of which lasts about an hour.

WHEN

The Upticker is required to initiate scheduling with the coach for the sessions, which occur roughly monthly.

WHERE

Uptick coaching almost always takes place by telephone or videoconference.

HOW

The client initiates telephone or Zoom call to their coach, with the client bringing the agenda for the conversation. See appendix seven, "Sample: Uptick Coaching Outline."

Coaching is a part of the Uptick Core network, but while it is preferred, it is not absolutely required. Those starting new Uptick

---

17 Tod Bolsinger, Upticker conversation, Richmond, Virginia, November 2018.
18 See https://coachfederation.org/. This body certifies three level of coaches: *Associate* (requires 100 hours of coaching experience, sixty training hours, and ten hours of mentor coaching with a Professional or Master Credentialed coach); *Professional* (500 hours coaching experience, 125 training hours, ten hours with Master Certified coach); and *Master* (1,500 hours coaching experience, 200 coach training hours, ten hours with another Master Certified Coach).

networks often face financial constraints that put coaching on the back burner, at least for a time. Uptick Entrepreneur substitutes yearlong coaching for a single orientation and consult with a coach, plus a mentor in business with whom the Upticker can meet throughout the year (and sometimes beyond).[19] Still other Uptick networks, again, often due to fundraising or budget considerations, substitute ongoing structured relationships with wise people who are "further ahead on the Square" than the Upticker.

Still, whenever possible, we love to expose Uptickers to the discipline of coaching. The necklace is stronger when you can hold the pearls together with two strings: huddle and coaching (or some substitute). When financially viable, coaching becomes one of the most critical tools to help many Uptickers process *Kairos* in their lives during the Uptick year, and to clarify vocational passion for robust, long-term Kingdom leadership.

VITAL FRIENDS

The Covenant relationship Jesus forged with his disciples formed the basis of the Kingdom breakthrough he was able to achieve through them. Jesus was growing his relational capital by investing his physical capital in his covenant relationships. The covenant relationship Jesus forged with his disciples formed the basis of the Kingdom breakthrough he was able to achieve through them. Interestingly, it appears that investing relationally in this way was one of the ways Jesus paid his bills.[20]

—MIKE BREEN AND BEN STERNKE

One of the strong hopes I communicate to Uptickers at the beginning of the year is that they will come out of the process with great friends. This is not merely a pleasant wish but lines up with our pedagogy of increasing participants' spiritual and relational capitals. If a candidate can come through the year with a better vertical relationship with

---

19 See appendix eight, "Uptick Entrepreneur Mentor Guidelines."
20 Mike Breen and Ben Sternke, *Oikonomics: How to Invest in Life's Five Capitals the Way Jesus Did* (South Carolina: 3DM Publishing, 2015), Kindle edition, Kindle location 744.

God (spiritual capital) and better horizontal relationships with peers, mentors, protégés, and networks (relational capital), then Uptick will have done good work in their lives.

One of the earliest focal verses in Uptick's history was Hebrews 10:24–25:

> And let us consider how to provoke one another to love and good deeds, not neglecting to meet together, as is the habit of some, but encouraging one another, and all the more as you see the Day approaching.

Because of our pace and our load, leaders tend to neglect meeting together. We neglect building relational networks around us, whether within our families, at work, in our neighborhoods, or even at church. It is difficult to encourage (or challenge) others—to spur them to love and good deeds—when you rarely or never meet with them.

Many young adults come out of college or seminary experiences where they were often surrounded by an endless supply of possible peers and friends, and into ministry/work settings where purpose overwhelms play, and where making friends is suddenly much more challenging—this can be somewhat of a shock to the system. Perhaps add a new marriage, children, low pay, student loan debt, and the pressure not to waste money on socializing, and you have a recipe for relational paucity or stress. Many Uptickers come into the year starving for an experience of community that is very difficult to find within their own setting. When we mention that the Uptick year will provide the opportunity to build enduring friendships, many appear ravenous for this.

Moreover, having good relational networks is not only correlated to quality of life; it is also vital for doing our work with excellence. Margaret Wheatley says:

> It is possible to prepare for the future without knowing what it will be. The primary way to prepare for the unknown is to attend to the quality of our relationships, to how well we know and trust one another [...] In order to counter the negative organizational dynamics stimulated by stress and uncertainty, we must give full attention to the quality of our relationships. Nothing else works, no new tools or technical applications, no redesigned organizational

chart. *The solution is each other.* If we can rely on one another, we can cope with almost anything.[21]

Tod Bolsinger helpfully asks leaders to consider, "Who are the Hebrews 12 people in your great cloud of witnesses who are reminding you to look at Jesus as the pioneer and perfecter of your faith rather than the travails of the race you are running?" Citing Heifetz, Linsky, and Grashow,[22] Bolsinger encourages leaders to "think politically" when they lead. Doing so means to work in relationally strategic ways with six types of leaders:

1. **Allies**—people within your organization who see your goals, have other (even competing) loyalties, are not friends but partners, are aligned on mission, can give perspective, and are loyal first on matters of *purpose*.

2. **Confidants**—people who are usually outside of your organization, see your heart, encourage you, serve more as friends than partners, are first loyal to *you*. Confidants and Allies are often confused.

3. **Opponents**—"stakeholders who have markedly different perspectives than yours and who risk losing the most if you and your initiative go forward [...] If you are leading a change process, opponents are not your enemies in the same way that allies are not necessarily your friends."[23]

4. **Senior Authorities**—those to whom we are accountable and with whom we must remain connected by passing on anxiety, urgency, and challenges in the system upward to them.

5. **Casualties**—people in change processes who "experience the change most personally and dramatically."[24] The leader assumes responsibility for these people.

6. **Dissenters**—"In true adaptive change, there are no unanimous votes."[25] These naysayers are the canaries in the coal mine. They help us see how opposition will form and what arguments it will raise, asking the toughest questions.

---

21 Margaret Wheatley, as quoted by Tod Bolsinger, *Tempered: Forming Leaders for a Changing World*, slide 56, PowerPoint presentation at Uptick, November, 2018, Richmond, Virginia. See Bolsinger, *Canoeing the Mountains*, 157ff, and Ronald Heifetz, Marty Linsky and Alexander Grashow, *The Practice of Adaptive Leadership: Tools and Tactics for Changing Your Organization and the World* (Massachusetts: Harvard Business School Press, 2009), Kindle edition, Kindle locations 1576–79.
22 As quoted by Tod Bolsinger, *Tempered*, slides 46, 47, 60–68.
23 Bolsinger, *Canoeing the Mountains*, 161.
24 Ibid., 162.
25 Ibid., 163.

Bolsinger concludes, "The way you manage #3–6 affects deeply #1–2." The genius behind this way of thinking about leadership is that it fundamentally understands that leadership takes place in a relational context.

Uptick teaches that it is possible to expand our notion of what constitutes friendship and relational capital. Bolsinger's list expands the notion of relational richness beyond simply the people we like. A Dissenter, for instance, can provide you with important perspective and insight that your buddy may not. Jesus teaches that disciples should "Come to terms quickly with your accuser while you are on the way to court" and to "Love your enemies and pray for those who persecute you" (Matthew 5:25, 44), in part because this is a wise way to operate relationally within systems of power.

We believe Uptick leaders need to develop skills that help them to diagnose and operate within systems of power, that is, among relational networks. To do that, however, is not simply to accumulate tactical political skills in knowing how to identify and work with different groups of people. It is also to build a thriving relational ecosystem around the leader.

It comes as no shock to an Upticker when we posit our primary relationship to be with God. Clearly, we teach habits to cultivate that fundamental relationship. And, none are surprised when we urge them to attend (if applicable) to the quality of their marriage and family relationships. However, when we begin to tie these core relationships to the wider range of friendship networks that can and should exist in the life of a leader and disciple, most Uptickers experience some form of *Kairos*.

Our primary way of helping Uptickers with this is through teaching Tom Rath's work in *Vital Friends: The People You Can't Afford to Live Without*.[26] This book explores how we can build friendships within (and beyond) the workplace, noting the correlation between work satisfaction and performance, when there are deep friendship networks in place. In Uptick, however, we use the book not just to address workplace dynamics, but longevity in leadership and satisfaction in discipleship.

For instance, one of Rath's core arguments counters the common assumption that you can't be friends with people with whom you

---

26 Tom Rath, *Vital Friends: The People You Can't Afford to Live Without* (1st ed.) (New York: Gallup Press, 2006).

work. He shows that those who have three or more friends on the job tend to stay longer, have greater enjoyment, and demonstrate better productivity. In Uptick, we take that line of thinking even further. We argue that those who build out powerful networks of Vital Friends will hear God more clearly, discern their call more distinctly, align with core relationships more powerfully, lead more effectively, and experience Kingdom life more robustly.

These friendships are marked by what Mike Breen calls "high purpose and high play." Here's Breen's depiction of the range of relationships:

HIGH PLAY

KINDERGARTEN
- Defined by friendship (let's have fun!)
- Breakthrough is sustainable but not terribly effective
- Lots of fun with little accomplished

FAMILY
- Defined by shared extended family life
- Breakthrough is frequent and sustainable
- Lots of fun and massive breakthrough together

HIGH PURPOSE

DEATH

STAFF
- Defined by partnership (let's get things done!)
- Effective for some breakthrough but unsustainable
- Little fun, high turnover, but many tasks are completed

27

These high purpose and high play relationships Breen calls *oikos*, the Greek/biblical word for "family" (by which he means not just biological family but spiritual family). Rath teases out these "family" relationships using the language of "Vital Friends," and he lists eight types:

1. **Builders**—People who invest in your development and achievement in non-competitive ways.

2. **Champions**—Loyal advocates who stand up and promote you in your presence or absence.

3. **Collaborators**—People who share your interests and passions in life.

---

27 Mike Breen, "The 'Secret Sauce' our churches are missing," December 5, 2011, https://mikebreen.wordpress.com/2011/12/05/the-secret-sauce-our-churches-are-missing/ .

4. **Companions**—First responders to your big life events; the people with whom you hang out.
5. **Connectors**—People who extend opportunities, networks, and resources to you.
6. **Energizers**—Your "fun" friends who make you laugh, and recharge you.
7. **Mind Openers**—People who make you receptive to new perspectives and opportunities.
8. **Navigators**—Pragmatists who help you at ambiguous crossroads.[28]

Building a network of Vital Friends first means to survey the landscape and assess where you are rich and where you have gaps. Second, it can mean understanding that you may be putting unrealistic weight on existing friendships to fulfill multiple roles and goals. (It is not uncommon for spouses to believe that their partner should meet every friendship role; this is unrealistic and places marital friendship at risk.) Next, we must learn how best to engage with each type of friend. A navigator, for instance, may be someone we connect with rarely and at key decision points. This type of relationship can cope with this level of infrequency. But if we rarely see companion friends, those relationships most likely wither. Then, we look for the gaps in our "friendship portfolio," and devise strategies for finding certain types of friendships that we are missing. (It is at this point that Uptickers sometimes realize the riches of friendship networks available to them through their Uptick network.) Finally, it is important that we not only learn to look for the friends that we need, but that we meditate on the kind of friend that we are to others. Friendships are, by nature, reciprocal and not merely utilitarian. We ask:

- Who are the friends we have?
- Who are the friends we need?
- What kind of friend am I to others?

Typically, this Vital Friends presentation takes place at the mid-point of the Uptick experience. It marks a pivot in the caliber of relationships within the group, and, when that spark lights, it catalyzes the group toward a transformational experience.

28 Adapted from Rath, *Vital Friends*.

"

I now know what types of relationships I need in order to move. For instance, currently I am in search of a mentor and a collaborator. Because I know this, I can be specific in my prayers.[29]

"

When Uptickers begin to build out their network of Vital Friends, they build relational capital and take critical steps toward longevity, effectiveness, fruitfulness, and joy in their Kingdom work.

In conclusion, we have tried to answer the question of how to create conditions in which Uptick environments flourish. Our experience has been that the answer lies in using most or all of these Uptick *vehicles*:

- *"Pearls on a string"* scheduling;
- *Huddle* personal space discipleship conversations;
- *Coaching* conversations; and
- *Vital Friends* work to build a more robust and relationally rich network

These vehicles can help anyone curate an Uptick environment.

29 Upticker Shanice Alexander, Norfolk, Virginia.

Section 4

BENCHMARKS AND OUTCOMES FOR UPTICKERS

We now transition the flow of the book from Uptick *ethos* to *execution* or application of Uptick principles. Here are the questions we now need to address:

Can we tell when an Uptick network is working? Is there an agreed-upon framework for ongoing assessment and evaluation?

Can we determine that an Upticker is making measurable progress in skills for discipleship and leadership?

Are there specific ways to train Uptickers in the critical relational competencies for leadership? Are there concrete ways to improve "soft" relational skills, which can be hard to define but can make or break a leader?

Of course, we believe the correct answer to these questions is "yes!" In this section, we describe desired outcomes and benchmarks of progress in Uptickers in three principal ways. First, in chapter seven, we sketch out Uptick's use of "five capitals" as an overall linguistic and evaluative framework for how we want to see Uptickers assess and track growth.[1] The five capitals function as sturdy, functional scaffolding for identifying what has already been achieved, as well as what is required to progress.

Then, in chapter eight, we move into detailed, concrete behavioral metrics of progress in Uptickers by means of the Uptick Leadership Pipeline. This pipeline can be useful

---

1 See Breen and Sternke, *Oikonomics*; Brandon Schaeffer, www.fivecapitals.net ; and Ben Sternke, "What are the Five Capitals?" May 5, 2014. https://bensternke.com/what-are-the-five-capitals/ .

both for measuring individual gains, and for describing, in a very granular way, the growth trajectory (or succession planning pathway) throughout the entire Uptick network. It can serve as a detailed checklist of competencies for concrete personal skills necessary for leading at increasingly higher levels.

Finally, in chapter nine, we move into the arena of interpersonal intelligences: emotional-relational, social, and societal. Daniel Goleman's description of *emotional intelligence*,[2] or *EQ*, accelerated how we have come to view the importance of interpersonal skills in leadership. In this light, Uptick uses different tools to help disciples grow in the path (discussed in chapter two) of:

self-awareness → **self-regulation** → **social awareness** → **social regulation**

Uptick aims to help young leaders identify their own inherent preferences and corresponding strengths and weaknesses (self-awareness) in order to modify reactivity and other negative responses triggered by those preferences (self-regulation). Doing so positions them to attend to the relational dynamics around them (social awareness and regulation).

Without good emotional, interpersonal, and social skills, the smartest leader in the world can be derailed into underperforming drastically below capacity. It is almost impossible for an emotionally and relationally clueless leader to overcome these deficits and gain societal impact.

2 Goleman, *Emotional Intelligence*.

7

Five Capitals: Ordering Your Whole Life in the Way of Jesus

There are five capitals we see in Scripture:
Spiritual: *How much faith do you have to invest?*
Relational: *How much relational equity do you have to invest?*
Physical: *How much time and energy do you have to invest?*
Intellectual: *What intellect, skill sets and competencies do you have to invest?*
Financial: *How much financial capital do you have to invest?*[1]

BEN STERNKE

The list above is in descending order from the most valuable and hardest to acquire (spiritual) to the least valuable and easiest to acquire (financial). In the world, and often even in the church, this list is reversed.[2]

In *Oikonomics*, Mike Breen and Ben Sternke refer to the wise disciple as being one who recognizes the most important of the five capitals and consequently makes savvy "investments." Because following Jesus is often at crosscurrents with the wisdom of this world, determining priorities of how we invest involves making value judgments on which capitals matter most:

> Our problem, then, is that our measurement of wealth is too small. It's not that we shouldn't look for a return on our investments—it's that we need to expand our definition of what kind of return we are looking for. We need a new way of evaluating and measuring what actually happens when we make these kinds of investments. We need to think bigger about prosperity and wealth. Our word wealth comes from an old Middle English word that means simply

---

1 Adapted from Ben Sternke, "What are the Five Capitals?"
2 See Breen, *Multiplying Missional Leaders*, Kindle edition, Kindle locations 2078–87.

"well-being." [...] We begin with the reality that true wealth is not just about money. It's about other kinds of capital that we need to identify and grow. And true wealth is not just about me—it's about my whole community flourishing. It's about the common good, not just my individual prosperity. *Oikonomics is about the economy of our oikos.[3] It's how we do everyday discipleship. Jesus was the most brilliant economist who ever lived.* Because, as Dallas Willard has said, "Jesus isn't just nice, he's brilliant."[4]

A disciple, by definition, is someone who follows Jesus into his practices. Discipleship is not merely a matter of believing what Jesus taught; to follow Jesus also involves doing what he did. Jesus prioritized investments in certain capitals (such as spiritual and relational capital) more highly than other forms of capital (such as financial capital). Uptick uses this language of different forms of human capitals to help leaders evaluate how they are ranking, prioritizing, and investing in the key capitals in the manner of Jesus.

Here, then, is what the Uptick framework of the five key capitals looks like, in compact form:[5]

Financial Capital—currency is *money*
This is simply the money we have available to invest, measured in dollars and cents, pounds and pennies, etc.
We are most familiar with this one, because we work with it every day. It's neither good nor bad; it's simply a resource we have available to invest. We can turn it into an idol, of course, if we are *relying on it* for significance or security. But when it is in its right place, it is simply a form of capital that allows us to invest in other capitals that are worth more.

3 *Oikos* is the New Testament Greek word for "household," referring to our most relationally dense community. In this sense, *oikonomics* refers to how we order our lives—and prioritize the five capitals—within the relational context of our shared lives.
4 Breen and Sternke, *Oikonomics*, Kindle edition, Kindle locations 293–98, 307–08, 310–12.
5 Adapted from Sternke, "What are the Five Capitals?" by Sarah Burnett and Anne Scruggs of MontVue Capital. Sarah has served brilliantly for many years as the chair of the Uptick board. MontVue, a financial services company, has adapted the framework of the five capitals as the defining value structure for their business. See www.montvue.com .

Intellectual Capital—currency is *concepts and ideas*
This is the creativity and knowledge we have available to invest, measured in concepts and ideas.
This is of higher value than financial capital, because you can't create ideas, or grow in creativity simply by spending a lot of money.

Physical Capital—currency is *hours and health*
This is the time and energy we have available to invest, measured in hours and minutes.
It comprises the time we make available for tasks, projects, and relationships, as well as the capacity we have to use that time. Our overall health comes into play here, because it greatly affects our ability to invest our time and energy. Health includes things like getting proper rest and living in a rhythm of life that allows us to both work hard and repose. These things are essential if we are going to steward our long-term physical capital, our use of time and space.

Relational/Social Capital—currency is *family and friends*
This is the "relational equity" we have available to invest, measured in family and friends, the quantity and quality of our relationships with others.
Having family and friends is extremely valuable, and the amount of relational capital we have accrues to us in many ways, from our overall sense of well-being and happiness to more tangible forms. In fact, none of the other capitals can actually grow without a relationship of some kind.

Spiritual Capital—currency is *wisdom, power, influence*
This is the "spiritual equity" we have available to invest, measured in wisdom and influence.
Some secular books refer to this as "purpose" or "values." The ability to look beyond one's self and see a bigger meaning.

Following *Oikonomics,* Uptick ranks the five key capitals in order of importance: spiritual, relational, physical, intellectual, and financial, and asks evaluative questions for each capital.

1. **Spiritual**—has this person grown as a disciple and does s/he have a clear path for future growth in discipleship and calling? How is s/he building spiritual capital in others?
2. **Relational**—is s/he intentionally developing a strategic network of mentor, peer, and protégé leaders from whom s/he can benefit and to which s/he can contribute, and consciously investing in the discipleship of other leaders?
3. **Physical**—is s/he living bodily with a discipleship perspective in relation to use of time, calendar, and space? Does s/he have a vibrant rhythm of life that makes for long-term leadership?
4. **Intellectual**—is s/he growing in the world of ideas and best practices? Is s/he learning from others so as to bring innovative disruption into the settings where s/he leads?
5. **Financial**—is this leader living generously and as a good steward, actively looking to grow in the ability to invest relationally and financially in Kingdom work, particularly in relation to reproducing discipleship networks?[6]

Over the course of the year, Uptick is structured around teaching, practice, and intentional investments in each of the five capitals. The goal is to create a mental framework around which leaders can reframe and reprioritize how they value and practice investing in different forms of capital. Using the Square LifeShape, this is generally a discipleship journey from:

*   **Unconscious incompetence**—Uptickers are unaware of how they have been following the "spirit of this world" (1 Corinthians 2:12) in prioritizing the five capitals; to
*   **Conscious incompetence**—Uptickers, through *Kairos* moments, becoming self-aware of their priorities, begin the journey toward self- and social-regulation in reprioritizing these five capitals; which can lead to

6 See "Sample: Uptick 'Metrics of Success' Survey" in appendix six.

- **Conscious and Unconscious Competence**—here, the lives of Uptickers begin to conform more closely to how Jesus valued and invested in different capitals.

It can be a challenge to reprioritize how we invest. The broader culture of the United States is diametrically at odds with how Jesus chose to invest. In our age, one can make an easy case that the order of priorities in wider U.S. culture are:

- **Financial**—how much money and how many possessions do you have? This cultural priority is so strong that each of the other capitals defer to how they increase financial capital.
- **Intellectual**—how smart are you and from where do you possess a degree (or, how did your ideas monetize into financial wealth)?
- **Physical**—how do you look, what clothes do you wear, and does your bodily appearance conform to what is culturally defined as beauty in advertisements (and often pornography)?
- **Relational**—are you well-networked (often viewed in terms of leveraging relationships for gaining greater financial capital)?
- **Spiritual**—do you have some deeper value framework to make sense of the meaning of life and legacy? (Again, legacy is often defined in terms of work and how much money you accumulate or leave behind rather than in terms of moral or spiritual character.)

In the United States, our question of what a person is "worth" is assumed to be referring to financial wealth. Is this what followers of Jesus believe and what we want to practice? This is the sea we swim in, and discipleship often means making a fish aware of this water! The language of the five capitals can function like a "detox," making us aware of how Jesus inverts and challenges the cultural defaults and values of the environment in which we live.

Even more startling is when Uptickers become aware of how their vocational settings (including self-described Christian contexts) uncritically mirror the surrounding culture in their prioritization of the five capitals. In the United States, churches and denominations often measure success in terms of the "ABCs—Attendance, Buildings, and Cash." In this framework, effective leadership means increasing physical and financial capitals. Those capitals matter, but wouldn't prioritizing growth in spiritual and relational capitals result in different metrics? What about "D"–Disciples made? In like manner, the Academy (including not only universities but also many seminaries and divinity schools) seems often consumed in prioritizing intellectual capital (what do students learn and know?) over spiritual capital (how are students being formed as citizens or disciples?).

The construct of the five capitals thus functions as an eye-opener for how we might choose to reorder our lives according to the values of the Kingdom of God as taught and practiced by Jesus. And here is where Breen offers a note of hope: "The good news is that spiritual capital is astronomically valuable and radically available!"[7] He offers a biblical illustration of this:

> (An) example can be found in 3 John 2, where John prays that the recipient of the letter would prosper in "all respects," that he would be in good health, "just as your soul prospers." The writer is giving us a holistic view of prosperity that is a helpful corrective against the myopic focus of the so-called prosperity gospel. John is saying that every area of your life should prosper, not just one or two [of the five capitals]. He describes prosperity in terms of multiple kinds of capital and currency.[8]

In other words, it is possible to reorder, re-rank, and reprioritize the five capitals in how we live and lead, resulting in a more robust form of prospering or well-being than simple financial accumulation.

STRUCTURING THE UPTICK YEAR TO INVEST IN ALL FIVE CAPITALS

The Uptick year is structured to give opportunities to invest each of the five capitals into the lives of Uptickers. Vehicles such as huddle become critical for ongoing deepening of spiritual capital. The work that we do throughout the Uptick year to create a Vital Friends network builds relational capital. Exposure to conversations with high-caliber Kingdom leaders and to ongoing coaching augment intellectual capital.

It requires a little more ingenuity to ensure there are Uptick

---

7 Breen and Sternke, *Oikonomics*, Kindle edition, Kindle locations 766–67.
8 Ibid., Kindle locations 617, 649–54.

investments in physical capital and financial capital. In certain Uptick networks, financial capital is a central point of focus. In nearly every in-person gathering of Uptick Entrepreneur, for instance, we discuss how disciples interact with money. These business leaders are accustomed to daily decisions around finances and need significant conversations about money in order to help them make business decisions with a Kingdom mindset. In Uptick Entrepreneur, we discuss topics such as tithing, building wealth without losing your soul, estate planning, strategic and spontaneous gifting, and retirement—all within a framework that treats financial capital as secondary to spiritual and relational capitals.

In other Uptick networks, such as ones focusing on pastoral leaders, the financial capital conversation might be far more basic. Often, we will bring in a financial planner who personally models Kingdom generosity and have them teach basic skills of stewardship. These discussions range from managing student loan and credit card debt, budgeting on a tight income, modeling generosity as a Kingdom leader, and creating habits that position you for substantial generosity over the entire course of your life (and estate).

It is not difficult to find people who can help you grow the financial capital capacity of those whom you lead in an Uptick group. There are scores of savvy disciples who deal with financial capital in shrewd, wise, and generous ways. You can ask them to share for an hour their most important insights; you may be astounded at the life-changes that an hour can prompt in the lives and trajectories of young leaders who have never received such helpful input.

Investing in physical capital can be a bit trickier. (Remember, we said earlier that physical capital pertained to use of time, calendar, and space, and asked if a disciple had a rhythm of life conducive to fruitful, sustainable leadership through attending to what the body needs.) Sometimes the group has people who do not have the fitness or health to withstand a substantial physical challenge within the Uptick year. Other times, factors like meeting environment and inclement weather can stifle opportunities. In these instances, even low-exertion physical capital challenges can bring about *Kairos* moments.

For example, during Uptick Voice (an Uptick group for those who lead networks of women), we customarily have Uptickers walk a simple Labyrinth.[9] Using the LifeShapes Circle as a lens through which to

9 See http://www.holytrinitygnv.org/media/28044/Labyrinth-tri-fold-brochure.pdf , for example.

process, Uptickers then reflect on this Labyrinth walk in comparison to the cultural norm of "climbing the ladder." They compare the different approach the Labyrinth offers—of non-linear progress; of enjoying the journey; of reflecting on where you have already been; of how you are moving forward toward the center of things, even when it seems, at times, like you are walking in the opposite direction; of the space in the center of the Labyrinth that can be shared with others. And the journey *out* from the center is as important as the journey *into* the center. All of this is opposed to our cultural "ladder" mindset, where everyone tries to climb the next rung of the ladder as quickly and as competitively as possible, and where only one person can be at the top of the ladder.[10]

In other Uptick networks, we have provided a moderate-to-strong physical capital challenge in order to grow not only that particular capital but other ones as well. In one memorable Uptick physical challenge experience, our group went rappelling down the side of a mountain. (We gave strong safety training and certified guides for the experience.) Having never rappelled before, I can personally attest to how my spiritual capital was tested and stretched by stepping backward off the side of a cliff! Processing the experience using the Circle afterward, one Uptick participant, who was especially gifted in intellectual capital, described how this moment of physical challenge terrified him—and also became a place of breakthrough in his faith.

In other physical capital challenge experiences, such as the following recounted by Upticker Lynette Hicks, the growth can be life-altering:

"

> Uptick was an amazing journey in discipleship formation.
> My natural instinct has been to isolate myself from all others.
> However, the wonderful friends of my Uptick experience became
> mirrors and forced me to face myself in a very real way that I
> couldn't have done alone.
>
> One thing I faced in Uptick was my fear. During our July retreat, the
> reality of what a 'high ropes course' actually meant did not strike me
> until we were headed up the mountain. When I saw the scrawny bits
> of rope and cable secured to the trees with simple bolts and wood,
> I completely lost my nerve. Even though I knew I would be wearing
> a helmet and harness, I just couldn't picture myself walking across

---

10 Here, we are in debt to Uptick teaching done by the masterful Laine Scales at Baylor University: https://www. baylor.edu/social_work/index.php?id=947236 . Thanks, Laine!

ropes and wooden boards high in the mountains.

I made up my mind that, at the very least, I was going to attempt this course. Other people were investing in me by making this opportunity possible, so I wanted to honor them and invest in my own journey. However, the more I watched others take on the high ropes, the more unnerved I became. I remember clearly one of my friends asking me, 'Lynette, what are you really afraid of?'

This question made me think deeper about what I was feeling. Dressed in my harness and helmet, accessorized with my rope clamps, I made my way up the ladder to the first tree. I secured my clamp to the first rope and stepped out on the cable. The uneasy feeling at the pit of my stomach was the fear of losing control. It wasn't the height but the feeling of being exposed, with no ability to save myself if I misstepped. The feeling of not having anything stable under my feet. What if I made a mistake or lost my grip? There was nothing else for me to hold on to, and this was my first time in this experience, so I couldn't rely on what I knew. I couldn't save myself.

Halfway through the course I was terrified, sweating, wobbling, shaking, and just praying it would be over. I remember repeating to myself, 'God, I'm so scared.' Then out of nowhere I heard, 'This is how you live your life, in fear.' I was stunned because I knew that voice very well, and I could not believe that God wanted to have a conversation with me while I was in the woods walking on ropes in the air. The dialogue went as follows:

Me: Really God? Now? Up here?!

God: Yes. Now. Right here. You live your life in fear every day. The fear of losing people, fear of being hurt, fear of not being enough, fear of losing control.

Me: Yeah, God, you're right; I definitely do that. I need to have some type of control.

God: You are always trying to save yourself when you get scared— as if I'm not enough. Shift your walk from fear to faith.

Me: Okay, God, thanks so much for that. I'll start working on that as soon as I'm safe on the ground.

God: No. Start now in this place of fear. With every step you take moving forward say to yourself, 'Lord I trust you.'

When I took my next step I began to say, 'Lord, I trust you.' I kept repeating those words with every step. After the third step, what I noticed was the walk got easier. The journey moved more quickly, and I wobbled less. I was not concentrating on how afraid I was, but I focused my attention on confidence in God to get me through the course. I made it to the end and realized God's way was safer than my way. At the end of the course, we had to ride the zip line down. I hesitated again because we had to just sort of hop off a wooden platform. One of the women in the group yelled, 'Just surrender Lynette!' and I let go and enjoyed the ride down.

Since this experience, I have worked hard to really trust in the Lord with all my heart. What I learned about myself is that there have been many times in my life where I have been so afraid of falling that I tried to control every aspect of the situation. I relied on myself, my strength, my way, my power and I ended up falling anyway, most times quite hard. However, just like in the trees in Virginia, all God ever wanted me to do was trust him with every step—the sure steps and the wobbly ones.

"

Investing in one of the five capitals can thus pay dividends in that capital as well as others. Here, Lynette's physical capital grew—but the real growth was in her spiritual and relational capitals.

EVALUATING EFFECTIVENESS IN THE FIVE CAPITALS

All of the capitals above financial take longer to grow, but they are also more valuable and last longer. Spiritual capital, the most valuable capital, lasts forever. But it also takes the longest to grow. [11]

—MIKE BREEN AND BEN STERNKE

One of the most useful Uptick applications of the five capitals framework is determining how to address a weak or missing capital in an individual or within a system. The core principle is that you can augment a missing capital by leveraging the capitals you already possess. For instance, if you are deficit in financial capital, you apply the other capitals you possess toward it:

---

11 Breen and Sternke, *Oikonomics*, Kindle edition, Kindle locations 838–39.

- **Spiritual**—pray, asking God for insight and blessing about your financial situation;
- **Relational**—utilize the networks of people you know to gain wisdom around financial matters;
- **Physical**—spend the requisite time and attention to monitor your money usage and goals;
- **Intellectual**—familiarize yourself with the best ideas for good stewardship, learning best financial practices, utilizing appropriate money management tools (such as apps and software).

When we do that, we frame financial capital appropriately as a matter of our life with God; we view money within a community-of-faith-context; we do our due diligence of devoting our time to the subject and leverage our education and intellect to the issue. Thus, by using the capitals we possess toward the one we need, we can grow the missing capital. There is strong biblical precedent for wise (and unwise) interaction of the capitals:

Adam and Eve gave away their relational capital with God for intellectual capital—"knowing good and evil."

Abraham left his family (relational capital) to obey God, going to the new land God had call him to (spiritual capital), letting Lot take the better land (financial capital), and being rewarded for it.

Peter left his nets (the financial capital of his livelihood) to follow Jesus (spiritual capital). Matthew did the same with his livelihood of tax collecting.

King Saul was chosen because of an abundance of physical capital (he was tall and handsome), while King David, his successor, had an abundance of spiritual capital. Saul ended his kingly career in ruin, while David is considered Israel's greatest king.[12]

12 Ibid., Kindle locations 510–11.

In this biblical manner, the five capitals provide a wonderful wisdom tool for evaluating where you are and where you want to go. One Upticker describes how she thus applied the five capitals framework to focus and evaluate her leadership setting:

"

Each year I get the opportunity to invest in a team of young adults. Uptick was a pivotal experience for many reasons; one of the main ones being in how it directly impacted my investment into the Summer Leadership Team. Before Uptick, I was constantly searching for resources and programs on how to invest in the team. However, Uptick taught me to focus more on intentional discipleship than a well-polished program. I focused on discipleship primarily by teaching and using the five capitals. I ceased worrying about checking off boxes or to-do lists of programs. And along with that, I wanted to let the people who come through the Summer Leadership Team know that I care for them relationally. I don't see them as projects or numbers I need to fulfill some type of requirement, but rather as real people with whom I am willing and able to give access to my life as I look to Jesus. The five capitals gave structure without creating harsh boundaries. This has shaped my outlook and implementation with the Summer Leadership Team, and a number of team members have expressed to me multiple times how they utilize the teaching of the five capitals, and how they have taught it to other people as well. To me, this is discipleship at its best, with people continuing to love and pour into others as we all try to embrace Kingdom 'here on earth as it is in heaven.'[13]

"

As this Upticker mentions, the five capitals can change the scorecard for how we assess our lives and leadership.

---

13 Upticker Melanie Lassiter, Hampton, Virginia.

8

Character, Chemistry, Capacity: The Uptick Pipeline

The way to change leadership results is to change what leaders are doing and thinking about. Leaders have to live the change they seek. This is not easy; it requires ruthless self-management [...]. This is where the scorecard discussions [...] will come into helpful play.[1]

REGGIE MCNEAL

SCORECARDS—OLD AND NEW

In the Baptist church of my youth, Friendly Avenue Baptist Church in Greensboro, North Carolina, I brought a "Six-Point Envelope" (carrying my offering) to church every Sunday. Alongside of a record of how diligent I had been with inviting people to Sunday school, I was to check dutifully the (graded) box beside each of the six I had completed that week:

JANUARY 1ST SUNDAY My regular offering for the unified budget of my church				61
NAME				
AMOUNT $				
CLASS		DEPT		

	Contacts	**Prospects**	**Members**	**Total**
☐ Present				
☐ Bible Brought	Visits			
☐ Bible Read Daily	Phone Calls			
☐ Lesson Studied				
☐ Giving	Letters & Cards			
☐ Worship Attendance	Total Contacts			

1 Reggie McNeal, *Missional Renaissance: Changing the Scorecard for the Church* (1st ed.) (California: Jossey-Bass, 2009), 158.

The Six-Point Envelope served as a type of scorecard. Using a scorecard is a signal of a high-expectation community of faith—and that is a good thing.

However, that particular scorecard would be incomplete in our post-Christendom culture. What you measure, you value. And so, the metrics of the scorecard in a post-Christendom era today must reflect this new missionary context and task. What might that new scorecard measure? For while measuring is important, measuring the *right* things is even more important.

Around the turn of the century, I attended an annual meeting with professional counterparts at the American Society for Church Growth.[2] There, speaker Reggie McNeal offered a blunt critique on the nature and name of the group itself, strongly suggesting that "church growth" was no longer the required target for the day. The correct target, he proposed, was *Kingdom* growth. Emerging goals were not to be institutional, but missional. New metrics should not reflect how many people are coming *into* churches, but rather how churches are moving *outward* in ministry to the world.

McNeal later turned his work into books exploring similar shifts and posing some tough questions for the church.[3] Much of his work crystalized around the metaphor of changing the missional "scorecard." Instead of measuring (and valuing) the ABCs (Attendance, Buildings and Cash—also sometimes called "Nickels and Noses," or, even less elegantly, "Butts in Seats and Dollars in Plates"), disciples today need a new "scorecard," which would include:

- Developing disciples instead of increasing numbers of church members;
- Fostering the rise of new, apostolic leadership;
- Shifting from planning ongoing programs in churches to preparation for the challenges of an uncertain world;
- Recalibrating from an internal focus to an external focus, ending the model of the church as an exclusive social club;
- De-emphasizing church programs and ministries as the core activity, in favor of developing people spiritually; and

2 See "American Society for Church Growth," *Wikipedia*, https://en.wikipedia.org/wiki/American_Society_for_Church_Growth . Founded by Donald McGavran and Peter Wagner in 1986 to build on practices of the Church Growth Movement.

3 See Reggie McNeal, *The Present Future: Six Tough Questions for the Church* (1st ed.) (California: Jossey-Bass, 2003) and *Missional Renaissance*. Interestingly, some of his prophetic predictions foreshadowed Uptick's emphasis on "equipping apostolic leaders with a discipleship orientation."

- Expanding from leadership by professional clergy/experts alone to leadership shared by everyone in the community.

One might quibble with McNeal on certain elements of the new scorecard, but as a whole, his core idea was sound. Ahead of the curve, he saw that the church was, and is, in a new day, with a new type of missionary work before us, and that new benchmarks would be required to measure how well (or poorly) we are doing.

Churches dating back to the 1980s had already been exploring this task of changing the missional scorecard. Famously, Willow Creek Community Church in Chicago had a "5Gs" scorecard, measuring participation in Grace, Growth, Group, Gifts, and Good Stewardship.[4] Rick Warren led Saddleback Community Church in California to adopt the "Baseball Diamond" of Membership, Maturity, Ministry, and Missions as its scorecard:

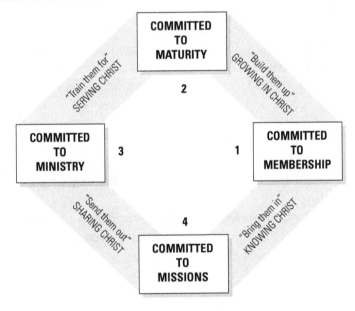

[5]

Both the 5Gs and the Baseball Diamond represent scorecards. You know where you stand on the base paths within the metrics and have an idea of the next steps you need to take. And people grow when they know the steps.

But we are no longer in the 1980s and 1990s, and, as McNeal pointed out at the turn of the century, we need new scorecards in today's missionary environment. Accordingly, many strategists in our day have sought to give new language to new scorecards. For example, distributing the discipleship task away from church committees alone and into the workforce, Amy Sherman brilliantly suggests four pathways:

1. **Bloom**: promote the Kingdom in and through your daily work;
2. **Donate**: volunteer your vocational talent outside your day job;
3. **Invent**: launch a social enterprise; and
4. **Invest**: participate in a church's targeted initiative.[6]

In like manner, speaking in regard to systems such as congregations or denominations, Paul Maconochie of 3DM uses the language of "slow track/fast track" to suggest strategies for building movements out of the local church.[7]

"Slow track" items in this scorecard suggest a steady, long-haul approach to changing the church or denomination toward movemental thinking and behavior. Tactics over time for doing this include steady, repeated, and sharpened messaging on philosophy of mission; creating shared language around the work; and developing a continuum for discipleship growth. Slow track elements include:

- Moving from being pastor-led to being team-led;
- Moving from single- to multi-site and/or engaging in church planting;
- Developing networks of churches in the city and region;
- Tapping into spiritual power through prayer, engaged worship, and spiritual gifts; and
- Developing intercessory and missional partnerships.

Over time, "slow track" behaviors such as frequent preaching on discipleship and mission, keeping emerging generations at the center of church or organizational life, and creating on-ramps for missional engagement with the poor and the wealthy will "warm the loaf" or

---

6 See http://www.vocationalstewardship.org/pathways/ and also Amy Sherman, *Kingdom Calling: Vocational Stewardship for the Common Good* (Illinois: IVP books, 2011).
7 In a year-long online huddle led by Paul Maconochie for an international, multi-denominational group of network or movement leaders.

slowly alter the ethos and scorecard of a community.[8]

However, simultaneously, a system will want also to engage in "fast track" behaviors which "add the yeast" to the system. Often this takes the form of identifying "people of peace" (high-capacity and highly eager leaders who model the lifestyle and practices of missional discipleship), and doubling down on equipping and empowering them to be pacesetting disciple-makers within the system. The system leader wisely calibrates both slow and fast track activities, increasing the temperature of the oven, as well as adding the yeast that causes the bread to rise.

THE UPTICK SCORECARD: LEADERSHIP PIPELINE

When asked to give the overall grand vision of Uptick in thirty seconds, I generally respond that I can do it in three: "Uptickers leading Upticks." There is quite a bit packed into those three words, but the gist is that the Uptick network wants to create high-capacity young adult disciples who are in turn able to reproduce similar strategic communities of disciples and leaders within and beyond their own contexts.

If "Uptickers leading Upticks" is the destination, then what are the mile markers that let you know you're getting there? It was clear early on that we needed to think concretely about benchmarking progress, of determining our scorecard.

To do this, we created the Uptick Leadership Pipeline. Since Uptick is grounded in "imitation" of leaders, and not just the dissemination of information, we needed to build an apprentice-type of model. Accordingly, the Uptick Leadership Pipeline is built on a model that loosely resembles how physicians are trained in the United States. The medical model has clear steps: from medical student, to intern, to resident, and often to fellow, to practicing physician. By the time a doctor has gone through this pipeline and into private practice, they have practiced plenty!

The heart of the Uptick pipeline is growth in *character, chemistry,* and *capacity*:

- **Character:** Being and becoming like Jesus (the interior world of a person);

8 For an example of how this is implemented in a local church, see https://www.gracegathering.com/about-us/ .

- **Chemistry**: The ability to work alongside other disciples fruitfully (APEST); and
- **Capacity**: The ability to extend and expand the work of the Kingdom through reproducing disciples.

Embedded in every segment of the journey is the teaching of *competencies*, which become the anvil on which the character, chemistry, and capacity are forged. The pipeline assumes that disciples are lifelong learners. The posture of a disciple is one who forever seeks to grow rather than posing as an expert who has "attained and arrived." Thus, disciples are forever learning new competencies, and the intensity of the Uptick year in introducing new discipleship and leadership competencies is akin to a "loading dose" of medicine. For this reason, the first trait we look for in a prospective Upticker is a strong *hunger* to grow as a disciple.

The three basic movements of the Uptick Leadership Pipeline are:

1. Upticker to Apprentice;
2. Apprentice to Associate; and
3. Associate to Network Leader.

One moves through the pipeline by mastering new competencies at each stage. As competencies accrue, capacity builds. While this book focuses mostly on competencies in the Uptick year, the pipeline helps to define how the trajectory of Uptick could look years down the road. In the same vein as using Future Stories, the pipeline gives Uptickers a path forward beyond the Uptick year. It has also enabled us to identify potential future staff and think in terms of planning and trajectory for the Uptick team. Ultimately, it was designed as a tool for succession planning for the Network Leader as well. The focus of this book, however, is primarily around the move from "Upticker to Apprentice." The ability to catalyze this step on a grand scale is at the heart of the movemental momentum possible through Uptick replication.

To the general principles governing pipeline movement, we now turn.

UPTICK LEADERSHIP PIPELINE: GENERAL PRINCIPLES

The leadership pipeline is the "internal architecture" for growing leaders within a company or system:

> Companies need an enduring architecture to focus human resource processes and programs. The architecture should set common standards for both performance and potential, differentiated by layer of management. It should also establish language and processes to address issues, identify problems, and exploit opportunities effectively.[9]

A detailed outline of the Uptick Leadership Pipeline can be found in appendix nine, "Role Descriptions and Assessments." Here are the key principles that give structure to the pipeline:

1. **Advancement from one level to the next assumes mastery and growth in competencies from earlier levels.** Of course, growth is never entirely linear and without occasional setbacks. But, as a rule of thumb, competencies achieved at one level should be matters in which leaders are "unconsciously competent" when operating at the next level of the pipeline.

2. **Behaviors that lead to success at one level may hamper leadership at another level.** For example, one-on-one discipleship skills at the Uptick leader/participant level may make managing networks of networks more difficult at the Uptick Network Leader level, where managing complexity and teams require skills better suited to leading teams than individuals.

3. **Leaders must grow when advancing from one level to the next, in:**
   - Skill set and management;
   - Time use and network development; and
   - Strategic thinking and implementation.

   Each manifestation of growth demonstrates growth in character, chemistry, and capacity. Better use of time, for instance, is evidence of a disciple's use of the Circle and Semicircle—a rhythm of life that makes hearing from and responding to God an ongoing and recurring divine-human conversation. Better management of skills and strategic thinking reflects having developed the

---

9 Ram Charan, *The Leadership Pipeline: How to Build the Leadership Powered Company* (California: Jossey-Bass, 2011), ix.

chemistry required with a broader and better implementation of APEST teamwork. And all of these practices should then result in leadership at a higher level of capacity, bearing more fruit, and demonstrating more effective Kingdom results.

4. **Advancement from one level to the next is determined by the following factors:**
   - Character, chemistry, and capacity;
   - Ability to work with current constituents (including the Uptick network board) and also extend Uptick's reach into new networks;
   - Demonstrated skill to lead existing networks and develop new ones;
   - Ability to fundraise for specific and overall network development;
   - Strategic vision for innovative disruption and ability to implement.

5. **Key markers in discerning "tipping point" transitions into the next level of leadership include:**
   - From **Upticker** to **Apprentice**: when we see leaders graduate from strong self-leadership to good mentorship of others. The first evidence of this is that the Uptick leader has been able to reproduce a viable, healthy Uptick network. We want every Upticker to advance to this level.
   - From **Apprentice** to **Associate**: when leaders move from managing new networks that they have started to oversee strategic development of self-reproducing networks. Evidence of this points to the person as potential Uptick staff and the networks they create as potential recipients of Uptick "Kingdom venture capital." Growth to this level will be rare (though encouraged) and vetted by results achieved in building the capacity of the overall Uptick network. These leaders contribute to the leadership culture of the entire Uptick network.
   - From **Associate** to **Network Leader**: When a key leader (who is unconsciously competent at creating Uptick networks) demonstrates vision and capacity beyond management of the current Uptick network of networks, and can also inject disruptive innovation, and possibly exponential growth,

into the entire system, then that person is a candidate to be the Uptick Network Leader. Growth to this level is rare but encouraged. It provides not only a robust pool for succession planning, but leaders at these highest levels elevate the overall caliber of Uptick network leadership.

6. **Progression along the Uptick Leadership Pipeline requires:**
   - Greater ability to lead in public events and settings;
   - More initiative and self-management, combined with reduced supervision;
   - Increasing acknowledgment that the role and requirements of the job will evolve and require new intelligences; and
   - An ability to manage the complexity of ever-shifting requirements of leading the work involved.

These general principles frame the internal architecture of the Uptick Leadership Pipeline. Again, for details of the character, chemistry, and capacity work (along with the very specific competencies associated with them), see appendix nine, "Role Descriptions and Assessments."

9

Relational, Social, and Societal Discipleship Intelligence

The first duty of love is to listen.

PAUL TILLICH

THEOLOGICAL FOUNDATION

The theological work of ordinary disciples is to hear from and respond to God. As we hear from God, we discern the truth of divine revelation. We respond to God by interpreting and applying that truth to everyday situations. Paul Tillich's "method of correlation" pictured the work of theology not merely as a "circle" (divine truth alone), but as an "ellipse" which contained both divine truth and the *situation* in which that truth is received. Because our situation changes from moment to moment, our lives as disciples require ongoing theological work, ongoing listening to and responding to God, ever interpreting truth as it applies to our life and situation at that given moment. In this sense, discipleship is always moving between two magnetic poles:

1. Eternal truth as revealed by God, and
2. The moment in which that eternal truth is received.

Divine truth doesn't change, but its interpretation and application to our life and context is ever-evolving. "The method of correlation unites message and situation, questions and answers, human existence and divine manifestation."[1]

Tillich was arguing his case against the approach of his mid-century contemporary, Karl Barth, who insisted on an exclusive focus on truth as divinely revealed, regardless of human context. Visually, Tillich's and

1 Paul Tillich, *Systematic Theology*, Volume 1 (Illinois: University of Chicago Press, 1956), 8.

Barth's theological approaches can be represented as follows:

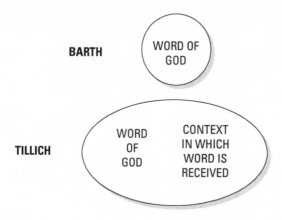

If this is the case—and I agree with Tillich here—then a disciple's leadership task is to learn, know, and come to understand the will of God, but not to stop there. Having understood, the task is then also to interpret and apply revelation of God's will to the context in which revelation is received, including:

1. Local and global **culture**;
2. The history, makeup, and aims of the **community** (your context, i.e. congregation, place of work, etc.); and
3. The nature of your own **calling**, gifts, and roles as a disciple and leader.

Somewhat akin to the Wesleyan Quadrilateral,[2] the ongoing interpretive work of the disciple is to interpret revelation from God in relation to *culture*, *community*, and *calling*:

---

2 See "Wesleyan Quadrilateral," *Wikipedia*, https://en.wikipedia.org/wiki/Wesleyan_Quadrilateral .

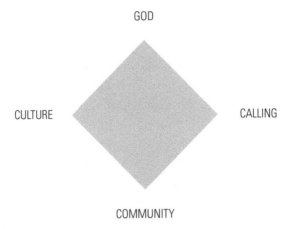

GOD

CULTURE   CALLING

COMMUNITY

Learning to interpret *culture, community and calling* in light of the will of *God* requires cross-disciplinary learning, a curious and investigative spirit, and a willingness to engage with introspective work. In each arena, disciples are responding to Jesus' pivotal words at the heart of the Lord's Prayer (Matthew 6:10), seeking to enact life "on earth as it is in heaven."

The biblical category that describes the totality of this work is *wisdom*. Where there is no clear law, commandment, ordinance, or decree, the Bible instructs those who follow God to use wisdom, under the guidance of the Holy Spirit.[3] Uptick therefore focuses on emotional, social, and societal intelligence functions under this broad biblical category of wisdom.

EMOTIONAL DISCIPLESHIP INTELLIGENCE: "PRESENCE" SKILLS

It's not uncommon for people to overvalue the importance of demonstrating their competence and power, often at the expense of demonstrating their warmth [...]. When we think of nonverbals, we think of how we judge others [...]. We tend to forget, though, the other audience that's influenced by our nonverbals: ourselves. Your body language shapes who you are.[4]

—AMY CUDDY

3 John P. Chandler, *Wise Southern Pastoral Leadership*, Fuller Theological Seminary, unpublished Doctor of Ministry dissertation, 1997.
4 Cuddy, *Presence*, 71ff, 226ff.

Wise leadership grasps the nature of ever-changing human dynamics. It is critical for disciples to understand that those dynamics are taking place *within* them as well as *around* them. For leadership, it is insufficient to be a good reader of the dynamics around you; you must first be aware of what is going on *within* you in order to lead well. Thus, one of the first "intelligences" of a disciple is emotional intelligence (EQ). And when a disciple has strong emotional intelligence, s/he can also build strong relational intelligence. Alluding to Daniel Goleman,[5] Tod Bolsinger puts it this way, "You get your job because of IQ. You keep it because of EQ. High IQ people fail when they are jerks and other people thus choose to let them fail."[6]

When a leader's EQ/relational intelligence is so low that they have run roughshod over the people around them, few lament when they are gone.

This emotional/relational intelligence consists of what we call "presence" skills.[7] Greater presence means being attuned, simultaneously, to internal and contextual dynamics, and to responding adeptly. As mentioned in the Uptick Pedagogy section, we call this the journey of:

self-awareness → **self-regulation** → **social awareness** → **social regulation**

To that end, Uptick participants take up to six inventory/assessments in the year, including (but not limited to) the DISC Personality Profile, Keirsey-Bates Temperament and Character Sorter, the APEST fivefold, Emotional Intelligence 2.0, Discipleship Dynamics Assessment, Enneagram, and StrengthsFinder/CliftonStrengths. Our experience is that at least one of these will "ring the bell" for every Upticker and increase their self-awareness significantly. In particular, this journey of emotional and relational intelligence dovetails nicely with self- and social-awareness regarding one's fivefold intelligence (what Alan Hirsch calls "5Q").

We don't use these instruments simply for self-understanding as an end unto itself; rather, we use assessments to help leaders make adjustments (self-regulation), particularly toward how they are perceived in social

5 Goleman, *Emotional Intelligence*, xv.
6 Bolsinger, Uptick conversation, November 2018, Richmond, Virginia.
7 Taken from Cuddy, *Presence*.

situations by others, and then adjust (social awareness and regulation). We are not interested as much in whether an individual is introverted; we want to help them understand how their introversion functions (or doesn't) in leadership and is interpreted by others in their context.

To give an example, using the DISC instrument, I have learned that I am a high "D" (Dominance) preference leader. I am aware of (and slightly proud of!) that style, which I have typically deemed to be "take charge." However, DISC testing revealed that I have potential blind spots in my "D" style leadership. Did I realize that I could be perceived as:

- Insensitive to those who act slower;
- Impatient with others;
- A selective listener;
- Argumentative and abrupt;
- One who takes on too much, too soon, too fast; and
- Someone who, in conflict, is quick to fight back?

Ouch! Not exactly all-star leadership. However, armed with the self-awareness that I can be perceived as argumentative (even when I don't intend to be), I can move from self- and social- *awareness* toward self- and social- *regulation*. Assessments can help us see ourselves as we are perceived by others, which helps us to interpret and respond to others with better leadership.

Elizabeth Jeffries describes emotional intelligence as having five hierarchical competencies:

Intrapersonal emotional intelligence
1. Self-Awareness
2. Self-Regulation
3. Motivation

Interpersonal emotional intelligence
4. Empathy
5. Social Skills

Core competencies of **self-awareness** include:
- Realistic self-assessment of strengths and limitations;
- Self-directed sense of humor; and
- Self-confidence, or a sound sense of self-worth and capabilities.

Key skills related to **self-regulation** are to:
- Handle feelings appropriately, especially the big three: anger, anxiety, and sadness. To redirect them, soothe yourself, shake them off;
- Suspend judgment and think first; and
- Maintain a sense of optimism, even in the face of failure.[8]

These competencies are critical to "managing relationships, building networks, and the ability to create and lead teams." Quoting Napoleon Bonaparte, Jeffries says they are what help us to "lead others by showing them a future," enabling us to become "merchants of hope."[9]

Finally, Tod Bolsinger captures in concise form some excellent core tactics and strategies we use in coaching Uptickers on the journey from intrapersonal to interpersonal intelligence.[10]

He says, "You are in an emotional system that must be navigated in order to accomplish the mission." To do so, he suggests the following four practices:

1. **Pay attention to your body.**
Are you sick? Exhausted? Is your body breaking down? While some people tend toward hyper-sensitivity (or even hypochondria), many leaders are alarmingly unaware of what is going on with their bodies. Some use practices like meditative or guided prayer, mindfulness or breathing techniques, or yoga to slow down and become aware of where they are carrying stress and tension in their bodies. Another tool is the "Feelings Wheel."[11]

---

8 Jeffries, *What Exceptional Executives Need to Know*, 191; also, corresponding PowerPoint presentation given with Uptick Voice in Waco, Texas, May 2019.
9 Ibid., 20.
10 Bolsinger, Uptick conversation, November 2018.
11 See https://imgur.com/tCWChf6 for one example of many.

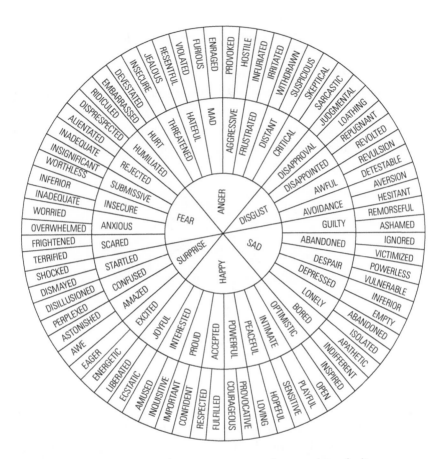

By simply locating and naming core and secondary feelings we are experiencing in the moment, with some refinement, clarity, and precision, we are often able to see how those emotions are working themselves out within our bodies. This is a great help in self-awareness that can lead to self-regulation.

2. Pay attention to where you are spending your time.

We sometimes counsel Uptickers that, if they are emotionally "off" for a sustained time, to conduct a simple time diary for about a week.[12]

Even the brightest people tend to be radically unaware of how much time they spend doing things which are unproductive and counterproductive. Besides helping with efficiency in managing

12 For one of many versions of this tool, see https://www.businesstrainingcollege.com/business/what-is-a-time-diary.htm .

workload, patterns in this diary often provide clues to whether we need to focus on intrapersonal or interpersonal leadership.

3. Focus on seeing over solving.
Bolsinger says, "Adaptation is 90 percent seeing properly." Borrowing from a common counseling mind-frame, one of the ways we try to encourage Uptickers to "see" is to ask within a demanding relationship or conversation, "What's yours? What's mine? What's ours?"

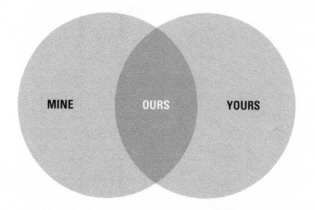

Using this simple lens, it's easier to determine when a situation is not mine to address; to be able to say, "I didn't break them, and I can't fix them." Romans 12:18 says, "If it is possible, so far as it depends on you, live peaceably with all." The trick is, much of it doesn't depend on me! When I can "see" what does and does not belong to me, and to us, I can lead myself—and then lead others—well.

4. Pay attention to what you are paying attention to.
Again, Bolsinger asks, "Who bothers you right now? What's the speck in someone else's eye that is aggravating the log in your eye?"[13] In the same manner as paying attention to what your body, feelings, and allocation of time reveal, noticing what is "sticking in your crawl" or what has your full attention can be illuminating and empowering. Often the very matter one notices in another person is a significant clue to some internal work that needs to be investigated

---

13 Matthew 7:3–5.

by the one looking.[14]

As mentioned in chapter two, growing in self-awareness and self-regulation enables leaders to move from leading out of the "Red Zone" of reactivity, and into the "Blue Zone" of leading reflectively.

RELATIONAL/SOCIAL DISCIPLESHIP INTELLIGENCE: SOFT RELATIONAL SKILLS

Trust is the conduit of influence, and the only way to establish real trust is by being present. Presence is the medium through which trust develops and which ideas travel.[15]

—AMY CUDDY

Closely related to emotional intelligence is the idea of relational or social intelligence. If *intrapersonal* emotional intelligence originates in the self- and social awareness quadrants, then relational or social intelligence generally lives in the realm of *interpersonal* work that involves self- and social regulation.

INTRAPERSONAL INTELLIGENCE
"Self Smart"

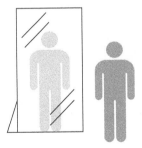

DEFINITION
The ability to access, understand and communicate one's own inner feelings.

INTRAPERSONAL INTELLIGENCE TRAITS
Self-knowledge, deeply aware of one's own feelings, good at following instincts, self-motivated.

14 Bolsinger, Uptick conversation, Richmond, Virginia, November 2018.
15 Cuddy, *Presence*, 74.

INTERPERSONAL INTELLIGENCE
"People Smart"

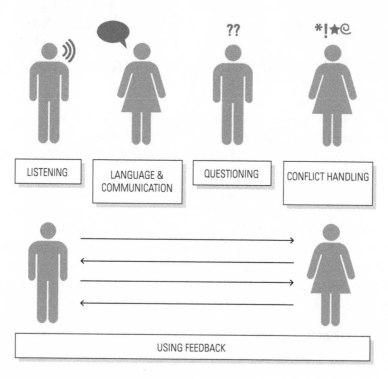

DEFINITION
The ability to understand and interact effectively with others with verbal and nonverbal communication.

INTERPERSONAL INTELLIGENCE TRAITS
Sensitivity to verbal and nonverbal cues, entertaining multiple perspectives, listening and question-asking, giving and receiving feedback, conflict management.

Uptick aims to build competencies, or what we call "soft relational skills," because much of what derails promising young leaders pertains to deficits in interpersonal behaviors. It is hard to measure soft skill growth, but we aim to increase leadership capacity in Uptickers by working on these practices of social intelligence. And, as Cuddy reminds us in an entire chapter of her book about how we can make our bodies "present" in social and public situations, "Tiny tweaks can lead to big changes."[16]

When we talk about Uptick being "intelligent but not academic," quite a bit of that training has to do with growing in social and relational intelligence. A good chunk of "the next 20 percent" involves how to behave in groups. As we have all experienced, a social faux pas can derail us substantially from larger leadership aims. An unintended insult can break a deal or make an enemy.

Yet Uptick also teaches that social awareness and regulation are more than matters of interpersonal savvy. They are also matters of discipleship, in the sense that social awareness and social regulation fundamentally help us focus and attend to the relationships around us—which is holy work. When "covenant relationship" is at the very heart of what it means to follow the God of Jesus Christ, then paying attention to the person or people in front of you is not just "nice bedside manner." It is at the heart of what you model as a leader who demonstrates what life in the beloved community is like.

I love the evolving term, "social graces."[17] Disregard older debutante, finishing school, cotillion, or charm school connotations of this term; we aren't interested in their class-based coding, gender expectations, or royal customs. But in the evolving sense, a person of any socio-economic standing could be said to practice social graces. In the newer sense, they are becoming matters of a sophisticated alertness to protocol, and to what is fitting, hospitable, and honorable. One who practices diligent attentiveness to the people nearby puts others at ease, making genuine interaction and conversation possible. In this way, social graces can build spiritual and relational capital and as such are part of the proper work of discipleship.

POSTURE MATTERS: SOLER

How do you know if a person is lying? If you're like most people, your first response will be something like, "Liars don't make eye contact." Judging a person's honesty is

---

16 Ibid., chapter ten, 249–71.
17 According to *Definitions* "social graces are skills used to interact politely in social situations They include manners, etiquette, deportment, and fashion. These skills were once taught to young women at a finishing school or charm school. The focus of social graces has changed over the last century recently with an emphasis on business etiquette and international protocol." https://www.definitions.net/definition/social+graces .

> *[...] about how well or poorly our multiple channels of*
> *communication—facial expressions, posture, movement,*
> *vocal qualities, speech—cooperate. When we are being*
> *inauthentic—projecting a false emotion or covering a*
> *real one—our nonverbal and verbal behaviors begin to*
> *misalign. Our facial expressions don't match the words*
> *we're saying. Our postures are out of sync with our*
> *voices.*[18]
>
> —AMY CUDDY

When our posture or presence is poor, we can be perceived as less than trustworthy—even when that is not the case. Being relationally aware is a matter not only of the true things we are saying, but also of how people *perceive* truthfulness, and how that is reflected in our posture. Therefore, fundamental to social awareness and social regulation are elemental posture skills such as:

- **Alertness**—knowing what has been "brought into" the room, and what is going on in and around the room;
- **Proprioception**—having a sense of where you are in relation to other people, things, and events in the room;
- **Presence**—mindful attentiveness to yourself in relation to others in the present moment, without undue attention deflected by the past or future;
- **Poise**—the ability to maintain presence and equilibrium and not be rattled by unexpected disruptions or distractions; and
- **Courtesy**—politeness, kindness, or gentleness that regards the well-being of those around you as greatly important.

Of course, there are many other skills, but these are basic ones, and most Uptickers already value them, as well as having some ability in them. However, many have never been given concrete instruction on how to practice them. This lack of training, combined with the ubiquity of our cell phones, often conspires to make us less than socially aware. Many haven't learned how to be fully present in social interactions.

Because of this, Uptick teaches some basic things about our social posture—how we position ourselves vis-à-vis others in social settings.

18 Cuddy, *Presence*, 37.

Whether in a "formal" leadership setting or not, we are always leading and modeling discipleship (or not) in any social setting. These posture skills help Uptickers to be "all there" in relation to other people.

The acronym "SOLER" was developed by Gerard Egan in 1986 to assist new counselors in how to put their clients at ease through body language.[19] Learning to do so is a straightforward skill in a therapeutic setting; what is trickier is how to be SOLER with an individual while within a larger social setting. Any Upticker can grow in social graces by regulating their sitting or standing posture to another person or group in this way:[20]

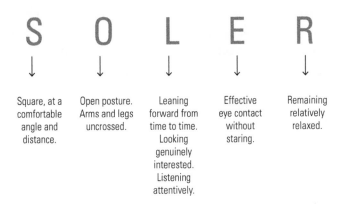

S	O	L	E	R
↓	↓	↓	↓	↓
Square, at a comfortable angle and distance.	Open posture. Arms and legs uncrossed.	Leaning forward from time to time. Looking genuinely interested. Listening attentively.	Effective eye contact without staring.	Remaining relatively relaxed.

- **Square**—Face the other person directly to signal that you are engaged, interested, and actively listening. Sit up straight if sitting and stand up straight if standing. Maintain proper distance for the nature of the conversation you are having and the surroundings. You may tilt your shoulders slightly (for instance, to a "five o'clock" position) to dispel any feelings of intimidation, but your face should be square onto the face of the other(s).
- **Open**—Uncross your arms and legs to convey a sense of transparency, honesty, and a willingness to receive or share.
- **Leaning in**—This communicates genuine interest and lets the other person know that your focus is to hear and understand them.

19 Gerard Egan and Robert J. Reese, *The Skilled Helper: A Problem-Management and Opportunity-Development Approach to Helping* (California: Brooks Cole, 2018).
20 Diagram adapted from https://atraineecounselor.wordpress.com/2016/02/27/counseling-basics-soler/ .

- **Eye contact**—Looking directly at another person (without staring) indicates that they are your top priority and that this current interaction is your top value. (Here is where a smartphone is an omnipresent competitor, ever tempting one to break eye contact.)
- **Relax**—Reduce fidgeting, which conveys anxiety. Nervous movements communicate you have something else on your mind, would rather be somewhere else, and/or you are not interested in them. Fidgeting also tends to lead others to imitate your restlessness.

Like many aspects of discipleship, being SOLER with people in social settings is simple to understand, but hard to implement. It is difficult to overstate the positive impact it can have when applied in social settings.

SOFT SKILLS BOOT CAMP: ETIQUETTE TRAINING

According to Harvard University, the Carnegie Foundation and Stanford Research Institute, 85% of job success is based on "soft skills" while only 15% is based on technical knowledge. Ninety percent of a first impression is based on nonverbal skills. Today much business is conducted at the lunch or dinner table, so don't just guess at table manners; know them.[21]

—KAREN BOWLES

Karen Bowles, Founder and Director of the Etiquette School of the Commonwealth, has worked with business executives, emerging academic stars, and children who grew up with little or no adult supervision. She is also a disciple of Jesus and is passionate about helping Uptick leaders thrive in social environments. Etiquette, she frequently says, is not about lifting your pinkie when holding a teacup; it is about being comfortable in the setting you are in so that you put your first and best attention on the person or people with you, making them comfortable.

Uptickers have at times approached etiquette sessions with suspicion. Some imagine etiquette to be trivial, decidedly unimportant when

---

21 Karen Bowles, Founder and Director, Etiquette School of the Commonwealth, http://www.etiquetteva.com/About.html . I am deeply grateful for Karen, and the skill and grace with which she has helped to equip hundreds of Uptickers toward greater social and relational discipleship intelligence.

compared to the weightier matters they are trying to address. Others view manners as primarily a class or race code, a socio-economic status signifier, or the mores by which the privileged maintain power and control over those who don't have it.

It is important to have these broader conversations, and in Uptick, we do. We also teach that etiquette is a matter of how to lead within social settings, thus adding spiritual and relational capital to the lives of those with whom we interact. Practicing good etiquette is akin to understanding the rules of the road, so that we may drive safely, efficiently, and effectively alongside other drivers. We have received frequent feedback over the years from initially wary Uptickers who later found etiquette training to be empowering. Many have described feeling far more confident in social situations after this instruction.

Here are a few key etiquette areas critical to social awareness and regulation to which we give attention:

Meals

> We (average person) have 10,000 taste buds—that's how much God loves us. Our 10,000 taste buds are a show of grace and an expression of God's love.[22]
>
> —KAREN BOWLES

As was true with Jesus in the Gospels, an incredible amount of discipleship and ministry today occurs at the table. Learning how to be attentive at the table is a form of practicing radical hospitality. Again, the point is not to learn how to act if you are invited to dine with royalty; you really won't need to know the proper use of a finger bowl in most situations. But it is important to feel comfortable with the rules of engagement at the table, especially when a social faux pas can injure more than your pride.

Bob Russell has helped to train Uptickers since 2007. Every year, he takes the group to an upscale restaurant. He provides advance guidance on proper attire and what to expect with the menu and venue. Bob often tells the group that over time they will encounter people who have the potential to fund ministry in significant ways. These upscale restaurants may not be typical for young leaders, but they are for many people—

22 Karen Bowles, Uptick gathering, Fredericksburg, Virginia, July 2019.

and it is important not to be so flustered by the menu and venue that you forget the ministry focus with the person.

This is great advice. We often role play etiquette meal training as a business lunch where the Upticker plans to ask a prospective donor for help with ministry. When you are in this situation, it helps to know which fork is used for the salad and which direction to pass dishes around the table. Doing so correctly may not visibly impress your tablemates; but doing so poorly may derail things you had hoped to achieve. It is important to be proficient at the table in order to utilize it as a space for building spiritual and relational capital.

Networking

Another area for etiquette training is how to network a room. Specific skills covered here include:

- How to meet and greet new people;
- How to get into and out of a conversation (in my opinion, saying hello and goodbye well is incredibly important in life, ministry, and discipleship);
- The proper way to shake hands;
- How to introduce yourself and others;
- Where to stand and what to say when you are trying to network a room full of strangers;
- Dealing with food and drink while standing in social or business situations; and
- Appropriate (and inappropriate) conversation topics.

Some Uptickers are naturally talented and charming and do these things well as second nature. Many, however, have benefited from concrete direction about the goals and means of "working a room."

Dress

"What to wear" can be tricky for a number of wider cultural reasons related to gender, race, socio-economic status, and generational differences. Uptick training has been to focus on contextually appropriate expectations for public environments. For instance, one piece of advice we give to those who are preaching is to dress as if you are dressed for work, even if congregation members are very informally dressed. Generally, if in doubt, dress one step higher than your hearers if you don't know what is expected in the social context. (It is easier to dress down a bit if you are over-dressed than to dress up if you are under-dressed.)

For leaders who happen to be female, the conversation about apparel can be a minefield to navigate. We take Uptick Voice groups of women to a local television station to have them interact with female news anchors, advertising managers, and station directors—all of whom receive frequent and pointed viewer commentary on what the women of their station are wearing on-air. These industry leaders are savvy about what (and what not) to wear, and some of these conversations have been quite lively and specific.[23] Upticker Jenn Leneus, writing soon after these interactions with etiquette training and television personnel, said:

> **"**
>
> *I'm reflecting and want to thank you for giving me an opportunity to experience these frank conversations in Uptick Voice. My life is being transformed from the inside out and I have a longing for more growth, a desire to experience Christ on another level, to minister on another level, to walk into my purpose with a boldness and a confidence that I did not have before. Based on last week I have a lot of work to do and a lot of adjustments to make, but this training has laid down a solid foundation for me.*
>
> **"**

Smartphone

I don't think there is a more pervasive, persistent, and omnipresent competitor to relational and social intelligence for disciples than the smartphone. Studies are evolving rapidly in this area, but in recent years, statistics indicate that the average person in the United States checks their smartphone fifty to eighty times per day, with millennials

---

23 I am deeply grateful to my friends at NBC-29 WVIR in Charlottesville for their generous and helpful sharing with Uptick leaders over the years: Harold Wright, Sharon Gregory, David Foky, and Terri Thelin.

averaging up to 150 times per day.[24] Many simultaneously report that such frequency improves communication and connection in their lives, while also (paradoxically) saying that smartphone use has been a significantly negative factor in some important relationships. Suffice to say that all of us would do well with better phone etiquette, and Uptick training includes concrete guidance and ground rules around common situations, such as when circumstances allow you to interrupt a meal to answer the phone.[25]

Thank You Notes

There is great power in a handwritten thank you note, and Uptick etiquette training includes instruction on how to write, what to say, and when to send one.

Improvisational Speech Skills

Public speaking remains one of the top fears in North American life,[26] yet many leadership contexts often entail being called on to "say a few words" to a gathered group. One Uptick exercise involves having participants pick a slip of paper out of a metal coffee can with a topic written on it. They are given thirty seconds to gather their wits, then asked to speak on that topic for two minutes. An observer stands in the back of the room with the can, and every time the speaker says, "um," "you know," "like," or other common vocal tics, the observer drops a hard bean into the can. With every "ping," the speaker becomes more aware of their own sloppy vocal habits. S/he also learns how to maintain poise in the face of distractions.

Social mores evolve, and these particular points of emphasis may not endure as the prime arenas for etiquette training in years to come, or in different cultural contexts. However, we have found it to be

24 See Todd Spangler, "Are Americans Addicted to Smartphones? U.S. Consumers Check Their Phones 52 Times Daily, Study Finds," *Variety*, November 14, 2018. https://variety.com/2018/digital/news/smartphone-addiction-study-check-phones-52-times-daily-1203028454/ ; and John Brandon "The Surprising Reason Millennials Check Their Phones 150 Times a Day," *Inc*, April 17, 2017. https://www.inc.com/john-brandon/science-says-this-is-the-reason-millennials-check-their-phones-150-times-per-day.html .

25 The answer (for those dying to know): almost never. If there is an anticipated emergency or need (such as a babysitter who knows to call if a childcare situation arises), you may inform your table-mates ahead of time that you may get a call from the babysitter that you will need to take. Apologize in advance, apologize again as you leave the table to receive the call, and otherwise put away your cell phone while at the table.

26 "The Top 10 Fears of 2018," The Chapman University Survey of American Fears. https://www.chapman.edu/wilkinson/research-centers/babbie-center/survey-american-fears.aspx .

significant within the general Uptick formation. First, it is (generally) gratefully received and something participants are glad they now know. Second, Uptick donors are often delighted to learn that Uptick includes this training in matters as basic as hygiene and professional demeanor. They perceive a deep need for instruction in protocol and comportment among young leaders and are grateful that Uptick is providing it. Finally, almost every Upticker is able to make a strong connection that practicing these social graces leads to a better ability to add spiritual and relational capitals to a group or relationship.

SOCIAL/SOCIETAL DISCIPLESHIP INTELLIGENCE: THE DISCIPLESHIP DYNAMICS ASSESSMENT

When talking about different discipleship "intelligences," Uptick clearly has far more experience in exploring and forming disciples in emotional, relational, and social intelligences than it does in societal intelligence and impact. (I am using "social" in the sense of interpersonal relationships, and "societal" in terms of how the individual relates to the sphere and concerns of the greater society.) Part of this is due to the relatively young age of Uptick. In addition, as a relatively young initiative, Uptick has only recently begun amassing enough graduates to enter any conversations about societal impact. While we forecast and pray for societal impact over time, it is still early in the game for Uptick to do so. I pray for the day when Uptickers begin Uptick networks in contexts where there are no nice hotels, restaurants, or air travel; where proper business etiquette concerns are replaced by matters of survival in contexts of war or starvation; where formal educational credentials are scarce or not a priority; where the poor receive proper Uptick discipleship training in contexts appropriate to where they are called to lead. We are not there yet—but this is where I pray that the native intelligence of future Uptick leaders will create ever-increasing Uptick networks among the least, the last, and the lost—just as Jesus did. It was central to how he changed the world.

As Uptick evolves in gaining societal intelligence for discipleship, four things give cause for hope:

1. Most Uptick candidates demonstrate great appetite for leadership conversations around societal impact and the discipleship skills required to lead in that.

2. Uptick's governing board identifies our overall Uptick network's primary fivefold gifting as prophetic (followed by apostolic and then teaching). Several key staff and board members are fivefold prophets. Over time, I believe the makeup of our leadership team will keep Uptick strategically focused on leading with a prophetic voice. (This will also keep the last, least, and lost before us.)

3. Uptick recently received a major grant to start several new networks in metropolitan areas of Virginia around themes of "intercultural intelligence." These "Uptick Catalyst" groups will explore discipleship themes vis-à-vis race, class, and socio-economic status in high-density areas populated by many people groups. What we learn from Uptick Catalyst will benefit overall Uptick societal intelligences for discipleship.

4. And finally, Uptick has had some success experimenting with the Discipleship Dynamics Assessment:

The Discipleship Dynamics Assessment (DDA) is a biblical, comprehensive, practical resource offering individuals and churches clear understanding of their current discipleship maturity in 5 Dimensions and up to 35 Outcomes that touch on all facets of the Christian life. There is no other resource available that integrates Spiritual Formation (loving God with all our being), Personal Wholeness (healthy self-respect), Healthy Relationships (loving our neighbor as ourselves), Vocational Clarity (having a clear sense of purpose) and Economics and Work (our labor at home or in the workplace). The DDA is not a curriculum or a program; it is a vision of whole-life discipleship that will inform both individuals and groups of areas they need to improve as well as strengths to develop. [27]

Scattered through these five discipleship categories are benchmark questions pertaining to societal intelligence and impact, such as:

- **Spiritual formation:** *do I pursue biblical principles for living?*
- **Personal wholeness:** *am I living with a clean conscience?*

---

27 https://discipleshipdynamics.com/about-the-assessment/ .

- **Healthy relationships:** *am I sensitive to the marginalized?*
- **Vocational clarity:** *am I seeking the common good?*
- **Economics and work:** *am I a steward of the environment?*

These are only a sampling of the forty discipleship categories which are tested several times throughout the Uptick year. More quantitatively comprehensive than any other instrument we have used, the Discipleship Dynamics Assessment tracks progress in the integration of faith and communal life. In this sense, it is a promising tool for helping Uptick leaders with metrics of growth in societal intelligence. Until now, we have used an "end of the Uptick year survey,"[28] tracking outcomes pertaining to personal and social growth. Eventually we hope to incorporate more tools like the Discipleship Dynamics Assessment so that we may track societal intelligence as well.

SUMMARY

In this section on benchmarks, we asked:

- How can we tell when an Uptick network is working?
- How do we determine measurable progress in discipleship skills?
- Are there ways to train Uptickers in "soft relational" competencies for leadership?

The "five capitals" serve as our overall framework evaluating Uptickers' growth. The Uptick Leadership Pipeline helped to describe checklists for how we track individual gains in very specific competencies. Finally, we noted that growth in the interpersonal intelligences (emotional-relational, social, and societal) can be difficult to quantify. However, as we have explored in this chapter, Uptick has experimented with some training and tools that we believe have helped to build soft relational skills in Uptickers. You can use them as well in making disciples through your Uptick network.

We now turn from impacting individuals through Uptick to how Uptick can impact larger systems.

---

28 See appendix six, "Uptick 'Metrics of Success' Survey."

10

Outcomes for Systems Through Uptick

Kingdom movements:
Are focused on making disciples of Jesus who can make
disciples who can make disciples;
Are scalable and sustainable;
Are highly reproducible on every level of group size;
Are lightweight and low maintenance;
Are about low control and high accountability;
Have strong and flexible leadership patterns;
Often find identity expressed through axioms and icons;
Live on the continuum of the organized and organic.[1]

MIKE BREEN

The "end game" for disciples of Jesus is to participate in and contribute to the Kingdom of God, and Uptick is one of many vehicles that can be used to give focus and momentum to that grand goal. As a process for disciple making, it can infuse "movemental thinking," not only into the lives of its participants, but also into wider systems and contexts. In other words, Uptick has the power to impact not only intimate, personal, and social spaces, but also public spaces. Specifically, it can influence organizational cultures and broader systems to tilt toward movemental leadership.

Now that we have explored at length how Uptick can impact individuals and build a collective of pioneering young leaders who encourage and challenge one another, we now pivot to discuss how such a collective might benefit the larger contexts of which it is a part. Your "system" may be a denomination or a congregation, a company or a department, a team or a youth group. The organization may be a startup that wants to build disciple making into its DNA. Or, as is the

1 Breen and the 3DM Team, *Leading Kingdom Movements*, Kindle edition, Kindle locations 1120–26.

case in Uptick's origins, your greater context within which you lead may be a system at or beyond organizational midlife and is therefore looking for ways to revitalize its leadership pipeline. If you are a leader within such a context, you can utilize Uptick as a vehicle to affect the entire system positively by both infusing a movemental ethos and by providing a vehicle for implementation.

As Edgar Schein puts it in his masterful *Organizational Culture and Leadership*:

> Culture evolves through the entry into the organization of people with new assumptions and with different experiences of different parts of the organization. Leaders have the power to enhance diversity and encourage subculture formation, or they can, through selection and promotion, reduce diversity and thus manipulate the direction in which a given organization evolves culturally. The more turbulent the environment, the more important it is for the organization to maximize diversity, therefore maximizing its chances of being able to adjust to whatever new challenges the environment creates by having a wider selection of hybrids available.[2]

As a healthy subculture, Uptick can enrich the environment of broader cultures or systems, widening their ability to move effectively, and with agility, to respond to new and changing circumstances. Uptick can do this by introducing new leaders (and therefore "hybrids") to the whole system. It can also serve as a vehicle which reliably delivers discipleship and leadership intelligences to serve within that wider context. Using an exercise analogy, Uptick can have the same effect that stretching, such as practicing yoga, has on the human body—increasing flexibility, range of motion, balance, and core strength.

Uptick can generate positive outcomes by:

1. Infusing movemental ethos into systems, raising its *spiritual capital* and the corresponding strategic focus on the Kingdom work of carrying out the Great Commission and Great Commandment; and
2. Increasing "bridging" or social capacities in systems, elevating its *relational capital* by making systems richer in networks of

2 Edgar H. Schein with Peter Schein, *Organizational Culture and Leadership, The Jossey-Bass Business & Management Series* (5th ed.) (New Jersey: Wiley, 2016), 250.

friendship, trust, and collaboration. Referring back to the Uptick pedagogy of building "bonding and bridging capital" in chapter two, this means that Uptick can:

- *"tighten the net"* through friendship-building exercises and environments that facilitate trust, vulnerability, and deeper in-group bonding; and
- *"widen the net"* by building bridges of relational networks with an increasing range of capable leaders.

The increase in bonds and bridges, in spiritual capital and relational capital, and the resulting expanded capacity to lead adaptively, are demonstrable and positive outcomes for systems. Uptick can create new ethos, "capitals," bonds/bridges, and vehicles for systems and organizations in the same way it can for individuals and small cohorts.

We now turn to five different catchphrases which capture how this works. Uptick can add value to wider systems through:

1. **"Adding a segment"** to the system's leadership pipeline;
2. **"Flooding the system"** with leadership talent;
3. **"Aiding succession planning"** in key leadership roles;
4. **"Infusing five capitals"** into systems; and
5. **"Creating sharing networks"** for talent development.

1. "ADDING A SEGMENT" TO THE SYSTEM'S LEADERSHIP PIPELINE

In the congregation and denomination of my youth, there existed a highly functional leadership pipeline:

- As an infant, you were placed in the church's database and sphere of care through enrollment in the "cradle roll," and included in family-wide worship rituals such as baby dedications.
- As a toddler, you might be part of the church's weekday preschool.
- As a child, you would be a member of an age-graded Sunday school class. (See the Six-Point Envelope from chapter eight for evidence of how you were held accountable by social pressure to be present and to grow.) You would also likely participate in

week-long Vacation Bible Schools during the summer. These camps were inundated with fun activities and snacks but were also intentional environments for biblical literacy, complete with "sword drill" (Bible citation and memorization) contests. They also taught you to invite non-churched friends to church.

- In junior and senior high, you supplemented your participation in Sunday school and worship with being a member of "church youth group." This was designed to be the center of your social life, replete with trips, retreats, fun activities, and service projects. "Youth Sundays" gave students their first opportunities for leading worship in various ways. (I preached my first-ever sermon at a Youth Sunday service.) In addition to core youth group, there were also optional groups such as youth choir or the church softball team.

- When you left for college, you joined your university's local Baptist church under "Watchcare" membership. (This augmented participation in your home church's collegiate ministries on visits home.) In addition, you joined the "Baptist Student Union" (BSU). This provided the collegiate version of your high school youth group, with more emphasis on mission and service work alongside the evangelistic emphasis to "invite your unchurched friends" to participate.

- All along the continuum, you were challenged each Sunday at the conclusion of every single sermon during the "invitation" (really, a challenge as well) to commit to one of the following:

  i Dedicate your life to Christ (*conversion*), followed by a new member's class and baptism;

  ii *Rededicate* your life to Christ (if you had "backslid" or become "lukewarm" in your spiritual journey, or if you had experienced an epiphany);

  iii *Move your membership* to this church (if you were part of another church);

  iv *"Surrender to the call of "full-time ministry,"* pledging to a vocation of congregational or itinerant ministry; or

  v *Give your life to full-time missions*, by becoming a career missionary ("home " or "foreign")—which was the peak spiritual response.

Every listener was expected to do numbers i–iii. Numbers iv and v were strongly urged but also considered "next level up." If a church generated any individuals who chose iv or v, the congregation celebrated it as a high-water mark. For those individuals who did answer the call to vocational ministry or missionary work, you would then:

- Enroll immediately after college into one of the denomination's six free seminaries (or a Bible institute, if you had no secondary education), where you would prepare for congregational work, itinerant ministry, or a missionary career;
- Upon graduation from seminary or Bible institute, you would begin a career in ministry vocation;
- Move, through the years, from smaller to larger congregations or to trans-local ministry work; and
- Retire having spent an entire career in ministry, with post-retirement often including part-time, interim, or "supply preaching" pastoral work.

Regardless of what you might think about specific segments along the way, *the pathway described above constituted a formidable, cradle-to-grave leadership pipeline.* It produced the largest Protestant denomination in the United States, as well as the largest missions-sending organizations and some of the largest seminaries in the world. Not every participant came through the pipeline from start to finish, but plenty did—and the result was scores of young adult leaders entering congregational ministry or becoming high-functioning disciples serving in other vocations.

That leadership pipeline today is a mere shell of its former self. For reasons denominational and cultural, and for reasons specific to particular congregations, that old pipeline sprang leaks and eroded decades ago, and is now missing (for the most part) entire lengths of pipe. To believe otherwise is a "pipe dream."

It seems obvious that a leadership pipeline today would look quite different than one from a half-century ago. Yet many denominations spend great energy and resources on trying to patch or recreate yesterday's pipeline. There are some successes, and some young adult leaders still make their way through the aging pipeline.

But what once flowed now trickles and leaks. Any denomination that conducts a serious cost-benefit audit will see that the financial and human resources cost-per-leader-produced (by the existing pipeline—if one even exists) has soared astronomically. It is becoming increasingly inefficient for churches, denominations, businesses, and other organizations to recreate yesterday. As Lyle Schaller once told a group of BGAV leaders at a strategy meeting, "The road from yesterday to today is not the same as the road from today to tomorrow."

Uptick does not pretend to replicate the entire cradle-to-grave pipeline described above; its aims are more modest. Uptick attempts to build a vehicle which serves as one sturdy component within a broader internal architecture that will produce disciples who lead. It is trying to "add a segment" to the larger leadership pipeline. By identifying and equipping one single life-stage group at a formative time, Uptick creates a vehicle that can be used within systems and for systems purposes. Beyond the specific deliverable of one segment of the pipeline, Uptick can also serve as a model for other parts of an organization to create similar vehicles for other life stages in the larger pipeline. In doing so, it can help reconstruct the overall leadership pipeline by augmenting additional segments.

2. "FLOODING THE SYSTEM" WITH LEADERSHIP TALENT

The greatest response to change agent effort occurs when opinion leaders adopt, which usually occurs at somewhere between 3 and 16 percent adoption in most systems. The innovation will then continue to spread with little promotional effort by change agents, after a critical mass of adopters is reached.[3]

—EVERETT ROGERS

As discussed in chapter one, our early functioning hypothesis for creating and launching Uptick was based on Everett Rogers' "Diffusion of Innovations" theory. Rogers articulates the need to mobilize 16 percent (the 2.5 percent of innovators + 13.5 percent of early adopters) of a system's most forward-thinking and effective leaders in order to tip that system toward positive innovation.

3 Rogers, *Diffusion of Innovations*, 222–23.

DIFFUSION OF INNOVATION CURVE

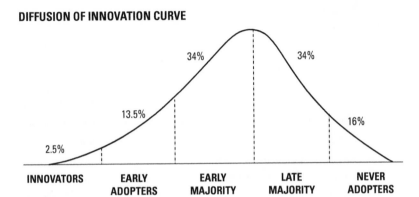

| INNOVATORS | EARLY ADOPTERS | EARLY MAJORITY | LATE MAJORITY | NEVER ADOPTERS |

4

Through Uptick, we first planned to find "innovators" and "early adopters" in our wider (BGAV) system and double down our investment in them. We used language of looking for the "top 3 percent" (young innovators within BGAV) as Uptick candidates. Early on, we said, "It only takes 16 percent!" (to impact positively the overall BGAV)—and a decade later, that has proven to be true. These were shorthand ways of saying that Uptick could contribute to the flourishing of a larger system by giving voice to a depleted class of innovators and early adopters, for the good of the whole. We reasoned that when there were enough Uptick leaders embedded within a larger BGAV social and congregational network, we would find hope for system-wide innovation and revitalization. In a BGAV denominational system of approximately 1,400 churches, this meant we forecasted the need to mobilize 222 well-equipped and well-networked leaders for critical mass.[5] We worked backward from this number to figure out how many Uptick networks we would need to create, fund, and resource. This became a significant goal and set of benchmarks for Uptick within our larger system.

In short, innovators and early adopters are missing or lacking as influencers in many systems. It takes intentional scouting, resourcing, and tenacity to identify, equip, and deploy them. It is necessary to create

4 Ibid., 281.
5 As discussed in chapter one, 222 represents 16 percent of 1,400. We attached the number 222 to 2 Timothy 2:1–2: "You then, my child, be strong in the grace that is in Christ Jesus; and what you have heard from me through many witnesses entrust to faithful people who will be able to teach others as well." For us, this captured the "pay it forward" ethos to sacrifice for the younger generation for the sake of the greater mission we all shared.

greenhouses for their incubation. By doing so, it is possible to flood the system with talent. Enriching the talent pool energizes impoverished or malnourished systems.

Consider two short analogies for "flooding the system" with talent:

- It is comparable to adding nutrients to a malnourished or vitamin-deficient body to nurse it back to health and strength. A common example today is a platelet-rich infusion or injection of blood to an injured or diseased part of the system to jump-start healing.
- It is akin to a Major League Baseball team that builds a strong "farm system"—developing young, inexpensive talent that can be patiently cultivated, and eventually develop players who become cornerstones around which a franchise can build.

John Upton, executive director of the BGAV, and former president of the Baptist World Alliance,[6] has publicly praised Uptick "for delivering more innovative and creative leaders to BGAV congregations and entities than any other partner." Upton is an ardent promoter of the "Uptick way" in numerous Baptist, evangelical, denominational, and international contexts: "I cannot state strongly enough how the BGAV is currently being transformed by the leadership of those who have come through the Uptick cohorts. Churches, institutions, governing bodies, agencies, are thinking more creatively, moving more boldly, and acting more fruitfully because of these leaders."

3. "AIDING SUCCESSION PLANNING" IN KEY LEADERSHIP ROLES

Has your governing board calculated all the various costs that would be associated with a poorly managed pastoral transition? If you are like the large majority of church leaders in the United States, your answer is no. When it comes to dealing with a pastoral transition, many strong leaders stop leading.[7]

—CAROLYN WEESE AND J. RUSSELL CRABTREE

6 "The Baptist World Alliance (BWA) is a worldwide alliance of Baptist churches and organisations formed in 1905 at Exeter Hall in London during the first Baptist World Congress. The organization counts 47 million people and is the largest organization of Baptist churches in the world," from "Baptist World Alliance," *Wikipedia*, https://en.wikipedia.org/wiki/Baptist_World_Alliance . John Upton served as president of BWA from 2010–2015.
7 Carolyn Weese and J. Russell Crabtree, *The Elephant in the Boardroom: Speaking the Unspoken about Pastoral Transitions* (1st ed.) (California: Jossey-Bass, 2004), 2.

There's a temptation to conclude that God is sovereign, and the church is in his hands; therefore, no transition plan is needed. That same line of reasoning could point to a person who didn't use a seat belt and yet survived a horrendous crash as a rationale for not using seat belts. It does occur, but the odds are not in your favor. For every church that has experienced a smooth transition with no plan, there are five that have really struggled.[8]

—BOB RUSSELL AND BRYAN BUCHER

I have fought the good fight, I have finished the race, I have kept the faith.[9]

—APOSTLE PAUL

The required competencies of a future Uptick "Network Leader," can seem daunting and challenging, particularly the ability to:

- *Be system-influencing;*
- *Be a content generator to influence public practice;*
- *Have the clout and courage to garner resources; and*
- *Expand Uptick trans-local influence.*

Some of these leadership competencies are generally attained through the long-term personal growth and effort of the leader. However, they more likely occur because of that leader's functioning within a spiritually and relationally rich environment, which has helped her or him to grow. To cultivate that sort of positive organizational culture requires at least three different components: a new kind of *valuing*; overall system-wide *depth* in talent; and a reliable *method* for generating new or improved talent. Uptick can be a tool in each of these, and in this way can contribute to succession planning in organizations—both at the top of the organization, and throughout the system in key positions. Here are the three components:

i. **Valuing new competencies for key leadership roles.** In the United States, leaders at the top of good organizations are given celebrity

8 Bob Russell and Bryan Bucher, *Transition Plan: 7 Secrets Every Leader Needs to Know* (1st ed.) (Kentucky: Ministers Label Publishing, 2010), 58.
9 2 Timothy 4:7 (the apostle Paul, speaking at the end of his life, to protégé Timothy and the churches who knew them).

status. It is not uncommon to hear them referred to as "rock stars." Praise for CEOs like Jeff Bezos, the late Steve Jobs, Elon Musk, and Bill Gates can border on reverential. Granted, it takes unique talent to lead innovative and complex companies to great success. But if these competencies reside only in a few chosen "rock stars" who have the rare and untransferable "it" factor of charisma, vision, courage, and focus, then the forecast for companies is bleak. Jim Collins refers to this situation as the "genius with a thousand helpers." The ideas of the genius are implemented by an army of good soldiers, but the genius fails to impart any of their competencies or decision-making processes to anyone else. So, when the genius leaves, the organization falls apart because its success relied on the competency of one individual.[10]

On the other hand, Kingdom leaders always value the *mission* of the organization more than the *charisma* of its organizational leader. Accordingly, the "successful" leader in an organization will sublimate ego and transmit their competencies to others who are younger in age or experience in the pipeline, ensuring even more success for their successors than they will see in their own day. This becomes a model for others in the organization to follow, and the senior leader will insist that all leaders at the highest levels will similarly learn to transmit their competencies.

The Uptick Leadership Pipeline thus encourages passing along the leadership of the mission not through celebrity or charisma, but by embedding key values and competencies all the way through an organization or system. As Jesus demonstrated (and the Square LifeShape explains), godly leaders at the "top" of the organization always humble themselves to fight for the fruitfulness of other younger leaders coming up the ranks.

ii. **Increasing the depth of the talent pool.** When top established leaders in a system invest deeply in the emerging leaders starting in that system, the whole system becomes richer, or in my word, more *talented*.[11] Some of this is a simple result of practicing polycentric, APEST-oriented, team-based leadership. It also, however, can be attributed to putting increasing numbers of strong players on the field of play.

Going back to the Major League Baseball illustration above, Uptick

10 Jim Collins, *Good to Great*, 45–48.
11 See Matthew 25:14–30, "The parable of the Talents."

can provide a "farm system" that develops talent over time. In baseball, a good farm team isn't engineered to produce the single celebrity superstar; rather it looks to produce a reliable stream of solid-to-great players that can contribute. A good system consistently generates rising talent, priced below market value, that can contribute meaningfully now or soon, and even more substantially down the road. Occasionally, one or more of minor-league candidates emerges as a top-of-the-organization player. It takes patience to develop this talent, but teams that do can become consistent long-term winners.[12]

One thing is clear in both baseball and organizational theory: when you have more candidates for key leadership roles, you have higher probability for a favorable outcome in choosing the right new leaders. You want a rich talent pool from which you can find many good leaders for different levels of the organization.

iii. **Providing a reliable method of developing competencies in younger leaders over time.** Naturally, a great (individual) leader is going to invest personally in mentoring younger leaders. But better results come when such *organic* mentoring is combined with an *organized* leadership pipeline running in tandem. Organized vehicles like Uptick's Leadership Pipeline give a steady, predictable, and repeatable way to create a clear and demonstrable growth path. In a company, congregation, staff, denomination, business, or team, this vehicle can infuse key values and competencies for already-capable young leaders who can be better prepared for increasing levels of leadership.

Succession planning is perhaps the top leadership task of a leader who is within the last five-to-seven anticipated years of a role—especially when that person holds a senior position within the organization. Uptick can be a valuable ally in making sure that when the succession conversations start, the landscape for new candidates isn't completely barren.

---

12 As a lifetime fan of the Oakland Athletics, this is the phenomenon behind "Moneyball" or sabermetrics, where under-resourced teams find efficiencies to outperform expectations. See "Moneyball," *Wikipedia*, https:// en.wikipedia.org/wiki/Moneyball . I once interviewed by telephone the A's director of scouting, Eric Kubota, about how their organization looks for promising young leaders. I also interviewed the legendary University of North Carolina men's basketball coach, Dean Smith, about scouting and recruiting young talent that fits your "program" or larger system. Similarly, I would encourage you to be bold in cold-calling leaders like this and mining their system wisdom. If you are patient and persistent, you may find that they can be more generous with their time and advice than you suspect.

4. "INFUSING FIVE CAPITALS" INTO SYSTEMS

We often notice that Uptick candidates are poor in some things—money, leadership experience, longstanding institutional knowledge, long track records of experiential wisdom, and abundant strategic relational networks. However, these same candidates are rich in other aspects—promise, ability, agility, a leadership horizon of many decades, native ability within emerging generations, optimism, new ways of thinking, to name but a few.[13]

Established leaders invest the five capitals that we have (our discipleship focus, extensive relational networks, time and presence, experience and wisdom, and ... *cash*) into the lives of the Uptickers. In response, Uptickers tend to return the favor, sharing with us their gifts, which are expressions of the five capitals that we lack: new ways of walking with God, different approaches to networking, fresh ways of thinking and problem-solving, eyes for different opportunities, etc.

The same scenario is true of organizations and systems; they can be rich in some valuable things (for instance, reputation, track record, stability, fixed assets, and human resources). At the same time, they can be impoverished in others (such as organizational agility, vision for the long-term future, ability to recognize new competitors and opportunities). When Uptick is available as a part of a larger system, a mutually enriching relationship can ensue. It is important to weigh these return-on-investments when considering the start-up costs of launching an Uptick network. Though the start-up costs of Uptick are not insignificant, over the long haul, Uptick networks provide a disproportionately high dividend on the initial investment. It simply requires the organizational will and discipline to delay gratification.

Here are some examples of specific benefits Uptickers can bring to systems, through the filter of the five capitals:

- **Spiritual:** Uptick can introduce pioneers into existing systems, tilting the system toward apostolic, prophetic, and evangelistic emphases, adding many of those types of leaders who are otherwise missing, rebalancing the APEST portfolio for the good. Uptick leaders can help organizations speak prophetically and without fear to confront issues of injustice.

---

13 For these reasons, I often counsel churches seeking pastors to look for a promising young candidate whose best years are still ahead; you would rather buy Amazon stock at its startup than its maturity or decline!

- **Relational:** Uptick can help systems build different kinds of peer networks. New young leaders provide a conduit to even more fresh, young, capable leaders. Some of those new leaders may eventually be high-value hires for organizations.

- **Physical:** Uptick has a track record of providing "candidates from the future" for local leadership in churches. Having accelerated their growth path, it quickly increases the pool of high-capacity candidates for leadership opportunities. This is a boon to organizations that might bring people on board whose best leadership days are ahead of them, not behind them.

- **Intellectual:** Uptick can provide prophetic voices and experimental communities to help the wider system explore hot conversations (e.g., race, sexuality). Because Uptick conversations take place in small communities of trust, by participants who generally consider such discussions normal, Uptick can serve as a laboratory for learning without the same high-risk or catastrophic explosions potential if these conversations were housed in wider public forums (e.g., at annual convention meetings, where they have split denominations). It adds natives from emerging generations to wider conversations about evangelism and mission. It brings young leaders, often hardwired to tolerate risk, into risk-averse organizations, helping them to get "unstuck." An example of this are Uptick Catalyst networks exploring racial, cultural, social, and societal dynamics of pastoral leadership in "minority majority" cities, where intercultural intelligence is essential.

- **Financial:** Sometimes, Uptickers are the ones who start new initiatives that no one else in the organization had the imagination to envision. Financially, some of these initiatives can add new income streams, different prospective donor pools, and gifts-in-kind of talent. Investing in Uptickers also creates and cultivates a cadre of grateful "repayer" future donors.

5. "CREATING SHARING NETWORKS" FOR TALENT DEVELOPMENT

We must, as part of APEST communities, teach young leaders how to be emotionally healthy. How to deal with loss. To develop reconciliation skills. To fight fairly and without drawing blood. Churches no longer know how to be a part of a movement (e.g., the Civil Rights movement) or a community that they are not the center of. Building broader networks of peers and mentors gives cross-cultural access points to keep people in ministry, to teach us to be good to each other, and to provide forums for task-focused collaboration.

—UPTICKERS JOSH HAYDEN AND VERNON GORDON

One of the great developments over the first decade of Uptick was the emergence of a network of key established and influential churches whose pastors served both to send and receive Uptick candidates. On the sending end, these pastors—all of whom were stellar leaders—had a great eye for talent and could recognize prospective Uptick candidates who had high potential and the "right stuff." They also had the organizational sway to ensure that these young leaders had the resources (such as time off) to participate fully in Uptick. On the receiving end, these same pastors were often the first to employ or give references for Uptickers to fill vacant or new church staff positions.

Carl George calls this a "feeder-receptor pattern."[14] In this application, key pastors both "fed" a steady diet of candidates into the Uptick process, and also "received" Uptick alumni/ae as staff once they had been through the process. Besides creating value for Uptick and for the individual church that received quality young staff, this feeder-receptor pattern, over some time, came to help the whole larger ecosystem of the BGAV. It created a "sharing network" for locating staff. It also encouraged churches to think differently about what they valued in prospective staff hires. Finally, it made the BGAV overall a more interesting and attractive option for young leaders to seek out. Word got out that the BGAV sought to call young ministers, not because they were inexpensive, but because they had competencies to lead churches in a different day—and the successful completion of Uptick to verify

14 Carl F. George, *Prepare Your Church for the Future* (1st ed.) (Michigan: Revell Publishing, 1991), 31–33.

it. It is a wonderful day for a denomination when bright young leaders actively seek to join your system.

Over time, this strengthened the relational bonds between emerging and established leaders across a much-broader system. At its best, this relational enrichment provides an organic "360 degree" dynamic of mutual learning between emerging and established leaders.

SUMMARY

To summarize, even when it is only a small part of a larger organization, Uptick can add value to larger systems by:

1. **"Adding a segment"** to the system's leadership pipeline;
2. **"Flooding the system"** with leadership talent;
3. **"Aiding succession planning"** in key leadership roles;
4. **"Infusing five capitals"** into systems; and
5. **"Creating sharing networks"** for talent development.

It takes time to get the flywheel turning and for these benefits to begin to appear. But with patient cultivation, Uptick can be a boon for an organization looking to inject new life via an influx of talent, by modeling a practical vehicle, and by strengthening its spiritual and relational capitals.

In the next chapter, we will move into greater detail about how Uptick can share these benefits across systems.

11

Launching Your Own Uptick: Up, In, Out, and Beyond

One of the gifts we have failed to give our churches is to teach the gift of repentance. As a result, we have held onto lots of obsolete systems that are undermining our movemental thinking.[1]

ALAN HIRSCH

Many leaders over-rely on their own instincts when they lead. The problem with this is it tends to lead to one-generation leadership initiatives, because things are too tied to the personal charisma of the leader. We need grounded, practical initiatives, clear principles, and multipliable practices that avoid the single-generation pitfalls and instead become multigenerational and movemental.[2]

RICH ROBINSON

It's time to move from the strategic to the tactical and give practical steps for launching Uptick networks in your own context. To return to our early analogy of a motorcycle rider's manual, you've read the manual, you understand the parts of the cycle and how to use them, and you are now sitting on the bike with your helmet on. It's time now to ride, and this chapter aims to give instructions about being on the road. What follows are some typical challenges and joys as you launch an Uptick network and how to address them. Motorcycle riders are taught early on that the safest way to ride is to anticipate obstacles, surprises, and dangers, and look beyond them to clear riding. Your bike follows your eyes; you move toward what you are looking at. So, to ride well, you need not only to anticipate

---

1 Alan Hirsch, 100 Movements leadership gathering, New York City, May 2019.
2 Rich Robinson, 100 Movements leadership gathering, New York City, May, 2019.

gravel in the road and see it from a distance, but you also need to learn to look *beyond* that gravel to ride around it. Focus on the obstacle itself, and you'll likely hit it. But look beyond the gravel to the far side of it, and your bike will follow your eyes around it to the other side. In the same way, we want to give you some tactics that will help you navigate the challenges of launching Uptick so that you can successfully ride past them. We'll discuss these challenges in a framework of, *Up, In, Out,* and *Beyond.*

UP: REPRIORITIZING SPIRITUAL CAPITAL

I'd rather fail at the right task—making disciples—than succeed in the wrong task, which will look successful but ultimately lead to disillusionment. You can't be disillusioned unless you had an illusion in the first place.[3]

—THE RIGHT REVEREND JUSTIN DUCKWORTH, BISHOP, ANGLICAN DIOCESE OF WELLINGTON, NEW ZEALAND

Without sounding too lofty or dramatic, the first obstacles to overcome in launching an Uptick network can be spiritual ones. Of course, this means praying deeply and broadly about Uptick. What such prayer often uncovers is that overcoming obstacles to Uptick may be a matter of moving "Up" (toward God) by valuing the spiritual purposes of an Uptick initiative more highly than other things that often occupy organizations, such as budget entitlements, legacy programs, staff pet projects, risk aversion, or dealing with employees unwilling to try new things. Jesus did his great work of inaugurating the Kingdom of God through countless meals, arguments with adversaries, practical works of restoring what was broken, and teaching. In the same manner, the practical, functional work of implementing an Uptick network may appear to be mundane—navigating organizational politics, massaging budgets, dealing with human resistance. But it is incarnational work, deeply spiritual, and thus "Up" work.

Frankly, unless you are supremely powerful, irresistibly charming, or financially rich within an organization, you'll have this sort of work to do in order to start an Uptick pipeline. Whether in a congregation, denomination, business, or other organization, here are some of the things you'll need to do to navigate beyond the obstacles to launching Uptick:

---

3 The Right Reverend Justin Duckworth, 100 Movements leadership gathering, New York City, May, 2019.

Help the organization learn (or re-learn) how to prioritize spiritual capital and outcomes over financial ones. As a rule, substantial organizations don't endure over the long haul unless they are rooted deeply in a mission upon which everyone agreed was important and urgent. What inevitably seems to happen to organizations, though, is "mission drift." Authors Peter Greer and Chris Horst offer this example of how institutions drift away from their original purposes:

> Consider this mission statement of a well-known university: "To be plainly instructed and consider well that the main end of your life and studies is to know God and follow Jesus Christ." Founded in 1636, this university employed exclusively Christian professors, emphasized character formation in its students above all else, and rooted all its policies and practices in a Christian worldview. This school served as a bastion of academic excellence and Christian distinction. This mission statement, however, is not from Dallas Theological Seminary. Neither is it from Wheaton College. It's from Harvard University – this statement described their founding mission. Harvard began as a school to equip ministers to share the Good News. Today, Harvard is an incredible institution with an unmatched reputation, but it no longer resembles its founding.[4]

The prophetic work of leadership in organizations is to help systems adjust back to their core calling and function, even when such course corrections result in pruning longstanding practices. It should be axiomatic in churches, for instance, that living as disciples is at the heart of following Jesus. Yet I have listened to countless pastors describe the uphill battle of helping people in their congregations to embrace this wholeheartedly:

> How do you transition consumers to become disciples of Jesus wherever they live, work, study, play, and shop? If you can get someone to take personal responsibility to be on mission with Jesus in these five arenas, then they don't have to become missionaries to Uganda. They can be missionaries who impact thousands right where they are.[5]

4 Peter Greer and Chris Horst, *Mission Drift: The Unspoken Crisis Facing Leaders, Charities, and Churches* (Minnesota: Bethany House, 2014), 16–17.
5 Jimmy Carroll, pastor, Journey Church, Raleigh, https://takeajourney.org/ .

Without belaboring the point, the first step to gaining critical support for launching Uptick within a system unaccustomed to such a mindset is to help the system reprioritize *spiritual* capital and outcomes above all other capitals—and especially over *financial* capital. This is a blunt statement but gets at the heart of what it takes to overcome mission drift and invest for the future instead of protecting the past. In many systems, the loudest and most reflexive protests to investing in pioneers are monetary. If the first and main objections an organization have to starting an Uptick network are budgetary, it is a dead giveaway that this kind of reprioritizing work is needed. To get things moving, you will have to reframe questions about *financial* "costs" under the wider perspective of the *spiritual* costs of failing to invest in emerging generations of disciples who lead.

Gain the enthusiastic advocacy of the key leader of the system. If a big part of the work you must do is to reprioritize *financial capital* beneath *spiritual capital*, then the chief means by which you do this is through the exercise of *relational capital*. Naturally, how this is applied varies from organization to organization, as well as one's role within it. But what is generally true is the need to gain the energetic endorsement of implementing Uptick from the pacesetting leader. You will need to work in relational harmony with that key leader in order to move things forward. This key leader, even if senior in his or her role, may not have direct means to authorize the changes and costs needed to start an Uptick network. But s/he must be sold on the need for doing so, and excitedly look for ways to make it happen. You need that leader's *relational* equity, and for her or him to exercise *intellectual* capital as a thought leader. You need the leader's *physical* capital of time spent attending to what it takes at the top of the organization to include Uptick. Rare is an organization that doesn't see the need for future leadership; yet far fewer fund and reflect those concerns directly in their budgets and expenditures. Unless you have a financial windfall, or the personal means to give or get the money it takes to lead an Uptick network, you'll need the senior leader on your cheerleading team, advocating for budgetary inclusion.

I love telling stories of how John Upton, executive director of the BGAV, did this for Uptick in our organization. John has a missionary perspective and vision for the organization that are grander and more enduring than his own personal agenda and tenure. It didn't happen overnight, but his enthusiasm for a vehicle to produce high-quality leaders and disciples was, over time, expressed in changes he approved to wider organizational budgets, staff, and priorities. He was willing and able to spend his leadership "chips" to run interference for Uptick. He took on blocks, shielded and defended, and took hits for reallocating resources from legacy initiatives toward new initiatives. He trusted an idea that had not yet been proven. Uptick would never have launched or survived without him. Everyone who wishes to start an Uptick network in an existing organization must leverage relational capital with a leader like John to get things done. I would also add that Uptick benefited from great board chairs in Jim Baucom and Sarah Burnett, who are not BGAV employees, and who could challenge and push John about Uptick from outside-the-system vantage points. The synergy of these great leaders working in harmony (on the inside and from the outside) has been invaluable.

Practice both *Pauline* (getting the message "out") and *Petrine* (continually interpreting what you're doing back home) vision-casting, leadership, and messaging.[6] In the book of Acts, the work of the apostle Paul could be summarized as helping the gospel reach Gentile territory beyond "Jerusalem and Judea" and out to "Samaria and the ends of the earth" (Acts 1:8). The work of the apostle Peter, on the other hand, might be summarized as ensuring that the founding church in Jerusalem and Judea didn't veto the mission as the church was moving out into Samaria and the ends of the earth (see Acts 15 and the Council of Jerusalem). Paul and Peter's work was complementary, with one extending the gospel to the edge, and the other making sure that the center held. One pushed to the frontier, the other gained approval and permission from home base. Both are necessary.

In the same way, launching Uptick means utilizing both a Pauline and Petrine approach. That is, one must consistently "pitch" or "message" Uptick to new and expanding audiences (Pauline) while also back-casting vision throughout the housing organization (Petrine). In both instances, it is a matter of casting vision for Uptick in formal and informal venues of influence; hallways, lunch tables, team meetings, boardrooms, and podiums all matter.

---

6 Many thanks to Paul Maconochie for this language and framework. Paul's sharing this with our Uptick board has been a tremendous help to our overall work, and to my personal work within that.

It may be helpful to think of how you can use the "four spaces" strategically to do this Pauline and Petrine Uptick work:

1. *Intimate* space:
   - Pauline: Use one-on-one conversations with potential Uptickers, referral sources, and prospective donors, to recruit candidates and grow support for the grand vision. Leverage personal relationships to meet people who can contribute talent, networks, and ideas to Uptick. Treat discussions with people who show interest about Uptick as potential partners or as possible opportunities to recruit future board membership.
   - Petrine: Think of yourself as a lobbyist within or alongside an organization. You have a cause that you are representing in every formal or informal individual conversation in your organization. Never forget to thank existing donors in formal and informal ways. Don't be shy in intimate space conversations to make specific financial or organizational requests. Become an accomplished and prolific thank-you-note writer.

2. *Personal* space:
   - Pauline: Never waste an opportunity in a group setting— whether an informal dinner (where someone asks you what you do) or scheduled team meeting to advocate for the Uptick cause. You are always "sowing seed."
   - Petrine: Utilize staff and team meetings, and committee work to represent advocacy for Uptick in terms of framing work responsibilities, budgets, and departmental or organizational aims. Don't be overbearing, but don't let your cause go neglected either, especially when decisions are in the works.

3. *Social* space:
   - Pauline: Take advantage of scheduled and spontaneous opportunities before larger groups to tell stories that highlight the work, accomplishments, and contributions of Uptickers.

- Petrine: Never miss an opportunity in front of a crowd to point out what "one of ours" is doing within our larger system. Repeatedly thank the home base for prioritizing spiritual gains, sacrificing financially, and for putting an emerging generation ahead of their own comfort.

4. *Public* space:
- Pauline: Continually speak in general terms of the need to invest in and sacrifice for the next generation, even when not talking directly about Uptick. (Do that as well, though!) Regularly cast vision for the call to lay down our lives for the mission of God. Preach, teach, and write with passion when given opportunities toward the bigger and broader needs that Uptick addresses.
- Petrine: Connect success stories of Uptickers and how they are making a difference in venues within the existing system. Thank stakeholders for taking risks, giving selflessly and generously, and thinking of others. Don't be shy about quoting Scripture that reflects these things. Connect strongly the specific aims of Uptick with the historic stated aims of the wider organization.

In sum, by helping an organization correct back to its core values or purposes, working with its key leaders, and casting vision both inside and outside the organization, one can do the "Up" work required to get an Uptick network off the runway.

IN: PUTTING TOGETHER THE UPTICK COHORT AND YEAR

If the "Up" work needed for launching Uptick is akin to clearing a wooded lot in order to build a house, then the "In" work is like designing the floor plan, laying the foundations, building the house, and then furnishing it so it feels like home. Here we will turn to the "In" matters of recruiting the right participants (and the right *mix* of participants), as well as designing both individual gatherings and the overall course of the Uptick year.

HOW TO CHOOSE CANDIDATES

At the end of the day, we don't want a small tree with a little fruit. We don't want a big tree with a little fruit. And we don't want just one big tree with a lot of fruit. What we want is an orchard. We want reproduction on every level. We want large, strong trees that bear tons of fruit, which can then bear tons of fruit, which can then produce more of the same. It's not about one tree, small or large. It's about producing an orchard with more fruit than we can wrap our minds around. That's what a Kingdom movement is like.[7]

—MIKE BREEN

One of the ways that you can think "orchard," rather than "tree," is to build consistent standards and processes in how you identify, screen, select, and mix candidates for an Uptick cohort. As Jim Collins made famous in his "first who, then what" adage:

> We expected that good-to-great leaders would begin by setting a new vision and new strategy. We found instead that they first got the right people on the bus, the wrong people off the bus, and the right people in the right seats – and then they figured out where to drive it. The old adage "People are your most important asset" turns out to be wrong. People are not your most important asset. The right people are.[8]

Once you have the right Uptickers selected, you are 80 percent of the way to a good Uptick year. If it took Jesus a whole night of prayer before selecting the twelve disciples (Luke 6:12), it will probably take you a little longer to pray for prospective Uptickers! Having done that spiritual legwork, though, here are some of the things we have learned that help in picking the right candidates:[9]

- **Select candidates by your recruitment and referrals from strong**

---

7 Breen and the 3DM Team, *Leading Kingdom Movements*, Kindle edition, Kindle locations 1509–10.
8 Collins, *Good to Great*, 13.
9 I have opted to bypass discussion of many of the assumed spiritual characteristics of high-quality Uptick candidates because there are plenty of excellent discussions of these traits elsewhere. One of my favorites is from JR Woodward and Dan White Jr. in *The Church as Movement*, 111–14, where they give examples of how to build a discipleship core team around criteria of *Character, Compatibility, Competency, Capacity,* and *Confidence,* elaborating on each point in helpful detail. I am trying to add points here that might build on their foundation.

leaders, not from participant application. As discussed in chapter one, a strong referral from a thought leader or pacesetting practitioner is golden. Sometimes, Uptickers who have completed the year and shown great growth can give good referrals. Screen these referrals, though; sometimes Uptickers have simply had a good experience and want to share it with their friends.

- **Assess potential for "exponential impact."** Does the candidate currently show strong potential for handling demanding or complex ministry? How would you assess that s/he responds to "scaling up" work? Is s/he able to take on (or initiate) growing responsibilities smoothly without becoming flustered? Can you anticipate multiple decades of influence from this person? You're not looking for finished products here, but people who are giving signals that their ceiling is very high, especially if they can exercise Kingdom influence over decades. Bob Russell has said that most leaders overestimate what they can accomplish in one year and underestimate what they can accomplish in ten. Estimate the ten-year (or, better, the thirty to forty-year) ceiling for a candidate. Uptick Entrepreneur leader Matt Paxson made this witty observation about potential candidates: "Uptick is looking for entrepreneurs, not 'want-trepreneurs.'" In other words, plenty of young leaders talk a good game, but a smaller group is beginning to show early indications that they might walk it. You are not necessarily looking for an airplane already flying at thirty thousand feet, but you want them at least to have gotten their wheels moving fast or even off the runway.

- **When possible, pick for system impact.** Find out what your larger system needs, and what is missing from the mission of God being carried out through it. Then look for candidates who can potentially help bring that. Again, avoid political appointments or picking people because of a noisy constituency. As in the case of the BGAV, often there is a lack of "APEs" (apostles, prophets, and evangelists), so scout for those if needed.

- **Assess teachability, gratitude, and hunger to grow.** Don't try too hard to talk the wary candidate into participating. Their hesitation can be a signal of a lukewarm interest or commitment that will bite you later in things like tardiness, lack of presence in group conversation, missing sessions, and failure to engage deeply with others. Look for folk who are humbled and grateful to be selected. They will more likely have a "pay it forward" heart at the end of the process. Do make sure that you understand the candidate's likely means of engaging; if they are all about texting and you are all about email, you may mistake their failure to notice your emails as their indifference to Uptick. Pay attention to your own instincts regarding likeability. If you intuitively bristle when interviewing and assessing someone, do some deep soul work on yourself to ponder "Why?"— but also be aware that it can be a signal of a deeper incompatibility that will affect their Uptick experience and the cohort.

- **Launch with high challenge.** While interviewing, and at the point of inviting, be "high challenge" with the candidate. Where applicable, make sure they have the full blessing of their spouse and boss before proceeding. Give them the schedule and tell them in advance what potential excuses will not be tolerated for missing gatherings. It is at this point that I tell a candidate on the verge of accepting that Uptick is not a "dog-ate-my-homework" kind of group. If Uptick is investing deeply in an individual, that individual needs to reciprocate. Because of this up-front challenge, we have only had two candidates start and then drop out of Uptick during the year since 2007.

- **Look for a "connectional" temperament.** Is the person a team player or lone ranger? Insist on love for the local church and respect for the sponsoring organization, even if they are frustrated with aspects of it. Don't mistake introversion or a quiet temperament for isolationism. Look for people who are eager to make new friends with other Uptickers.

GETTING THE RIGHT MIX: CHEMISTRY OF THE COHORT

While it is true that if you get a bunch of high-potential leaders together in an Uptick cohort, you have done the heavy lifting, it is still important to pay attention to the *dynamics* of the group when you are recruiting. Do consider the chemistry of the cohort. In one of the early years of Uptick, I inadvertently picked a group with all evangelists. It was lots of fun but completely disorganized! We didn't maximize potential in that group because it was missing key APEST voices.

When putting together an Uptick cohort with strong chemistry, the adage sometimes attributed to Augustine holds true: "In essentials unity; in non-essentials liberty; in all things charity." That is, make sure every participant is first united by a *fervor* for Kingdom discipleship and leadership practice. Then, to the degree that it is possible, bring liberty and breadth to the group by maximizing diversity—men and women, race and culture, socio-economic status, types of leadership roles and positions, APEST intelligence. It is particularly helpful to have women and men together in an Uptick cohort.[10]

This can be slow, difficult work, especially if you are from a largely monolithic system. But it is incredibly worthwhile. I often say that it is possible to make water run uphill, and the fact that you took a shower proves it. Diversity is worth building the plumbing that will make water run uphill. If variety is not a high reality or value of your system, it is even more important to give the system a sign and foretaste of what could be. This is a place Uptick can make a major contribution to the larger system of which it is a part—to model the future.

Finally, build activities into the Uptick year that help participants to build friendships. When the friendships and corresponding trust ignite, the degree of diversity and variety in the group will correlate to the overall brightness and richness of the Uptick experience.

SCULPTING THE YEAR

Having previously discussed the Uptick "pearls on a string" means of scheduling in chapter six, we will simply add here a few practical ideas to consider when designing your annual schedule. Of course, schedules may vary widely by context—if you are in a university setting, the academic calendar will impact when you do what you do, for instance. Or, an Uptick for pastors wouldn't schedule gatherings during Holy Week. Nevertheless, here are some general tips to help you sculpt your Uptick year:

- **Embrace the hybrid.** Education studies are demonstrating that a "mixed modality" model of in-person and online education yield the best student outcomes.[11] You may encounter initial resistance from Uptickers about an online huddle, for instance.

10 If, during the Uptick year, there are conversations that are best suited for women alone or men alone, there are natural ways for those to occur (such as among roommates), and you can also structure some huddles to be gender specific. But it has been our experience that men and women together in Uptick have sharpened each other in unmatched ways that accelerate discipleship growth.
11 See Mark Lieberman, "Blended is Best," *Inside Higher Ed*, April 12, 2018. https://www.insidehighered.com/digital-learning/article/2018/04/12/online-programs-can-contribute-better-outcomes-lower-costs-and .

Most of that tends to disappear once they've experienced one. If your Uptick year is more online than in-person, then try to front-load an in-person gathering at the beginning of the year. (We have not yet experimented with an all-online Uptick.) Do be sure to set online etiquette expectations up front.

- **Give them a starting "handle."** Assign pre-reading so people will come to the first conversation with some sense of preparation and thoughtfulness. We use *Building a Discipling Culture* (and the LifeShapes app) for this—it helps with participant comfort and engagement level and gives a game plan for those who appreciate that structure.[12]
- **Take advantage of time and location efficiencies.** Choose meeting locations that are as easy to get to for the most people possible. If you don't think local exploration or experience is on topic, you should see the overall impact it has on group engagement!

To give you a sense of how to schedule a year, here is the 2018 Uptick Core schedule of in-person gatherings. (Online huddles and coaching calls are not listed on this schedule but generally are organized while the group is convened, and occur in between gatherings every 4–8 weeks.) This particular group was made up mostly of Virginia residents, which is reflected in the locations for gatherings.

SAMPLE ANNUAL UPTICK SCHEDULE

In 2018, the "in person" schedule of Uptick convened as follows:

January 15–17 – Discipleship gathering with British leader Paul Maconochie, coaching orientation, prophetic prayer, Lynchburg, Virginia.

March 14–17 – Leadership conversations with Alan and Deb Hirsch, followed by participation in www.freshexpressionsus.org gathering, Alexandria, Virginia.

---

12 Breen and Cockram, *Building a Discipling Culture*; LifeShapes App, Chris Henderson.

June 8–10 (women only) – Discipleship gathering with Averett University President Tiffany Franks, Averett University, Danville, Virginia.

July 11–14 – Leadership assessments and exercises, Sweet Brier College, Amherst, Virginia. *Includes Keirsey-Bates and emotional intelligence assessments, storytelling skills, Vital Friends, APEST/5 Gears, physical challenge, Enneagram, financial capital instruction, etiquette training.*

September 10–13 (men only) – Mentoring retreat with www.bobrussell. org/mentoring-ministers/, DISC assessment, Louisville, Kentucky.

November 14–16 – Discipleship gathering with Tod Bolsinger, Future Stories, prophetic prayer, Richmond, Virginia.

DESIGNING EACH GATHERING

Once again, we have already spoken extensively on creating an "environment" conducive to Uptick formation and don't need to belabor the point of how important setting is (see chapter five). Here then are a few final practical points to help you plan in-person gatherings.

Give instructions in advance about social media and telephone distractions, prayerful framing, and careful instructions about dress code. This raises expectations, helps people transition well into the unique Uptick space, and reduces social anxiety about what to pack, wear, and expect. Don't underestimate those factors! It is helpful to send an email detailing all this information approximately two weeks before the gathering.

Start on time, finish on time, and do contingency planning for travel difficulties. Early on, emphasize the gift of valuing one another through punctuality, and, as leaders, honor that by keeping your word on start and stop times for sessions. Understand that things like airlines and interstate traffic don't always cooperate. One way we mitigate group disruptions is to begin with a "soft start" meal, so that if someone is thirty minutes late because of a flight delay, it is not disruptive to the conversations initiated by the presenter.

Don't skimp on meals, snacks, and hospitality. I am a bit of a foodie and have taken my fair share of ribbing over the years for overly focusing on strong dining experiences. But I will defend this point vigorously: giving strong attention to quality mealtime experiences is critical in forming the relational bonds that make an Uptick network work. Reading through the Gospels, you will be amazed to note how many of the encounters with Jesus take place around meals and tables. Eating well is a form of building physical capital. Dining during the Uptick year is not an "intermission" from the real work; it is part of the "soft" formation of communal bonds. Introverts, who in group settings can be very slow to reveal anything in-depth, can suddenly light up in table conversations and make and receive huge contributions.

Pay attention to things like seating comfort and configuration, and the rhythm of teaching inputs and breaks. Make sure there are good snacks and beverages; if you're going to provide coffee, make it *good* coffee! Honor the table experience by insisting that everyone puts away phones. Assess how noisy dining spaces might be and whether they are conducive to conversation. Ask in advance about allergies or dietary restrictions, but also stretch the group in terms of types of food. Nothing about this kind of hospitality is particularly difficult; it simply requires attentiveness, thoughtfulness, planning, and diligence in execution. Many great leaders understand the value of helping their groups eat well as part of cultivating cultures of appreciation.[13] Uptick experiences are cemented with joy by dining together and dining well.

Go as "local" as possible where you are (and have some local fun!). To the extent you can, make your gathering something people *want* to be a part of, particularly by doing something that helps them experience and appreciate the unique setting. Curate local intelligence to find hidden gems. Take a couple of hours in the schedule to do something fun that is unique to the area. Whenever possible, try to include experiences of fun, adventure, or interest. Plato said that we can learn more about a person in an hour of play than a year of work. We have seen laughter over an evening game that accelerates the progress of an entire group. We have taken groups rappelling, to a chocolate factory tour, to the Library of Congress, to Monticello, to civil rights and art museums. Are these superfluous to disciple making? Not if you believe enriching relational and intellectual capitals is mission critical.

13 See, for instance, Baxter Holmes, "Michelin restaurants and fabulous wines: Inside the secret team dinners that have built the Spurs' Dynasty," *ESPN*, April 18, 2019. https://www.espn.com/nba/story/_/id/26524600/ secret-team-dinners-built-spurs-dynasty .

SAMPLE SCHEDULE OF AN UPTICK IN-PERSON GATHERING

This was a gathering in July 2018 of the Uptick Core network at Sweetbrier College in central Virginia. each gathering has its own rhythm, this should give a sense of the topics, intensity of engagement, and overall rhythm of formation.

Wednesday: Dress for today—dress pants and polo or button-down for guys; women, "what you would wear out to business lunch"
    11:30 a.m. – Arrive, lunch in Burnett home
    1:00 p.m. – John Chandler teaching 5 Gears
    3:00 p.m. – Karen Bowles, The Etiquette School of the Commonwealth —Soft relational skills: Mocktail, dress advice, phone skills, "donor dinner"
    5:30 p.m. – Dinner at Burnett home
    7:00 p.m. – Wise Development of Financial Capital in Your Life for Maximum Generosity (Sarah and Tim Burnett)

Thursday: Dress for rest of gathering—super-casual (shorts, jeans, tees), with walking/hiking shoes for Friday
    8:00 a.m. – Breakfast at Sweetbrier
    9:00 a.m. – Laura McDaniel teaching "story" skills
    12:00 p.m. – Lunch, then continue "story"
    3:00 p.m. – Laura McDaniel instruction on emotional-social intelligence, Keirsey-Bates
    6:00 p.m. – Dinner at Vitos
    After dinner: Uptick group contest, fun and games

Friday
    8:00 a.m. – Breakfast at Sweetbrier
    9:00 a.m. – John Chandler teaching on Vital Friends
    10:30 a.m. – Huddle
    12:00 p.m. – Bag lunch
    1:00 p.m. – Hiking Crabtree Falls trail, meditation/yoga-style exercises/ reflection with Carey Sims, Saunders ice cream stop
    4:30 p.m. – Optional session (Seven Faces of Philanthropy) or rest
    6:30 p.m. – Dinner at Main St. Eatery
    7:00 p.m. – Group walk/talk/pray

Saturday

    8:00 a.m. – Breakfast

    8:30 a.m. – Takeaway & Leave-Behind: Visual Explorer

    10:00 a.m. – Carey Sims leads in prophetic prayer

    12.00 p.m. – Dismiss with lunch to-go

OUT: RESOURCING MULTIPLICATION

Like it or not, if you want to launch an Uptick network, you'll need to figure out how to provide the financial backing to make it possible. As discussed previously, we believe that it is imperative to scholarship Uptick participants in order to transcend a transactional relationship and create a "pay it forward" culture. But if that is the goal, then it is the responsibility of those launching Uptick to find the "Kingdom venture capital" to get the network off the ground.

"Out" (toward the world) signifies moving an Uptick network off the blueprint and into construction. It also refers to expanding the number of Uptick networks outward, treating Uptickers as future Uptick starters and leaders. In this sense, then, "Out" is about resourcing the multiplication of Uptick networks.

MAKING IT WORK FINANCIALLY

We need to create economic engines that will release Kingdom movements. We need economic engines that are not good at making money simply for the sake of making money, but good at making money for the sake of releasing successive generations of movements. Where are the movement leaders who will take us to this new (and old) reality?[14]

—MIKE BREEN

Funding is a big deal. I was fortunate to have the BGAV as a parent organization to pay a salary for my role. From inception, the Uptick board and I were challenged to raise our own financial support for Uptick initiatives. Once an existing modest interest income stream disappeared (within the first year of my leading Uptick, due to a downturn in the economy), the need to raise money became a source of focus, stress, and

14 Breen and the 3DM Team, *Leading Kingdom Movements*, Kindle edition, Kindle locations 1421–24.

challenge. I had plenty of ideas of what the first Uptick class should do. But I had to match those ideas with ways of figuring out how to pay for them. For my first three to five years, that was a dicey proposition. During that time, our board functionally operated with the knowledge that we could be out of business within a year unless we figured out funding.

Over time, we moved beyond this "survival" stage, not because of a single breakthrough gift, but through:

- Steadily building a stronger and more cohesive strategic board;
- Broadening our institutional, congregational, and individual donor base; and
- Launching and completing an Uptick network which could then provide encouraging "first fruits" stories back to current and prospective financial sponsors.

Remember, I had a supportive boss from the beginning. Without him, I would most likely not have survived some of these start-up challenges.

In hindsight, Uptick was well served by our having to scramble to finance our own work. It helped to shape us as a hungry, pioneering, frontier entity. We learned by experience that "You eat only what you hunt!" But the stress of the hunt was substantial.

Early on, I often felt frustrated by having to spend so much time raising financial capital. All the scrambling for survival-level funding felt like a diversion from the spiritual, relational, and intellectual work I hoped to accomplish to develop Uptick. But there is no getting around it; if you don't find a way to fund the network, you won't get one started.

The moral of the story is that those who hope to start Uptick networks—unless they are independently funded or wealthy—must attend both to finding and developing the Uptick leaders they hope to grow, *and* to building the financial and relational base of those who will pay to make it possible. Starting an Uptick cohort is not simply designing a cool, new process and finding cool, new prospects. It is the hard work of building an ecosystem of donors, board members, institutional allies, referral sources, and the right Uptick candidates. We never get the simple luxury of focusing on building only one thing.

I believe that we learned some *strategies* and *tactics* that helped us get from concept to launch to multiplication to movement. Perhaps some of these will apply to your work of starting Uptick.

Strategic—Building Funding Streams

Over time, and out of necessity, we figured out how to cobble together multiple funding streams, each of which provided partial funding for Uptick. The pathway to building connections with funding streams was *always* a matter of leveraging spiritual and relational capital. We prayed deeply for God to provide funds. We fantasized about a single major gift to underwrite the whole initiative. And then we rolled up our sleeves and leaned into the unrelenting work of cultivating long-term key relationships and ministry partners who might help. Some provided ideas and encouragement; over time, others began to add funding.

To inspire you with possible places for finding funding streams, here are some of the places we looked for, and found, financial help for launching and expanding Uptick "Out":

- **Denominational sourcing.** Our first, biggest, and most consistent supporter has always been the BGAV, who essentially contributed to my salary, as well as administrative support. Your parent organization may not be able to invest at this high level. But if you have the support of the key leaders, then it is a small step from there to find some budgetary support as well. If you are starting an Uptick as part of a denominational or congregational initiative, you may want to start here.
- **Partner organizations.** At inception, the Woman's Missionary Union of Virginia[15] (who historically works closely with BGAV) became a champion and financial contributor for leadership development through Uptick—especially as we emphasized growing leaders who happened to be women through the process. The broader lesson is to look for institutional partners proximate to existing supporters; often these partners will also quickly get on board with support, as Uptick can be framed as a win-win.
- **Board member giving.** There is only one correct answer for what percentage of your board should be financially contributing to

15 See www.wmuv.org . I am grateful to previous WMUV Executive Director Earlene Jessee for her founding vision for the network that became Uptick, previous Executive Director (and current Uptick Network Catalyst) Laura McDaniel for her incredible work as a champion to accelerate, shape, and expand Uptick growth, and current Executive Director Valerie Carter Smith for her ongoing work on the Uptick board. I am also grateful for the grassroots strategic leadership of so many women of WMUV to establish, sustain, and grow Uptick networks among women. They stand in a long line of WMUV leaders who were trailblazers for leaders who happened to be women, and who continue to do so with Uptick networks today. Thanks be to God!

your network on an (at least) annual basis: 100 percent. Our Uptick board members, over the years, have been pacesetting givers. In recent years, we have challenged each Uptick board member to "give, make, and/or get" 5,000 dollars of financial support for Uptick annually. The Uptick leader must absolutely set the pace for modeling this personally for the board.

- **Church support.** Many congregations quickly experienced the benefits of being led by an Uptick alumnus/alumna and began to put Uptick in their church budget or special offerings. Early on, I also (humbly but directly) challenged and requested financial support for Uptick from pastors and churches with whom I had a relationship. I continue to do that regularly. Many of these congregations are annual givers, which is a huge help in building a financial base of support.

- **Individual donors.** In the early days, we probably focused too much on looking for individual "home run" donors who could give breakthrough financial gifts. However, over time, and as Uptick has born demonstrable fruit, we have encountered generous people of means who are impressed by the results and track record they see in Uptick. A growing number of these generous people fund Uptick at a level that makes a difference. Our experience is that it is unwise to bank your early hopes on a single (or very few) donors; rather, build your financial base steadily and add individual major donors over time as you have something successful that you can show them. Most major donors don't respond to desperate pleas or starving organizations; they instead feed the rising stars to help them grow faster.

- **Alumni/ae giving.** Teaching Uptick grads to be Uptick donors is part of creating a "pay it forward" culture. We have sometimes calculated the cost for an individual to receive a scholarship for Uptick and asked that Upticker to lead her or his organization to make it possible for a future Upticker to participate by donating the same amount. Alumni/ae giving is a slow-track source of income. Uptickers are young, often saddled with debt, struggling financially, and a long time away from the peak-earning years of their life. We have not yet seen this as a substantial funding stream. Over time, though, we anticipate growing income from graduates. We are currently trying to encourage this by teaching

Uptickers best practices of charitable giving and helping them to identify their "giving personality.[16]

- **Grant writing.** For the first decade, we flailed away unsuccessfully at this. What we learned over time is that the granting world is highly relational (should this have surprised us?). We built relational capital and referral sources over time. We focused on creating something that demonstrated tangible results and a track record. And then, in 2018, much to our surprise, we received the most substantial grant by far in our history. The grant was given for starting new Uptick Catalyst networks for growing intercultural intelligence in metropolitan Virginia regions. We believe this initial grant achievement may be an entrée to future grant writing success. As with prospective high net-worth individual donors, our experience is that, early on, one should not over-rely on grant funding for start-up costs. Better to get a few successful networks under your belt, and then come to grantor organizations leveraging a track record of early "wins" that can be accelerated through grants.

- **Endowment income.** Many organizations, businesses, churches, and family foundations, with whom you already have strong relationships, have endowments or charitable giving arms. Most are required to spend 5 percent of their principal annually. It can be a quicker and less competitive path to request start-up grants from them than from major philanthropy organizations. Utilize that relational capital! Find out who are the decision-makers in disbursements or budgets in these endowments and focus there.

- **Inherited assets.** One of the first acts as leader of Uptick was for Mary and me to change our personal estate planning in order to bequeath substantial funding to Uptick's ongoing work. There are people who have experienced transformation through Uptick to the point that they would be willing to do the same. Don't be afraid to challenge people to be followers of Jesus by what they leave behind after this life. Many who insist on tithing in life have essentially pagan wills that cede their legacy stewardship to the state.

16 In particular, we teach concepts from Russ Alan Prince and Karen Maru File, *The Seven Faces of Philanthropy: A New Approach to Cultivating Major Donors* (California: Jossey-Bass, 1994). This is not only helpful to some Uptickers where they currently lead, but also helps them identify their own personal donor profile and core motivations for being generous. Our annual conversation on financial capital also contains a strong challenge to align financial goals with the spiritual capital Uptickers desire to grow, which includes estate planning.

- **Matching gifts.** In recent years, we have benefited from donors who offer matching gifts for new Uptick networks. It is a great tool for someone who needs to raise cash for starting an Uptick network to be able to approach an organization, saying they have half the amount promised "contingent upon your donor gift." This has helped some slower-moving organizations speed up their timeline for investing, particularly if the matching gift is first-come-first-served.

Tactical—Capitalizing on Efficiencies

Over time, we figured out how to fund Uptick by becoming more efficient in how we operated. If we are teaching Uptickers to be adaptive leaders, then we must model this by being an adaptive organization. We do this through asking for participant feedback, trying "betas" in most new Upticks to test out potential new components, and generally morphing how we do Uptick from one year to the next. If building funding streams are *strategically* required to move Uptick "Out" into the creation of new networks, then here are a few things that might help *tactically*:

- **Schedule Uptick gatherings adjacent to other partner/ institutional gatherings.** Often you can capitalize on proximity as a win-win. For instance, we schedule our final Uptick Core gathering every year next to the BGAV annual meeting in November. BGAV constituents love seeing in their midst the Uptickers in whom they have invested.[17] In addition, we are able to split travel and honoraria costs for prominent speakers who will "stay over" after speaking at the BGAV meeting to then lead Uptick.
- **Find free hosting sites.** When you can avoid it, don't pay high fees for meeting rooms in hotels and conference centers. Use your network to find a church, business, or institution to host instead. Recently, we were hosted by a church who loves Uptick. Every day, the proverbial "little old ladies" of the church lavished our group with homemade treats. And chefs from the church catered

---

17 At times, we have had a group of Uptick artists lead worship for the BGAV annual meeting, which has been a time of mutual blessing.

dinners for us that would have cost hundreds of dollars. There are gifts-in-kind all around you for hosting, lodging, dining, etc. Don't poor-mouth, but don't deprive people who are eager to give to you in these ways.

- **Utilize Uptick board members, prominent friends, and local experts as speakers and as connectors to local presenters for Uptick gatherings.** You honor Uptick board members, friends, and donors by inviting them into the work, and their enthusiasm for the shared work always increases as a result. And by utilizing local presenters, you realize cost efficiencies and capitalize on strengths close at hand. For instance, because of strong relational partnerships, we have often traveled to Truett Seminary at Baylor University in Waco, Texas for Uptick gatherings. It would be silly to fly in presenters from the East or West Coast to Waco instead of utilizing fantastic Uptick presenters who can simply walk across campus.

- **Find ways of thanking people profusely.** If you do not have the budget to pay a market-rate honorarium to a speaker, tell them what you are able to pay (and do offer as much as you can afford). They will let you know whether it is possible at that level; don't say "no" for them, though. We have learned to supplement financial honoraria with sincere thank you notes, local delicacies, and thoughtful gifts. You would be amazed to find out how appreciation can be conveyed without adding zeroes to a check.

COST CENTERS

Finally, a word about budgets. It is impossible to answer the question about how much it costs to launch an Uptick network anywhere, because of contextual factors. Where will you meet? Will the candidates all be local? Will people need to drive? Or fly? How many times per year will there be in-person gatherings? (This can range from three to ten.) Will there be a conference as part of it? If so, what will be the costs of attending?

Better than offering a sample budget, here are some of the major cost centers you will need to account for as you put together a budget:

- Lodging—frequency, location, and length of gatherings?
- Travel—local, state, national, international?
- Meals and snacks
- Conference fees
- Site hosting fees
- Books[18]
- Speaker honoraria and gifts
- Coaching fees and/or mentor gifts (if applicable)
- Administrative costs (if not provided by organization; can include things like postage, fees for videoconference applications, etc.)
- Personality assessments

MULTIPLYING NETWORKS

Beyond building the financial base to expand Uptick networks "Out" into the world, it is important to create conditions consistent with movemental multiplication. We are only at the front edge of this and thus cannot speak with the same level of experiential authority as we have with other matters. Nonetheless, here are some early keys we have detected in helping Uptick move "Out" through multiplying Uptick networks:

- **Uptickers leading Upticks.** The fundamental model is not to grow Uptick by employing centralized staff; it is to create a pathway for Uptick graduates to become Uptick network generators and leaders. As discussed earlier regarding the Leadership Pipeline, Uptick graduates will know by experience how to create networks with Uptick DNA, regardless of the context or specialization of their cohort.
- **Ongoing support.** While every Uptick shares DNA, obviously each context requires leadership sensitivity, nuance, and finesse. To multiply networks, senior leadership will need to find ways of supporting and coaching those who are leading new Uptick networks. Recently, some of our most enterprising Uptick alumni/ae identified three primary areas of focus for supporting Uptickers who are leading Upticks:

18 In Uptick Core, we have provided copies of Breen and Cockram's *Building a Discipling Culture*, Rath's *Vital Friends*, Kubicek and Cockram's *5 Gears* and *5 Voices*, and copies of my books, which our network has been able to donate. Occasionally, we will add another book or two.

i *Communication*—building channels through which Uptickers across networks can share stories and best practices;

ii *Training*—creating modules for addressing Frequently Asked Questions, offering coaching videoconferences periodically with teaching inputs, and hosting in-person summits for those who are leading Uptick networks for idea-sharing, networking, and best-practice sharing; and

iii *Development*—at our board level of leadership, continuing to seek ways to find venture capital, and to help Uptickers find venture capital, in order to launch new Uptick networks. This means building a financial model that incentivizes local and ever-expanding funding streams for the work in each context.

Uptick alumni/ae are currently developing strategies and vehicles for communications, training, and development ... stay tuned.

- **Building a shareable model.** Ultimately, the hopes of this book are to capture some of the key gains that will make Uptick understandable and adaptable in your setting. As mentioned, our tag line has been, "Transforming Leaders Through Sharing." The key word in that phrase is "Sharing." Our heart is to codify what we've learned by experience and share it with interested partners so that they may know how to generate, sustain, and multiply Uptick networks in their own contexts.

BEYOND: CONSOLIDATING MOVEMENTAL GAINS

In the "Up/In/Out/Beyond" framework, to push Uptick "Out" is to *add* networks. To push Uptick "Beyond" is to work strategically so that Uptick networks reproduce naturally, eventually multiplying exponentially until they attain the momentum of a self-regenerating movement. We are not there—yet. But this chapter discusses the foundation of what Uptick is doing now with the intention of capturing learnings for movemental gains. Our current and ongoing work that may be useful for helping others take Uptick "Beyond" includes four categories:

1. Building a strong board;
2. Codifying instinctive successes into transmittable forms;
3. Strategic sharing; and
4. Ensuring continuity.

1. BUILDING A STRONG BOARD

Over time, the initial WIIFM (What's in it for me?)
motivation can be converted to a desire to work together
with an organization to make a difference in an area of
mutually perceived importance.[19]

—KAY SPRINKEL GRACE

As the Uptick board matured, we learned some things about board composition and focus that might be useful as you put together the strategic team behind the Uptick networks you will start.

First, start with the basics: you need a board. Don't try this alone. Model APEST. Build a team.

Second, set your criteria for the type of people you need on the board. When we started Uptick, our inherited criteria for board members at that time were that the board should include:

- Pastors and institutional representatives;
- Representation from regions of Virginia;
- People who represented one of the (then) five areas of interest of the board;
- Women and men; and
- Some businesspeople or people of financial means.

As might be expected with an inherited founding board and a new, first full-time leader, there were early hiccups (to say the least!) in clarifying strategy in the new network.[20] As was said of the Jerusalem Council in Acts 15:7, "After there had been much debate," we arrived at a focus on Uptick as the singular goal of our board, and began gradually to replace board members who rotated off or resigned. As these transitions occurred, so did our criteria for new board member selection:

19 Kay Sprinkel Grace, *Beyond Fundraising: New Strategies for Non-Profit Innovation and Investment* (2nd ed.) (New Jersey: John Wiley and Sons, 2005), 4.
20 During the first few years of this turbulence, the strong leadership of John Upton, Vice Chair Jim Baucom, and WMUV Laura McDaniel were particularly critical. I will be forever grateful.

- Selecting only a few pastors and institutional representatives;
- Eliminating geographical representation as a criterion for selection;
- Adding board members based on competencies needed for our board at this stage of its development (including legal, business plan development, accounting procedures, partner cultivation);
- Adding cultural diversity to the existing focus on having both women and men lead; and, most importantly,
- Assessing whether candidates were spiritually clear, relationally compatible, and strategically gifted.

In short, our board evolved over time from a **representative** board, to a **competency**-based board, to a **fundraising** board. I should mention that our emphasis on fundraising does not overshadow our board's valuing of the five capitals:

> Fundraising is the process of giving people opportunities to act on their values [...]. To be innovative and attract long-term donor investment, organizations in the non-profit sector must define and apply their values. They should organize their internal systems, marketing and communications programs, and community outreach to maximize the understanding of, response to, and impact of those values. Only then can organizations attract supporters for the right reasons and engage them in a lasting and mutually satisfying relationship.[21]

Board members' primary contributions to Uptick are adding spiritual, relational, and intellectual capitals. Having said that, they apply physical capital (time and attention) toward these ends through making sure the work is resourced with financial capital. Kay Sprinkel Grace calls this moving "beyond fundraising," and teaches a particular posture toward financial capital (though she doesn't use that language). Boards like ours that want to move "beyond fundraising" must:

> Position themselves as organizations that meet needs, not as organizations that have needs

> Know that a gift to them is really a gift through them into the community

---

21 Grace, *Beyond Fundraising*, 1–2 , 12.

Focus on program results, not just financial goals

Remember that the process of asking and giving is based on shared values

View our organizations, and encourage others to perceive them, as vital additions to communities whose services and enhancements must be balanced and strong

Engage non-profit leaders and donors at all levels in a process that will convert them to donor-investors, committed to a long-term relationship based on shared values and vision

Position all contributions to non-profit organizations as social investments and all contributors as donor-investors

See the process of revenue generation and constituency involvement as a much larger, inclusive, and energizing process called development.[22]

Today, as we continue to learn to do these things, our Uptick board is incredibly vibrant, healthy, and strategic. It includes members from other states (which both reflects our growth and helps Uptick to expand beyond state borders). There is tremendous strategic input and consensus among the board and with the staff leaders. There is mutual submission and discipleship. Recently, board member Josh Hayden challenged us to monthly fasting and prayer together as a board at set times to seek God's leading voice in some particular areas. These shared times are rich.

I should also mention that our board meetings are more fun than any board I have ever known. They are marked not only by intense and frank strategy conversations,[23] but also by laughter, friendship, good food, storytelling, prayer, and sincere care—I would even say *love*. I recruit new board candidates by telling them that if they join the Uptick board, the best thing that will happen to them is they will enter a network of Vital Friends and fellow disciples who can deeply enrich their lives. They have enriched mine, for sure.

---

22 Ibid., xii–xiii.
23 For an excellent summary of the appropriate functions of a strategic fundraising non-profit board, see Grace, *Beyond Fundraising*, 33–35.

Our current focus on recruiting Uptick board members is to retain the present ethos of our board while simultaneously:

- **Becoming younger**—we want the board to be more in step with the generation of Uptickers we are trying to resource;
- **Increasing cultural diversity**—we want the board to look more like the generation and world we are seeking to impact, and less monolithic than our parent organization; and
- **Paying greater attention to APEST makeup and chemistry**—we want board leadership to remain primarily pioneering (apostles, prophets, evangelists) without neglecting key shepherd and teacher voices. This is critical for setting strategic "tone" for the whole network.

With great joy, we are beginning to see Uptick alumni/ae mature in their leadership to the point where they are becoming board candidates and members. Like Uptick as a whole, board development is a long, slow process and requires steady, diligent, patient leadership to stay the course.

2. CODIFYING INSTINCTIVE SUCCESSES INTO TRANSMITTABLE FORMS

An activist bent will lead to over-reliance on instinct and a "just get it done" mentality. We need to crucify the impulsivity of leading by instinct by codifying what we do in forms that we can pass along to others.[24]

—RICH ROBINSON

As a grandparent, I have become increasingly aware of my own leadership horizon. Most startups have a shelf life linked to the energy, ability, and tenure of their founding leaders. For example, research shows that:

88 percent of current FOBs [family owned businesses] think their family will still be running the business in five years. Only 30 percent of these businesses survive into the second generation and an alarming 12 percent make it to the third. If you were wondering about the fourth generation, that statistic is even bleaker at 3 percent.[25]

---

24 Rich Robinson, 100 Movements leadership gathering, New York City, May, 2019.
25 Dan Scouler, "The Frequently Fatal Family Business Flaw: Denial," *Entrepreneur*, February 25, 2014, https://www.entrepreneur.com/article/231757 .

How, then, does Uptick not follow the same pattern and instead move into multi-generational impact? Rich Robinson offers this helpful matrix and interpretation:

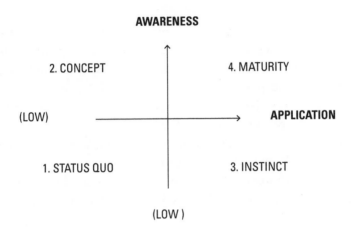

i. **Low awareness, low application:** everything stays at *Status Quo*.
ii. **High awareness, low application:** things remain at the level of *Concept*. This is the phenomenon of "death by 1,000 conversations." It is characterized by lots of talking, thinking, planning, and writing—but never by significant action. It lacks a journey of incarnation and must be solved by higher applications—things like pilot runs, betas, practice groups, and experiments that help you to fail fast and learn.
iii. **High application, low awareness:** this is the realm of leadership by intuition, charisma, and *Instinct*. Here, leadership is natural, embodied, and intuitive. Often, things are working, but no one can explain *why* they are working, besides the personal characteristics of the one leading it. *Its chief pitfall is that it is one-generational.* Its duration never outlasts the singular leader, founder, or initiator. *It requires getting what is in the leader's head into the heads of others, through codifying the ideas.* This can happen through writing, intentional mentoring of successors, and development of training vehicles that can prepare future leaders to

---

26 This matrix and subsequent explanations are derived from Rich Robinson's presentation at the 100 Movements leadership gathering in New York City, May 2019.

know how to respond to what the original leader may have known intuitively.

iv. **High awareness, high application:** organizational *Maturity* and movemental growth.

Uptick currently stands at the key juncture of this journey as it seeks to move from "instinct" to "maturity," or multiple-generational leadership and expansion. As highlighted above, this growth will only happen if key concepts and practices can be codified to the point that they are transmitted out of the heads of initial practitioners, and into repeatable forms that can be practiced by others.

We have begun recording short training videos to address FAQs for those who are leading their own Uptick networks.[27] It is, of course, the purpose of this book (and our deepest hope) to consolidate movemental gains in transmittable form for the benefit and use by others as widely as God sees fit.

3. STRATEGIC SHARING

And let us consider how to provoke one another to love and good deeds, not neglecting to meet together, as is the habit of some, but encouraging one another, and all the more as you see the Day approaching.

HEBREWS 10:24–25

Early on, our board came to believe that the Holy Spirit had given us this New Testament verse to capture the essence of Uptick work. Through Uptick, those who previously lived in separation and isolation from peers and mentors begin to form Christian community, by the simple act of habitual *meeting together*. It is all too easy to get out of the habit of meeting together. Uptick attains many gains simply by providing a structure for this! When this discipline is part of the warp and woof of everyday life, disciples both *provoke* (another translation is *spur*) and *encourage one another*. This is the stuff of "invitation to relationship" (encouraging) and "challenge to responsibility" (provoke/spur). It is how people share life robustly. The resulting *love and good deeds* receive their urgency from the approaching *Day*, when the Kingdom finally comes fully on earth as it is in heaven.

27 See www.uptick.org .

The equation looks like this:

Sharing (provoking + encouraging) **x Meeting = Transformation**

We saw—and see—in this, the magic of Uptick. It is through the habitual meeting together to provoke and encourage, to invite and to challenge, that transformation occurs. It is through this sort of holy sharing that "small dense networks change the world." Our job as a board then, is to enable or resource this kind of meeting to happen as widely as possible. We are trying to multiply *meeting* capacity by infusing resourcing. Or, as our tag line puts it: "Transforming Leaders Through Sharing."

As with a fractal, what is true of the micro is true of the macro. This means the same idea of transformation through sharing can occur not only within an Uptick cohort, but also as we think about how to resource a wider Uptick movement. Resourcing comes from an ethos of *sharing*. It asks, how do we share resources to catalyze a movement?

We hope to share "Kingdom venture capital" in a way that catalyzes new Uptick launches now, and incentivizes recipients to "pay it forward" with generosity later. Of course, this looks like sharing the five capitals:

- **Spiritual:** we multiply disciple-making capacity exponentially and consider it our calling to share whatever we have learned about doing so with those who pray and work to do the same;
- **Relational:** we catalyze reproducible communities of Kingdom purpose and love;
- **Physical:** we are openhanded in offering whatever time, conversation, and expertise we have gained to help Kingdom partners create Uptick networks;
- **Intellectual:** we are codifying our adaptive learning and sharing those ideas on the best platforms we can; and
- **Financial:** we are providing start-up grants (often matching) to doers (not dreamers or "wantrepreneurs") who are creating new Uptick networks.

Our board works diligently to find ways of resourcing movemental growth by helping us to grow a variety of income streams that we can share. Some of these streams are project-focused and specific; others aim more generally to undergird required infrastructure for Uptick network costs, staffing, and administration. Channels for generosity include:

- So-called "**passive** income"
  - gifts that renew/recur from relationships with endowments
  - annual, ongoing board member contributions
  - interest income
- Ongoing **partner** streams
  - denominational and ministry partners
  - significant and recurring individual donors
  - contributing churches who have put Uptick in their budgets, and/or who take special offerings for Uptick generally or for specific Uptick initiatives
  - Uptick alumni/ae giving
- Continued cultivation of **in-kind gifts**
  - presenters who offer their leadership to Uptick at rates below what they might receive on the open market
  - generosity from hosting sites
  - scholarship/travel help for candidates
- **Matching** gift opportunities
- **Estate** gifts[28]
- In the future, potentially a **capital campaign**

We have begun to see glimpses of sustainable sourcing for an expanding Uptick movement. Receiving a significant national grant has opened doors to explore similar infusions of major gifts. Similarly, in recent years, we have been given several substantial gifts from individuals. These people are not only generous in terms of how freely they share their financial capital; they are also helping us to be more astute about how we engage with other similar donors who have great capacity to give generously.

Finally, we have begun to see emerging examples of how to catalyze expansive growth. Laura Matthews finished her Uptick Voice year with a passion to create, share, and build the Uptick process with a new network of leaders in the greater Toronto area. She began with low financial capital to fund this new network but was strong in the other four capitals. Leveraging her spiritual and relational capitals with Canadian Baptist Women of Ontario and Quebec (CBWOQ), she

---

28 Here, it is worth noting that Uptick leader Laura McDaniel, a practicing attorney, has historically offered free estate planning work to any Upticker. She will, at no cost, draft a will for an Upticker. In the course of estate planning, Laura discusses with them their hopes for a Kingdom legacy of generosity and discipleship/stewardship beyond the grave.

convinced leaders of the value of a new Uptick network. When Laura received the promise of an Uptick matching grant, CBWOQ leadership was willing to provide the remaining 50 percent, and together they are underwriting the costs of the new Uptick network. Laura also utilized her strong relational capital to recruit co-leaders and candidates, receiving enthusiastic help from CBWOQ leadership.

Similarly, Virginians Matt O'Rear (Charlottesville area) and Brian Greene (Hampton) have a heart to start and lead an Uptick for worship leaders. By leveraging the promise of matching funds, they have been able to persuade their respective churches to fund the remaining 50 percent of costs for a new Uptick Worship Leaders network. They are also using their strong professional and personal networks to recruit presenters who are giving strong gifts in kind.

We believe these examples give a window into the future for resourcing shareable models.

4. ENSURING CONTINUITY

I challenge pastors to be minister developers, and then to measure every other effect in the church by that standard—not by how impressive the sermon is but by how many ministers are made.[29]

—CARL F. GEORGE

Ultimately, as a disciple-making network that teaches the Square LifeShape, Uptick itself must reproduce leaders who steward the network overall. I often say, "We have to eat our own cooking!" A Network Leader who does not curate the path for the leader who will succeed him or her will have failed at a core level of responsibility. Far sooner than one might suspect, it is wise for executive leaders to begin succession planning. Here are several key things you can do to help with this:

- **Bring on high-caliber people as board members who could be potential candidates to be the Network Leader.** Doing so assures a high-quality leadership voice on the board team. Then, you have lots of time and space to vet the person's character, chemistry, competency, and capacity as a leader and disciple-

29 Carl F. George, *How to Break Growth Barriers: Revise Your Role, Release Your People, and Capture Overlooked Opportunities for Your Church* (Michigan: Baker Books, 2017).

maker. Finally, this makes it likely that, when the time comes, the selection will come from a pool of qualified candidates rather than one or two, which increases the odds of a strong pick.

- **Make sure the Network Leader evolves in the role** as succession draws closer. By the time the current leader is five to ten years away from passing the torch, s/he should be recalibrating time spent on each side of the Square LifeShape:

  D1– spending minimal time

  D2 – spending decreasing time

  D3 – spending solid time

  D4 – spending increasing time

  Along these lines, Upticker Doug Paul suggests an excellent exercise for the Network Leader from time to time: to evaluate the percentages of time spent in each side of the Square both *now* and *next*, evaluating where you are and where you want to go.[30]

- As a new candidate emerges, the predecessor leader must initiate **titrating the point leadership** from the existing Network Leader to the emerging Network Leader. I have envisioned this passing the baton as shifting from a "parent" to "grandparent" role as Network Leader. Mike Breen once told me that there are two stages of grandparenthood—first, when still mobile and active, the grandparent travels to the grandchildren. Later, there comes a day when the grandchildren come to the grandparent. As the new Network Leader assumes parental responsibility, Gramps can stay home and be a grandparent for the network.[31]

My friend Jimmy Carroll, speaking of his heart to influence ordinary disciples to take personal responsibility for the mission of Jesus three or four generations from now says, "They don't have to know *me*, but they have to bleed what I bleed." We can look at photos of great-grandparents and still see their family resemblance reflected in us. In the same way, wouldn't it be amazing to ensure the continuity of movemental DNA three or four generations of Uptick into the future?

---

30 Conversation with Doug Paul, June 2019.
31 See appendix nine, "Role Descriptions and Assessments" for a strong list of duties that come with the role.

Next Steps

I recently heard a podcast featuring University of North Carolina men's basketball strength and conditioning coach, Jonas Sahratian. When the interviewer asked him to explain his perennial success in forming world-class athletes, his deep love of the players was evident, as was his ability to confront and push them (reflecting "invitation-challenge"). He talked about learning techniques from peers in parallel disciplines, for example, what strength coaches are doing to give soccer players more short-area quickness, high jumpers more explosiveness, gymnasts more flexibility, football linemen more balance. His approach was to take the best ideas from parallel sources and amalgamate a pathway that is right for North Carolina basketball, right for the team, and right for the individual player. His motto is "We want to do today what others will copy tomorrow."[1]

This reminds me of how Uptick came to be. It also captures what I hope you'll do as you start your own Uptick network. Take the counsel of this book that applies to your context and learn from others as well. Create something now that someone else can copy later. It's how moments morph into movements. I hope this book offers a solid blueprint for you as you "plot the revolution" of starting an Uptick network in your setting. I also hope the guidance offered in this book gives you the confidence to launch Uptick and that you now have an idea of where and how to begin. The issue of the young adult leadership pipeline is, in a word, solvable.

"Solvable"
\ ˈsäl-və-bəl , ˈsȯl-\
adjective
susceptible of solution or of being solved, resolved, or explained.

Recently, the Rockefeller Foundation helped launch a podcast, Solvable,

1 "UNC BB S&C Coordinator Jonas Sahratian, Baseball hosting a Regional and more," May 31, 2019, in "Carolina Insider," podcast, https://art19.com/shows/carolina-insider/episodes/5073d4a2-1623-4b36-b322-143d884fc2b7 .

a series of conversations tackling some of the world's great problems, such as xenophobic politics, workplace gender equality, access to vaccines, and chronic homelessness. I love some of the Solvable slogans and their tone:

"We believe the world's biggest challenges are solvable."

"Expertise about what is possible, optimism to make it happen."

"Accelerating breakthrough solutions around the world."

"Making big bets on catalytic, early-stage innovations for outsized impact."

"A global collaborative for systems change focused on improving the lives of millions of people around the world."[2]

What you hear in each statement is the strong (and biblical) theme of *hope*. Each podcast is characterized by a belief that, "This issue really can be addressed successfully, if we take the right approach, collaborate, and work hard." The podcast series is billed as "interviews with the world's biggest thinkers who are working to solve the world's biggest problems." Each episode has a title that states the issue they believe is solvable, for example, "Homelessness is Solvable"; "Political Demonization is Solvable"; "Refugee Poverty is Solvable" etc. And the thinker leads with the line "My solvable is ... 'ending food waste'; 'to get one million women and girls to learn how to code by the year 2020'; 'to take energy to where communities are'" etc. Well, I do not pretend to be one of the world's biggest thinkers, but my "solvable" is "to find and form the next generation of pioneering Kingdom leaders." The issue of identifying, equipping, and deploying promising young leaders, whose discipleship will lead to a Kingdom movement, is *solvable*, and Uptick is one of the tools that can be utilized as part of the solution.

Let me make three short suggestions about cultivating a "solvable" attitude as you start:

---

2   https://www.rockefellerfoundation.org/solvable/ . Their purpose statement: "The Rockefeller Foundation advances new frontiers of science, data, policy, and innovation to solve global challenges related to health, food, power, and economic mobility. As a science-driven philanthropy focused on building collaborative relationships with partners and grantees, The Rockefeller Foundation seeks to inspire and foster large-scale human impact that promotes the well-being of humanity throughout the world by identifying and accelerating breakthrough solutions, ideas and conversations."

1. **Be playful as you take risks.** There are risks in starting a new Uptick network, risks with engaging with Uptickers, as well as financial and organizational risks associated with launching new initiatives. There is an interesting cultural conversation occurring in the U.S. now about "free-range parenting" (encouraging less parental "helicoptering," "snow-plowing," and overprotection of children so that they learn to work things out for themselves). Within discussions about balancing protection against the value of unstructured play is what some call the *dignity of risk:*

   > By protecting our children from life's inevitable setbacks, we reduce their opportunities to learn things for themselves; by sheltering them from failure, we also get in the way of their chance to succeed. If we want our children to become thoughtful, independent, flexible, self-aware adults, we have to be willing to let them make mistakes and take a fall sometimes. When we protect them, we are teaching them that they are not capable of making and dealing with their own decisions.[3]

   Your Uptick candidates will be more resilient than you might first think. So are organizations. Approach your emerging network with playful hope. Allow mistakes and learn from them; don't freak out when there are hiccups. Think antifragility,[4] and as Martin Luther said, "Sin boldly, but believe even more boldly in Christ, and rejoice!"[5]

2. **Be non-anxious as you move in hope.** As New Testament scholar Wayne Meeks said, "The idea that the Christian faith offers hope and attracts people who have hope was one of the dominant characteristics of New Testament churches."[6] Lyle Schaller also pointed out long ago that the most important thing churches could do to attract people to the faith was to "offer a

3 See Anna Stewart, "Free-Range Parenting Balancing Protection with the Dignity of Risk," *Empowering Parents.* https://www.empoweringparents.com/article/free-range-parenting-balancing-protection-with-the-dignity-of-risk/ .
4 See "Antifragility," *Wikipedia,* https://en.wikipedia.org/wiki/Antifragility .
5 Fred Sanders, "Sin Boldly!" *The Scriptorium Daily,* August 1, 2009, http://scriptoriumdaily.com/sin-boldly/ .
6 Wayne Meeks, *The First Urban Christians: The Social World of the Apostle Paul* (Connecticut: Yale University Press, 1982), 181–91.

note of hope."[7] People around you will take their cues from you. If you are worried, preoccupied, risk-averse, and scared of failure, you'll infect others around you with the same malaise. As Fred Craddock often quipped, "Seriousness of purpose does not require heaviness of manner." Try stuff, don't worry if it's not perfect, learn from it, and move on.

3. **Be curious as you ask questions.** Edgar Schein speaks of practicing "humble inquiry."[8] You will have as many questions as answers. Enlist mentors, peers, and especially Uptick protégés on the "solving team." A movement is fueled by lots and lots of people driving innovation because they are asking how to improve.

Here's a great list of questions to help you begin hopeful, humble inquiry:

What is your purpose, passion, and problem?
- What is your big question you are seeking to answer or problem you are seeking to solve?
- What, if you solved it, would make the greatest Kingdom impact?
- What is your most significant battle?
- What is the place that is broken within your system?
- What is missing in your community and the deficit in your culture?
- Where is the main struggle for your movement?
- What could "sink the ship" or "blow you off course"?

What is your personal priority?
- Where is there a need for greater personal depth for your spiritual growth?
- Which area of spiritual life needs more intentionality or intensity?
- What's the revelation God is speaking to you about currently?
- Where is God's conviction?
- Where is God giving you encouragement or challenge to step out further or to go deeper.

7 Lyle E. Schaller, *44 Ways to Increase Church Attendance* (Tennessee: Abingdon Press, 1987), 23.
8 Edgar H. Schein, *Humble Inquiry: The Gentle Art of Asking Instead of Telling* (California: Berrett-Koehler Publishers, 2013).

- What's your personal faith adventure at the moment?
- Where are you hiding (or self-protecting) from God and others?
- What's the priority for deepening intimacy, character, and maturity as a disciple for you—and how are you aware and accountable in that place?[9]

THE LAST AND MOST IMPORTANT QUESTIONS

At the end of the day, coming full Circle (as we do!), we end this book by asking the two questions that make up the DNA of the Uptick experience. These are the two final questions that should govern your next steps:

How is God getting your attention?; and
What are you going to do about it?

As long as you keep asking these two questions, there's a good chance that an Uptick will happen. And we will do everything in our power to share with you as it does.[10]

Let this be recorded for a generation to come, so that a people
yet unborn may praise the LORD
PSALM 102:18

---

9 Adapted from Rich Robinson questions, 100 Movements leadership gathering, New York City, May 2019. Many thanks to Rich for his insight and open handedness.
10 Visit www.uptick.org for more information.

Appendix 1
Prophetic Prayer

*The Bible sustains a thoroughly consistent warning
against the centralization of power in a few individuals
and concentration of it in inflexible and impersonal
institutions. Prophetic religion also warns against the
ritualization of the relationship between God and his
people [...]. We should rather understand it as a form of
"holy rebellion" based on the loving critique of religious
instituition modeled by the original apostles and prophets
– "holy rebels" who constantly attempted to throw off
encumbering ideologies, structures, codes, and traditions
that limited the freedom of God's people and restructured
the gospel message that they are mandated to pass on.
This is prophetic religion in practice, and it remains
one of the essential elements of a true experience of
Christianity. It is rebellion because it refuses to submit to
the status quo. But because it is a holy rebellion, it directs
us toward a greater experience of God than we currently
have.[1]*

—ALAN HIRSCH

Uptick has increasingly benefited from the leadership of fivefold prophets Paul Maconochie and Carey Sims in recent years, who have added spiritual and relational capitals to our networks by leading cohorts in exercises of prophetic prayer. The Bible is rife with warnings about how immature or false prophets injure God's people and split churches; however, to marginalize prophetic practices out of existence does violence to biblical formation.

It has been helpful to give Uptickers opportunities to practice and experience healthy expressions of prophetic prayer. Hirsch has said of movements, "We need prophetic intelligence to go along with apostolic architecture."

1 Hirsch, *The Forgotten Ways*, 55–56.

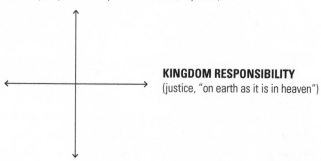

COVENANT RELATIONSHIP
(worship, experience of presence of God, mystical)

KINGDOM RESPONSIBILITY
(justice, "on earth as it is in heaven")

The prophetic *vertical* axis evokes our covenant relationship with God; its horizontal axis points to the expansion of the Kingdom of God (the just reign of God and the call to "be holy, for I the LORD your God am holy" (Leviticus 19:2).[2] Practicing prophetic prayer has been the source of spiritual breakthrough for an increasing number of Uptickers.

PROPHETIC PRAYER

*By Paul Maconochie, National Leader, 3DM U.S. and
Carey Sims, Uptick Strategist and Trainer*

There is an increasing recognition among Christians that prayer must be a two-way conversation with God. As part of that, there is also a growing willingness for disciples to expect God to speak, and for disciples then to respond to the promptings of the Holy Spirit. Even churches that would not consider themselves charismatic are becoming aware of the value in teaching ancient Christian practices such as lectio divina and listening prayer. Yet, many are still suspicious of prophetic prayer, and it is therefore often held at a distance.

Our hope is to help demystify the topic of prophetic prayer. There are three distinct applications of the prophetic:

1. The prophetic witness of God's people as they embrace the radical and countercultural ways of Jesus;
2. The prophetic ministry of listening to God and acting in obedience; and

2 Alan Hirsch, Uptick gathering, Reston, Virginia, March 2018.

3. Developing the gift of prophetic prayer that allows us to hear God for others.

In general, Uptick aims to equip disciples to embrace all three aspects as normative, distinct, and cooperative.

Listening to and discerning God's voice in prayer, and in the midst of our daily lives, is simply normal Christianity. It is what Jesus talks about in John 10:27 when he says, "My sheep hear my voice. I know them, and they follow me." Uptick equips leaders to engage the spiritual gifts according to Paul's instructions in 1 Corinthians 14:1 to "Pursue love."

HEARING GOD FOR OTHERS

For the purposes of this section, we will focus on identifying and developing the prophetic gift referred to by the Apostle Paul in his first letter to the Corinthians, which we will define as *hearing God for others*.

Robbie Yeaman, an Uptick board member, tells the story of his journey into a deeper experience of God through prophetic prayer. He was in the habit of meeting with others to listen to God for one another but was struggling with this practice. One day, a little frustrated, he confessed, "I just don't hear anything." The facilitator asked a simple, yet profound question, "Do you *expect* that God is going to speak to you?" When he answered, "No, not really," it was a revelation. As Christians we should expect to hear God's voice and delight in his words, so we might live according to God's Spirit. Robbie has seen great breakthrough in this area since adjusting his expectations that God will speak when we listen.

Another Uptick board member remembers a particularly tough season of ministry, saying, "I credit my bi-monthly prophetic prayer huddle as the gift that sustained me. Every two weeks I expected to hear from God, to gain divine wisdom that would inform my leadership." James 1:5 reminds us that, "If any of you is lacking in wisdom, ask God, who gives to all generously and ungrudgingly, and it will be given you."

There are several specific ways prophetic prayer has been important for Uptick. The most obvious benefits are for the edification of the community, to gain divine wisdom, and sometimes to receive warnings. The practice of prophetic prayer in community builds intimacy with God and with others. And this is of great value to Uptick.

"

Uptick gives the space to hear what God is calling us to do as pastors in our own spaces, and the community of encouragement to live into what we've heard. Exodus 19:5 says 'If you will listen obediently to what I say and keep my covenant, out of all peoples you'll be my special treasure' (MSG). When God tells you to listen it is generally a good idea to obey. The five times of gathering with Uptick which take me away from my normal schedule and routine and include times of deep prayer and reflection have been irreplaceable. I've heard how God wants me to shape and lead my ministry, and I wouldn't have heard those messages without the time away.

Uptick has also given me a community that encourages me to obey what I have heard from God. Sometimes as pastors we know the direction God is pointing us to lead the congregations we serve. We can take the time to listen but feel like we are not able to obey. The community of Uptick has helped me to obey what I've heard from the Lord. Because of Uptick I am more able to listen and obey.[3]

"

The entire Uptick process is grounded in a posture of listening. First, we must know how God speaks and then create the space to listen. Corporately, we do this through devotional times, using lectio divina, a holy listening to Scripture that invites participants to interact with God about what God's Word is saying and asking of them in that moment. At other times, we ask God to speak through pictures, as participants choose a printed image that helps them engage their imagination and illustrate how God is bringing invitation or challenge in their circumstances. It is a priority to allow plenty of room to process the *Kairos* moments experienced during our time together.

At the end of the first retreat, we all take a risk together. The final two hours are reserved for practicing prophetic prayer, defined as "listening to God for others." It is a time of stretching for everyone, as we embrace the (sometimes) awkward silence and enact our belief that God will speak in surprising, clear, and supernatural ways. Practically speaking, this is the model we use:

1. Create a safe space for people to step out in faith and emphasize the importance of confidentiality.

3 Matt Boschen, Uptick Core 2018.

2. Explain ways we have seen God speak at these gatherings: for example, bringing to mind a Scripture, a song, a word or phrase, an image, through the five senses or a gut feeling.

3. Give some (anonymous) examples of ways God has spoken in other Uptick groups to normalize the process and build a sense of expectation within the group.

4. Invite people to share anything that comes to mind, even if "it seems unrelated or irrelevant." Remind them of Paul's teaching, "On the other hand, those who prophesy speak to other people for their upbuilding and encouragement and consolation" (1 Corinthians 14:3). The words shared must be for the building up and encouragement of the whole community.

5. Open the time with a prayer of expectation but also protection, that any undue cynicism would be silenced so we only hear the voice of the true Lord Jesus, and that God would remind us of the authority he gives us to hear from him and be used as his messengers.

6. Spend a few seconds asking God what he might want to say to the person we are praying for, what he wants them to know, then invite the group into one full minute of silence as we all seek to hear from God (Scripture, song, word or phrase, image, etc.) on this person's behalf.

7. Wait for two or three people to share and allow the person to weigh their words along with the community. Here are several criteria we use to weigh these words:
   - Do they line up with Scripture?
   - Are they representative of what we know is true about Jesus?
   - Are they in line with the truth of the gospel?
   - Do they bring encouragement and edification to the person?
   - Are they being given from a place of love?

These criteria are important so that what is taking place is more than an exercise in free association.[4] Instead, it is a matter of communal discernment of how God is speaking (which, again, we treat as normal for disciples).

---

4 "Free association is the expression (as by speaking or writing) of the content of consciousness without censorship as an aid in gaining access to unconscious processes." See "Free association (psychology)," *Wikipedia*, https://en.wikipedia.org/wiki/Free_association_(psychology) .

The language we use is also important. Instead of using definitive statements such as "God showed me," or "God said," we model a response such as this: "As I was praying for you, I had an image of you sitting by a fire warming your hands ... I'm not sure of what this might mean, or if it was from the Holy Spirit, but does this image have any meaning for you?" Be prepared for the person either to confirm or question what they have heard. Sometimes there is no resonance. Other times, there is powerful confirmation. It is important to be open to either. It is also important to maintain an orderly process, where two or three people share what they have seen or heard, and then have a conversation about it, using the criteria listed above.

Unfortunately, as Christians, we often make two key mistakes in relation to prophetic prayer:

1. We engage with it, but it is misused;
2. We don't engage with it at all.

Many individuals have stories about how they have seen prophetic prayer misused. The most common occurrence seems to be the increased power of a few individuals, and the abuse or manipulation that ensues. Yet, the other extreme is a refusal to explore or engage with prophecy, which is one of the gifts Paul exhorts us to "strive for" (1 Corinthians 12:31). Uptick models a third way that helps leaders engage with prophetic prayer:

"

> *I came into our time of prophetic prayer with skepticism. I did not grow up in a tradition in which this practice was common, and I had only met the rest of the group the day before. A couple of people went before me and as it came to be my turn, I was not really expectant of what I would receive. We prayed, the floor was opened for response, and maybe a few people said a few things. I assumed we'd move on to the next person. Just as we were about to start someone else, Paul Maconochie stopped us and encouraged us to not move on too quickly. He felt there were people who had something to share, but we hadn't given it enough time. We spent the next few minutes in silence and Paul said to me, 'I have an image of a tree.' Maybe it was a family tree, he thought, or was a metaphor for legacy. Someone else chimed in that they saw a tree,*

*too. They saw the tree's roots, breaking through the ground—
groundbreaking. Someone else added that they too saw a tree
with a tall trunk and deep roots. This tree was only tall because it
had deep roots. Finally, John Chandler offered up Psalm 1 to me:
'Happy are those who do not follow the advice of the wicked,
or take the path that sinners tread, or sit in the seat of scoffers;
but their delight is in the law of the Lord, and on his law they
meditate day and night. They are like trees planted by streams of
water, which yield their fruit in its season, and their leaves do not
wither. In all that they do, they prosper' (Psalm 1:1–3). At that
moment I remembered how years ago a woman I had dismissed
as a 'crazy charismatic' had given me a similar word about a tree.
I was stunned and moved. It was through words of strangers,
in a moment where I was skeptical, that God spoke words of
encouragement, challenge, and affirmation to me. It was incredible
to me the way the images and messages spoke directly to multiple
things with which I was struggling: parenthood, how to balance
ministry and family, and how to appropriately harness ambition.
Those images and words continue to form my leadership and
identity.*[5]

"

Listening together to discern God's voice is an authentically biblical practice, following Paul's instructions in 1 Corinthians 14:29. Listening together provides a check and balance so that no one individual can claim to have a personal "hotline" to God. Rather, any believer can receive revelation through the Holy Spirit, but this must be weighed, in the context of Scripture, and interpreted through a community of gathered believers. Revelation can come to an individual, but interpretation and application are done together with others. This allows us to be open to the leading and prompting of the Holy Spirit without allowing a culture of manipulation to develop. We have found that as we practice this in Uptick, the participants are encouraged and built up, with increasing confidence in their relationship with the Lord.

5 Andrea Ackerman, Uptick Core 2018.

Appendix 2
Uptick "Lean Canvas"[6]

1. **Primary People**—Uptick candidates, participants and alumni/ae, referral-receiver network, investors, trainers who share, cheerleaders.

2. **Problem**—Inadequate pool of high-capacity pioneering leaders, lack of discipleship orientation in leader formation, challenges of being young in older systems.

3. **Solution**—Front-end investment in reproducible discipleship processes, spiritual and relational capital enrichment, language and a pathway for lifelong growth and multiplication that can impact individuals, congregations, and systems.

4. **Unique Value Proposition**—Early venture capital investments "pay it forward" by elevating high-impact leaders who engage for years/decades.

5. **Revenue Streams**—BGAV giving/infrastructure, individual and corporate donors, gifts-in-kind shared by trainers/board, spiritual/relational capital sharing economy.

6. **Channels**—Cultivated referral network, Uptick alumni/ae, word of mouth, BGAV publicity, testimony from others about Upticker growth, social media, trainer cheerleading, investors.

7. **Key Metrics**—How many growing missional disciples formed, how often they replicate within/beyond their ministry context, numbers of leaders involved, quality of life for leaders and systems involved, impact on BGAV and other systems.

8. **Cost Structure**—Fixed: Personnel, event costs (travel, lodging, food). Flexible: Physical space, trainer costs, sharing economy.

9. **Unfair Advantage**—BGAV backing and context, raving fans, decade+ track record of results, a shareable and repeatable process, original materials, networks willing to share resources, growing donor base.

---

6 "*Lean Canvas* is an adaptation of *Business Model Canvas* by Alexander Osterwalder which Ash Maurya created in the *Lean Startup* spirit (Fast, Concise and Effective *startup*). *Lean Canvas* promises an actionable and entrepreneur-focused business plan. It focuses on problems, solutions, key metrics and competitive advantages." See https://canvanizer.com/new/lean-canvas .

Appendix 3
Sample: Uptick Memo of Understanding

Uptick is a referral-based network of leaders who are typically aged 23–34 and who have already demonstrated significant potential for leading high-impact ministries in the future. The purposes of the track are to:

1. Give "backstage pass" access to experiences and networks, otherwise inaccessible to leaders of this age;
2. Fast track high-potential young leaders toward being able to lead high-impact ministries within three to ten years.

Uptick participants have a deep heart for congregation-based ministries, whether they are formal congregational leaders or exercise their Kingdom leadership in non-congregational settings. Candidates are identified through referral from established leaders and are interviewed by the Uptick team. Each annual cohort of Uptick consists of six leaders of each gender.

Here is the profile of a typical Uptick candidate:

- Age 23–34;
- College graduate (seminary or graduate degree optional);
- Maturing in and driven by a deep faith in Jesus Christ;
- A demonstrated heart for the local congregation and leadership;
- Potential for apostolic-level Kingdom impact over the course of decades of leading;
- Preference given to pioneering leaders of apostolic, prophetic, or evangelistic calling;
- A solid referral from a trusted, established transformational Kingdom leader;
- A teachable spirit and a connectional and relational (rather than independent) bias;
- Respect for and appreciation of the BGAV, whether Baptist or not; and

- A "pay it forward" intent of appreciating investment and reinvesting dividends.

As Jim Collins would argue, the most important component leading to the success of an Uptick cohort lies in "getting the right people on the bus." We accept only trusted referrals under the premise that "talent recognizes talent, and leaders recognize leaders." Selection and vetting of candidates to form a class of high capacity and good chemistry is critical.

Candidates to this invitation-only network are selected largely because of our evaluation that they will innovate beyond their experience, multiplying Uptick networks in and beyond their own leadership settings to spark a multiplicative movement of future Uptick networks.

Appendix 4
Sample: Covenant—Uptick Entrepreneur

(BENEFITS AND EXPECTATIONS)

- Personal mentoring and group discipling through intensive interaction with high-quality leaders who have been where you are and have gone where you are trying to go;
- Training in how to lead your business through the lens of discipleship, using your work as a platform for ministry in a way that integrates faith/work, sacred/secular, marketplace/calling;
- Clear vision on what it is like "to be on the other side of you"— heightened awareness of how you lead and how it impacts your family, team, clients, etc.;
- Concrete counsel on spiritual disciplines, personal habits, and marriage/family dynamics to prevent common young leader derailers;
- Executive coaching to address individual issues/hopes;
- The opportunity to learn from and "look under the hood" of successful start-ups/businesses that lead with Kingdom mission, vision, and values;
- Skill development in public and social savvy, development/ fundraising, networking etiquette, and personal financial health and stewardship; and
- A chance to form the habits that will prevent major life/leadership mistakes and get you to the top of your game early, instead of having to crash and make mid-course corrections.

All costs associated with Uptick are paid for with funds raised by the Uptick network. In exchange, participants are expected to engage fully and completely in all scheduled activities. All participants must secure permission to be absent from work and must commit to fully attend all gatherings in advance in order to be considered for Uptick. If married, they need the full blessing of spouse/family to join. Participants are expected to arrive on time, not depart early, and be unplugged from multi tasking addictions during forums—in short, full and total engagement. In these ways, we set the tone for high invitation/high challenge from the onset of Uptick.

Appendix 5
"Leaders Who Happen to Be Women"

As mentioned previously, disciple making is a function of the whole church, and to fail to include women fully in that work would mean failing to obey rigorously the Great Commission of Matthew 28.

Having said this, disciples who happen to be women face specific leadership challenges in North American contexts. Maria Teresa Gastón has helped Uptick to walk through specific challenges women face:

Maladies of Christian Women Leaders March 2018
Facilitated by Maria Teresa Gastón, PhD
Focus Question: What leadership maladies or temptations do Christian women suffer from?[7]

TWICE AS HARD, HALF AS FAR	PRESSURE, INSECURITY, FEAR (FEAR OF HUMANKIND, NOT GOD)	SCARCITY MINDSET	"MASK"-ULINITY	SUPER WOMAN	FORCED/ FALSE HUMILITY
Reality of lack of delegation of female pastors	Feeling the need to prove ourselves	Us vs them hierarchies	Downplaying expertise to make men more comfortable	Do/Be it ALL! Perfection-ism, trying to do it perfectly	Not to say the hard stuff
Having your opinions weigh less than men's	Fear of not breaking the glass ceiling	Competition with other women	Adjusting our demeanor to achieve our agenda	Idolatry of the nuclear family	Excessive Apology/ies
The need for extra educa-tion to get in the door	To live by others' dreams	Comparison (positively or negatively with what others are doing)	Ambition to be the female leader prototype	Reducing ministry to marriage/ family	Too willing to stay backstage
Longevity –shelf-life of women ministers less than men	Expectations high by liberal men	Not receiving peer approval (therefore perfection)	"Honorary men"	The leadership re-sponsibilities vs. family	Enabling through silence
	A fear of failure	Jealousy and competition (among other women)	Being impulsively emotional	To do it all!	Always the helper, never the leader
	Fear of speaking up	Manipulating situations for own agenda	Angry black women needing to be overly sweet		I'm not taken seriously (because of my gender)
	Fix it all				Being paralyzed by others' opinion
	Acting out of fear				
	To function in isolation				
	I have to prove myself				

7 Maria Teresa Gastón, https://www.faithandleadership.com/maria-teresa-gastón , presented at Uptick Voice in March, 2018, Durham, N.C. See also "Address of His Holiness Pope Francis," December 22, 2014, https://w2.vatican.va/content/francesco/en/speeches/2014/december/documents/papa-francesco_20141222_curia-romana.html ; and Gary Hamel, "The 15 Diseases of Leadership, According to Pope Francis," *Harvard Business Review*, April 14, 2015, https://hbr.org/2015/04/the-15-diseases-of-leadership-according-to-pope-francis .

We have found that gender-specific opportunities within the Uptick year can be helpful, within the larger framework of having men and women together in discipleship contexts.

Appendix 6
Sample: Uptick "Metrics of Success" Survey

Timing: survey before Uptick, during Uptick, post Uptick—immediately, one year, three years, five years

Method: Survey Monkey that will compile the results

Questions: both objective and subjective evaluation to yield quantitative and qualitative analysis

Demographics:
1. Name
2. Uptick Year
3. Current place(s) of service
4. Married or single
5. Male or female
6. Age

Post-Uptick Evaluation Questions
For the first five questions, Uptickers select a response from one of the following categories:
- Weakness—needs improvement
- Some improvement
- Considerable improvement
- Strength—breakthrough

Please provide a specific example or Kairos moment at the end of each question.

Evaluation of Uptick Discipleship Process: **Five Capitals**

1. As a result of the Uptick experience, rate your **spiritual** capital:
   a. I am a vibrant disciple as a leader in my context
   b. I am seeking opportunities to create innovative Kingdom initiatives
   c. I am leading a life that imitates Christ
   d. I am actively engaged in making disciples, i.e., I am helping people to become more like Jesus

2. As a result of the Uptick experience, rate your **relational** capital:
   a. I have a continued connection to the life of the Uptick tribe
   b. I am calibrating invitation and challenge to develop community around me
   c. I use Matthew 18 principles when necessary in my community
   d. I am sharing with and investing in others, what I learned in Uptick
   e. My network is vibrant and growing
   f. I am connecting with other Uptickers for investment

3. As a result of the Uptick experience, rate your **physical** capital:
   a. I am paying forward the Uptick investment in me to others
   b. I am maintaining a healthy rhythm of life between rest and work
   c. I am moving toward a healthy, sustainable lifestyle
   d. I am encouraging others in my community to maintain health in spirit, mind and body

4. As a result of the Uptick experience, rate your **intellectual** capital:
   a. I am living into my fivefold (APEST) profile of base and phase ministry
   b. I am actively recruiting and/or generating Uptick candidates
   c. I am actively developing my practical skills in my ministry context
   d. I am sharing my skills, abilities, talents with others in my ministry/community context
   e. I am sharing my skills, abilities, talents to help the extended Uptick networks

5. As a result of the Uptick experience, rate your **financial** capital:
   a. I am functioning as a better Kingdom steward of my financial resources

b. I am making better plans for giving, debt-reduction, saving, and spending
c. I am likely to seek financial investors for Uptick
d. I am likely to directly invest financially into Uptick for a future network

6. Rank in order of priority (1 being the most and 5 being the least) where you are investing your time and energy:
   a. Spiritual
   b. Relational
   c. Physical
   d. Intellectual
   e. Financial

Evaluation of Uptick Discipleship Process: **Coaching**

1. Was this an effective tool to help you gain clarity for leadership trajectory?
2. Was this an effective process to navigate through specific issues?
3. Are you likely to add coaching as a tool in your leadership
   If yes to any of the above, please provide insights as to why coaching was effective
4. What aspects of the leadership coaching process worked for you?
5. What upgrades to the leadership coaching process would you suggest?

Evaluation of Uptick Discipleship Process: **Huddle**

1. Did the use of LifeShapes strengthen your spiritual journey?
2. Did you experience *Kairos* that led to leadership breakthrough?
3. Are you using the tool of huddle to make disciples?
   For any yes answers, please provide insights as to why huddle was effective

Evaluation of Uptick Process: **Gatherings**

1. Did the large group gathering at ____ provide meaningful ideas and encounters to shape your ministry?
2. Did Uptick access to Kingdom leaders challenge you to make changes to your life?
3. Did Uptick access to Kingdom leaders challenge you to make changes to your ministry?
4. Did Uptick leaders provide insight and challenges for your life and ministry?
   For yes answers, please provide insights as to which events and conversations were effective, and why.
5. What upgrades to the Uptick process would you suggest?

Evaluation of Uptick Process: **Future Story**

1. Are you living into your Future Story?
2. What adjustments do you need to make to live more intentionally into your Future Story?
3. Do you need to re-write your Future Story?
4. As a result of Uptick, what are you doing differently in terms of thinking, being, and doing as a pioneering leader?
5. When do you plan to start a new Uptick group? What would that new Uptick network look like in your context?

Appendix 7
Sample: Uptick Coaching Outline

Purpose:

- To provide high-impact coaching services to set participants in the Uptick leadership development process on a path to transformational ministry leadership.
- To prepare participants for the post-graduate growth phase of the Uptick process with clear objectives and development plans.
- To maximize the impact of the Uptick process in the life and formation of these unique ministry leaders.

Coaches:

Certified Christian Leadership Coaches have a passion to help young leaders fulfill their potential for transformational ministry that impacts the world. Additionally, these coaches have backgrounds in vocational ministry, which makes them familiar with some of the particular challenges facing young ministry leaders. Each coach is committed to excellence in coaching standards and ethics and is pursuing additional certification through the International Coaching Federation, the largest certifying organization in the coaching industry.

Coaches are trained in and/or have experience with the use of the following tools that may enhance the coaching process:

- Leader Self-Assessment
- Personal Systems
- Boundaries and Standards
- Goal Setting
- High Performance Patterns
- Future Story writing
- Personal Mission Statements
- StrengthsFinder assessment

- Needs and Values
- Other tools to help leaders leverage their strengths and develop their potential

Time Frame for Coaching: Participants will commit to one coaching session per month for ten months for a total of ten sessions. Coaching sessions typically last forty-five minutes to one hour. Participants will have the opportunity to re-contract with Uptick coaches on an individual basis for a period of one additional year at the initially contracted Uptick rates. Additional coaching beyond the two year "Uptick" timeframe may be negotiated with individual coaches, independent of the Uptick Leadership Coaching Process.

Fees: Coaching fees are typically $100 per coaching session but are by paid for by scholarship by Uptick. Coaching sessions will take place via telephone. Uptick participants have the responsibility of placing the phone call and paying any personal expenses related to the call. Calls may be rescheduled with twenty-four hours advanced notice at no additional charge. If advanced notice is not given, normal session fees will apply.

Coach Selection: Each participant will receive a packet containing coach bios and a form to indicate coach preferences. Coach/client matches will be based on participant requests and coach availability. Uptick participants will be invited to change coaches after six months but may choose to work with the same coach for the entire year. Coach changes will be made on an as-needed basis at any point in the process for the benefit of Uptick participants.

Management and Accountability: Uptick leaders and coaches will collaborate as needed to ensure that Uptick participants gain the maximum benefit from coaching. The success of Uptick Coaching will be evaluated by the following criteria:

- Growing understanding and commitment level of participants to the coaching process;
- Development of appropriate objectives/action plans by the participants;
- Readiness of participants for post-Uptick growth phase;
- Participant feedback and evaluation of coaches; and
- Uptick convener feedback and process evaluation.

Appendix 8
Sample: Uptick Entrepreneur Mentor Guidelines

Thank you so much for serving as a mentor to a young Uptick Entrepreneur. Your investment in this leader will be a critical part of his or her ability to apply discipleship to the whole of life—work, home, heart, marriage—*all* of it.

Here are some guidelines for what is expected of mentors:

- **Spiritual capital.** See the attached "five capitals" paper[8] to understand our metrics for the effectiveness of this Uptick Entrepreneur network. Your main work is to sow into the soul of this young leader. Pray for her. Guide him like a father or mother in the Lord. Support or challenge in wise but not patronizing ways.
- **Confidentiality.** Please treat your conversations with the Upticker as personal and confidential. You may secure permission from the Upticker to share conversations with your spouse or with an Uptick leader; assume that all is between only the two of you unless explicitly told otherwise.
- **Relational capital.** Make your best networks available to the Uptick protégé. Building a strategic network of mentors, peers, and protégés is vital for them. You can help by connecting them with people in your network.
- **Initiative.** While we will instruct Uptickers to make the first move toward you, please offer your availability to them as you are able. Don't wait for them to get in trouble before contacting you. Find out what style of communication works for them (in-person, phone, text, videoconference), and work to meet them part of the way in that. Schedule time together in advance and figure out what sort of level of check-in from you is most helpful to them.
- **Preparation.** Please read in advance Breen and Cockram's *Building a Discipling Culture* in order to understand the language and framework for discipleship in this network. It will make you

---

8 The "five capitals" paper is a simple definition and summary of the five capitals.

conversant with the Upticker. We also recommend downloading the free "LifeShapes" app for a CliffsNotes-style summary.

- **Rigorous honesty and vulnerability.** You will have wisdom and success stories to share, and please do so. But remember that leaders often learn from the mistakes and struggles of others, especially of those whom they admire. Tell them yours. Don't be shiny. Let your authentic struggles be part of the conversation as well. It will make growth accessible to them.

- **Presence.** Plan on attending the first reception and dinner on (date/time) at (place) in (city). Get to know your Uptick protégé face to face. Dine with them. In fact, while not required, you are welcome to attend as many of the dinners as you are able to attend; just let us know when you are coming. Generally, stay in the background in group discussions so that the Uptickers may have the floor, but use the before/after time to process with the protégé what was happening in the session.

- **Time and availability.** Plan on *at least five sessions of sixty to ninety minutes* during the year with your Uptick protégé. Local mentors may want to prioritize in-person contacts. Distance mentors may have to meet in other formats some or most of the time (i.e. videoconference). Move early in the relationship to schedule the calendar and format of your meeting together. Invite them to visit where you work, "look under the hood" of your business, and learn some of your best operational lessons.

- **Model the way.** Demonstrate by example what discipleship can look like. Let your speech and example set the pace. Open your family life to them so they can learn from that. Talk openly about how and why your church matters to you.

We have also attached a schedule that will let you know what the Uptick Entrepreneurs are working on at different points. Be aware of those topics, though you are not asked to attend the sessions.

Signed

_____

Date

_____

Appendix 9
Role Descriptions and Assessments[9]

1. Uptick Leader
2. Network Apprentice
3. Network Associate
4. Network Leader

1. Uptick Leader

These are high-potential young leaders, typically age 23–32 for men and 23–35 for women. They are often apostolic, prophetic, or evangelistic, and love the local church. They value the five capitals. They require imitation-based investment and are often not yet clear on their final ministry direction. They contribute by developing capacity in their current ministries and by becoming candidates for filling larger platform ministries and creating new ones.

Term and scope: one year; functions in intimate, personal, and social space.

Chief Outcomes
- Valuing the five capitals (spiritual, relational, physical, intellectual, financial);
- "Imitate me as I imitate Christ"—self-leadership and development of capacity for Kingdom leadership.

Character/Competencies
- Hunger to grow as a disciple of Jesus and leader of others;
- Humility, teachable spirit, holy confidence, relational, values the local church, values BGAV life;
- Loves Jesus, respects Kingdom mentors and fellow Uptickers, passionate for the transformation of people and systems.

9 These descriptions can be tweaked to match your context and provide templates for job/role descriptions for Uptickers as well as current and future Uptick staff.

Chemistry
- Fundamentally teachable, valuing practitioner and mentor input;
- Is learning to invest in strategic relational networks with mentors, peers, and protégés.

Capacity
- Is learning to make and keep commitments;
- Adopting professional standards, including planning and goal setting, punctuality, reliability, initiative and follow through, time management, work ethic, etiquette and personal habits;
- Evolving clarity about priorities and calling;
- Growing capacity to make disciples in personal, social, and public space;
- Commitment to "pay investment forward" through personal practices and via Uptick.

Required reading: *Building a Discipling Culture, Praying* series, *Vital Friends.*

Self and mentor evaluations are first done individually and independently, followed by a conversation together. One can use any agreed-upon scale (one to ten, A to F, etc.) for measuring.

UPTICK LEADER ASSESSMENT		
CHARACTER/COMPETENCIES: SPIRITUAL GROWTH AND SELF-MANAGEMENT	SELF-EVALUATION	MENTOR EVALUATION
1 Learning to hear from and respond to God		
2 Valuing the five capitals		
3 Growing discipline in engaging with the Bible		
4 Clarity in APEST base/phase ministry		
5 Clearer picture of one's Future Story—calling/vision/purpose		
6 New practices of intentional disciple making		
7 Growth in fruit of the Spirit		
8 Hunger to grow as a disciple and leader		
9 Teachable spirit, appropriate humility and self-confidence		

10	Loyalty to and gratitude for one's investors		
11	Growing faithfulness in use of money, sexuality, and power		
CHEMISTRY: RELATIONSHIP MANAGEMENT			
12	Values input from Kingdom leaders		
13	Cultivating long-term relationships/partnerships		
14	Intentionally searching for Vital Friends		
15	Dependability, reliability, availability to others		
16	Vigilantly recruiting protégé candidates		
17	Being a good team member		
18	Negotiating relational capital to get Kingdom work done		
19	Initiates ongoing and strategic contact with mentoring senior leaders		
20	Honors BGAV		
21	Encouraging others and contributing positive energy		
22	Relating appropriately across gender		
23	Relating appropriately across ages		
24	Relating appropriately across chains of command		
25	Able to ask for and offer assistance		
CAPACITY: GROWTH AS A LEADER AND DISCIPLE-MAKER			
26	Growing professionalism—dress, hygiene, etiquette, demeanor		
27	Growing work ethic and financial responsibility		
28	Increasingly generous, committed to growth		
29	Able to receive feedback/input and grow from it		
30	Intentional in leading strategic networks		
31	Growing in leadership in social and public spaces		
32	Commitment and strategy to "pay it forward"		

2. Network Apprentice

These are often young staff, typically Uptick graduates and apostles, prophets, or evangelists. They require hands-on supervision. They have a limited term of service. They contribute by recruiting and mentoring individual networks in ways that meet larger Uptick objectives. Their skill requirements are primarily imitation-based, with some creative contributions.

Term and scope: one year, potential to renew, based on evaluation; functions in personal and social space.

Chief Outcomes
- Ability to recruit and lead a new or existing strategic network;
- Input for next-stage development of new strategic networks.

Character/Competencies: All of the character/competencies of an Upticker, plus:
- Competent to implement network, including navigating tasks/events, relationship management, ability to work within budget;
- Goal setting, follow through, work ethic development, time management, including ability to juggle part-time role with Uptick alongside of other roles/jobs;
- Ability to give, solicit, and receive feedback.

Chemistry
- Ability to plan collaboratively with Uptick Network Leaders, yet work independently as needed;
- Skill to communicate to Uptick board and current stakeholders in clear, compelling ways.

Capacity
- Willingness and ability to search for funding streams for particular networks and the Uptick network overall;
- Contributes to strategic and creative input for green-edge new networks;
- Ability to navigate evolving part-time work responsibilities artfully and responsibly as vocational clarity continues to unfold.

Required reading: *Multiplying Missional Networks, The Starfish and the Spider, Managing the Millennials.*

NETWORK APPRENTICE ASSESSMENT		
CHARACTER/COMPETENCIES: **GROWING AS A NETWORK LEADER**	**SELF-EVALUATION**	**MENTOR EVALUATION**
1	Consistent in "winning the first battle of the day"		
2	Learning to lead intentionally out of what one hears from God		
3	Creating networks that value and teach the five capitals		
4	Leading clearly out of APEST base/phase ministry and calling		
5	Intentional disciple making undergirding the things one leads		
6	Commitment to lifelong learning and growth as a network-maker		
7	Fidelity in money, sexuality, and power		
8	Able both to follow direction and offer strategic input		
9	Strong management of details of running a single network, including event planning, budgeting, and communication		
10	Consistent professionalism—dress, hygiene, etiquette, demeanor		
11	Growing work ethic and more strategic in using time		
CHEMISTRY: NETWORK MANAGEMENT		
12	Mobilizes human and other resources to establish network		
13	Initiates updating supervisors about victories, challenges		
14	Begins to cultivate prospective investors/donors		
15	Prepared to communicate persuasively to stakeholders		
16	Initiates strong and consistent mentoring within networks		
17	Ongoing scouting and recruiting of Uptick candidates		
18	Forecasts next stage of network development		
19	Expands trans-local network for Uptick network gain		
20	Able to plan independently after initial supervision		
CAPACITY: GROWTH AS STRATEGIC NETWORK DEVELOPER		
21	Captures testimonies and stories of network outcomes		
22	Contributes strategically to origins of next Uptick/network		
23	Navigates part-time Uptick work well, among other responsibilities		
24	Clear and intentional about communicating future aspirations		
25	Consistent, effective communicator in social and public spaces		
26	Maturity to grow from supervisor input		

3. Network Associate

Brought on board because of existing professional competencies, track record, education, and wisdom. Significantly apostolic, prophetic, and/or evangelistic. Able to supervise and coach. Contributes by planning, leading, and supervising multiple networks in ways that meet Uptick network objectives. Offers strategic input to overall Uptick network direction.

Term and scope: open, full-time; functions in all four spaces.

Chief Outcomes
- Ongoing recruiting and leading strategic network(s);
- Creates and supervises portfolio of existing and new strategic networks.

Character/Competencies: All of an Upticker and Apprentice, plus:
- Exemplary personal discipleship and disciple-making skills;
- Strong overall management skills, including ability to supervise and help others succeed;
- Competent to implement multiple networks and navigate calendar management;
- Ability to set and follow overall budget and priorities;
- Strategic planning and collaborative thinking to contribute to overall Uptick network direction.

Chemistry
- Complementary skill sets with Network Leader that enable independent and collaborative work;
- Strong relational skills of invitation/challenge for team planning;
- Ability to communicate/lead well to Uptick board, current stakeholders, and larger Baptist family, in presence or absence of Network Leader;
- Significant role in board management and communication.

Capacity
- Major roles in managing networks, supervising apprentices, strategic goal setting, and donor cultivation;
- Contributes to strategic and creative input for green-edge new networks;

- Consistent recruiter of Uptickers, Apprentices, and successor leaders.

Required reading: *Good to Great and the Social Sectors, Great by Choice, Outliers, Courageous Church Leadership.*

NETWORK ASSOCIATE ASSESSMENT		
CHARACTER/COMPETENCIES: GROWING AS A NETWORK LEADER	**SELF-EVALUATION**	**MENTOR EVALUATION**
1 Imitation-worthy personal discipleship		
2 Consistent leadership out of what one hears from God		
3 Strong and ongoing practices of disciple making		
4 Creating/leading multiple networks that value the five capitals		
5 Facility in leading alongside other strong leaders		
6 Demonstrated lifelong learning and growth as a network-creator		
7 An example to others in use of money, sexuality, and power		
8 Strong management of details of running multiple networks, including event planning, budgeting, and communication		
9 Reduces waste, bureaucracy, redundancy in organization		
10 Fluent leadership in all four spaces		
11 Able to end networks well once they are finished		
CHEMISTRY: NETWORK DEVELOPMENT		
12 Mobilizes human and other resources for network portfolio		
13 Manages relationships with major vendors, key leaders		
14 Major role to discover and cultivate donor relationships		
15 Strong gifts in Uptick infrastructure development		
16 Able to supervise strategically		
17 Ongoing scouting and recruiting of Uptick, Apprentice candidates		
18 Servanthood in Uptick problem-solving		
19 Expands own trans-local network for Uptick gain		
20 Values "wins" in others and captures stories for Uptick gain		
21 Publicly loyal and personally challenging to Uptick leader		
22 Manages "up" and "down" and values accountability		

CAPACITY: STRATEGIC UPTICK DEVELOPER			
23	Major contributor to innovative disruption in Uptick		
24	Key voice in board leadership and succession planning		
25	Consistent, effective communicator in all four spaces		
26	Manages details needed for success while prioritizing leadership		
27	Develops networks for key leader recruitment		
28	Strong ability to communicate vision and work to Baptist family		
29	Accomplishes key gains through networks—more so than one-on-one		
30	Leads in developing non-congregational leadership networks		

4. Network Leader

Brought on board due to widely recognized accomplishments, including professional accomplishments, practitioner credibility, graduate education, entrepreneurial skill set, fundraising fluency, and publicly known contributions to the leadership field. Significantly apostolic, prophetic, and/or evangelistic. Able to cast credible and compelling vision and function as a "face" of the Uptick network. Contributes by creating the board and staff teams and key networks that can make Uptick successful and spur success in others. Offers lead voice in overall Uptick direction.

Term and scope: open ended; functions in all four spaces.

Chief Outcomes
- Being the "face" of the organization;
- "Buck stops here" decisions to set strategic direction, fuel strategic networks, end networks, and deploy Uptick resources to best effect;
- Personal and professional modeling for other leaders and organizations;
- Managing "up" to Uptick board and denominational leadership;
- Positioning Uptick as contributor within own system, nationally, and internationally.

Character/Competencies: All those of an Upticker, Apprentice, and Associate, plus:
- Above-and-beyond personal discipleship and disciple-making practices;
- Building the team that ensures success (board members, Uptickers, Apprentices, Associates);
- Setting clear and compelling vision for the network;
- Key voice in state, national, and world Baptist leadership and among evangelical centrists beyond Baptist life.

Chemistry
- Able to build and lead a high-functioning board and staff team;
- Commands respect from team and maximizes their contributions;
- Recruits successor candidates that enable Uptick to evolve toward future success.

Capacity
- Strong public representation of Uptick to board, current and future stakeholders, BGAV leaders and congregations, the world Baptist family, and evangelical centrists;
- Major roles in resource and donor cultivation;
- Contributes to strategic and creative input for green-edge new networks;
- Able to discern and deploy which Uptickers, Apprentices, Associates, and board members have ability to multiply impact and position them to do so.

Required reading: Should be reading all the time and writing books from time to time!

NETWORK LEADER ASSESSMENT		SELF-EVALUATION	MENTOR EVALUATION
CHARACTER/COMPETENCIES: **TOP LEADERSHIP WITHIN AND BEYOND UPTICK**		**SELF-EVALUATION**	**MENTOR EVALUATION**
1	System-influencing personal discipleship		
2	Pacesetting point leadership out of what one hears from God		
3	A five capital life that is widely influential		
4	Courageous and timely decisiveness		
5	Ability to build and lead a powerful team		
6	Content generator to influence public practice and Baptist life		
7	Willingness and ability to be the "face" of Uptick		
8	Contributor and influencer in key Baptist and national circles		
9	Clout and courage to garner resources for Uptick		
10	Theological and spiritual articulator of vision and mission		
CHEMISTRY: NETWORK DEVELOPMENT			
11	Key role in mobilizing resources for network success		
12	Manages relationships with key (inter)national leaders		
13	Major role to discover and cultivate donor relationships		
14	Ensures DNA in Uptick expressions		
15	Able to lead key Uptick leaders		
16	High-level risk management		
17	Servanthood in Uptick problem-solving		
18	Expands Uptick trans-local influence		
19	Establishes key partnerships		
CAPACITY: STRATEGIC UPTICK DEVELOPER			
20	Brings energy and hope to Uptick and Kingdom enterprises		
21	Commands a following in many spheres of influence		
22	Recruits and grooms successor candidate(s)		
23	The lead public communicator and "face" of Uptick		
24	Understands and sets major leadership and cultural trends		
25	Prioritizes 10 to 30-year picture over the urgent distractions		
26	Major contributor to innovative disruption in Uptick		
27	Responsible for architecture of leadership pipeline		

Glossary of Key Terms

Adaptive Leadership
"A concept deriving from chaos theory [...] in which a living system faces the challenge to find a new reality (due to) a situation of (1) significant threat or (2) compelling opportunity [...]. Adaptive challenges set the context for innovation and adaptation."[10]

APEST
The acronym describing the fivefold missional intelligences of disciples listed in Ephesians 4:11: apostle, prophet, evangelist, shepherd, and teacher. Also sometimes called *APEPT* ("pastor" replacing "shepherd), or *fivefold*.

Apostolic
The mode, energy, impulse, and genius of the New Testament church and its leadership as it is compelled to move outward into the world with the gospel.[11]

Appetite, Ambition, Approval
The core temptations of disciples, as addressed by Jesus in the wilderness at the beginning of his ministry. (Mike Breen also calls these, *Consumerism*, *Competition*, and *Celebrity*.[12] JR Woodward and Dan White Jr. name them *Soul pressures*: Be *productive*, *powerful*, and *popular*.)[13]

Capacity
The ability to extend and expand the work of the Kingdom through reproducing disciples.

---

10 Hirsch, *The Forgotten Ways*, 273.
11 Hirsch, *The Forgotten Ways*, 83, uses the term "Apostolic Genius" or "mDNA" (missional DNA), made up of six elements: at the center, the confession that "Jesus is Lord," surrounded by Disciple Making, Missional-Incarnational Impulse, Liminality and *Communitas*, APEST Culture, and Organic Systems.
12 Breen, *Multiplying Missional Leaders*, Kindle edition, Kindle locations 895–1084.
13 Woodward and White, *The Church as Movement*, 79ff.

Character
Being and becoming like Jesus (the interior world of a person).

Chemistry
The ability to work alongside other disciples fruitfully.

Christendom
The expression of the church and mission formed from the time of Constantine (AD 312) to the twenty-first century, which differ significantly from the expression of church and mission as described in the New Testament. Marked particularly by institutionalization.

Circle
LifeShape representing the "repent/believe" core questions of discipleship: How is God getting your attention? How are you going to respond to that?

Competency
Doing the things Jesus could do (the external world of a person).

"D2"
An extended season in the formation of a disciple marked by awareness of one's own struggles and shortcomings. It results in a) a naïve attempt to return to a more infantile faith; b) opting out of the discipleship journey; c) stubborn prolongation of this difficult phase; or d) progression in discipleship, where friendship with and trust in Jesus becomes natural.

Disciple
A person who learns to be like Jesus and to do what Jesus did.

Five Capitals
The key assets one might possess, lack, order, or invest: spiritual, relational, physical, intellectual, and financial.

Fivefold
Another name for the APEST (apostle, prophet, evangelist, shepherd, teacher) mentioned in Ephesians 4:11.

Four Spaces

Social structures in which discipleship can be experienced and transmitted: intimate (1–4 people, in which we can give and receive "vulnerability"), personal (5–12, where we can experience "accountability"), social (15–70, which offers "availability"), and public (70+, in which there is "visibility").[14]

Huddle

A discipleship vehicle consisting of a small group (generally six to ten people) and a leader or two who facilitates conversation around how God is getting our attention and what we are doing about it. Provides support, challenge, accountability, and a forum for imitation-based formation.

Invitation/Challenge

The discipleship calibration of a leader who extends to followers a deep relationship while also calling them to serious responsibility.

Kairos

A breakthrough moment when the Holy Spirit gives to a disciple revelation, wisdom, and truth.

LifeShapes

Visual representations of the core competencies of following Jesus.

Missional

A mode of church, leadership, or Christian faith whose primary commitment is to the missionary calling of the people of God to take the gospel out on the frontier and into the world, and which organizes its life accordingly.

Movement

The self-regenerating results and momentum that come from the work of a missional church or leader and impacts communities and cultures in significant ways. Movements are spurred when individual experiences are mobilized into communal expressions, resulting in a groundswell of exponential breakthrough.

14 Woodward and White, *The Church as Movement*, 155–61.

"Pay it forward"
Uptick signature phrase capturing the grateful and generous attitude of wanting to make discipleship growth possible for others in the same way it was made possible for you.

Person of Peace
A person with whom one has good relational chemistry, whose receptivity and referrals make evangelism, discipleship, sharing, and partnership natural, organic, and fruitful.

Post-Christendom
The current era of Western civilization, marked by the loss of primacy of Christian faith and its expressions in civic, cultural, and intellectual spheres, resulting in shifts in how that faith is perceived, valued, practiced, and transmitted.

Prophetic Prayer
The practice of hearing the Holy Spirit speak on behalf of others within a discipleship community.

Proxemics
The body of knowledge regarding the amount of space that people believe is necessary to set between themselves and others, and what can be accomplished within each of those four types of spaces (intimate, personal, social, and public).

Rhythm of Life
The framework of how disciples calibrate rest and work. Contrary to a static and elusive "work-life balance," it is a dynamic and responsive way of ordering days, weeks, and seasons of life in step with the ordering of creation, the way of Jesus, and the prompting of the Holy Spirit.

Semicircle
The LifeShape that helps disciples explore and grow in matters of Rhythm of Life.

"Simple but hard"

A phrase which captures the overall challenge of growing as disciples, which is not about acquiring endless information, but enacting and imitating the ways of Jesus.

Square

The LifeShape that describes the leadership stages of growing as a disciple and reproducing other disciples.

Triangle (Up/In/Out)

The LifeShape that describes the three great loves of Jesus and thus the dimensions of his disciples' lives. Up: deep connection with God and attentiveness to the leading of the Holy Spirit. In: constant investment in relational capital, especially with nearest communities. Out: entering the brokenness of the world and sharing the Kingdom for individual and systemic transformation.

For Further Reading

Bolsinger, Tod. *Canoeing the Mountains: Christian Leadership in Uncharted Territory.* Illinois: InterVarsity Press, 2015.

Brafman, Ori, and Rod A. Beckstrom. *The Starfish and the Spider: The Unstoppable Power of Leaderless Organizations.* New York: Penguin, 2006.

Breen, Mike. *Covenant and Kingdom: The DNA of the Bible.* South Carolina: 3DM Publishing, 2015.

———. *Multiplying Missional Leaders: From half-hearted volunteers to a mobilized Kingdom force , 1st ed.* South Carolina: 3DM Publishing, 2012.

Breen, Mike, and the 3DM Team. *Leading Kingdom Movements: the "everyman" notebook on how to change the world.* South Carolina: 3DM Publishing, 2015.

——— *Leading Missional Communities: Rediscovering the Power of Living on Mission Together.* South Carolina: 3DM Publishing, 2013.

Breen, Mike, and Ben Sternke. *Oikonomics: How to Invest in Life's Five Capitals the Way Jesus Did.* South Carolina: 3DM Publishing, 2015.

Breen, Mike, and Sally Breen. *Family On Mission: Integrating discipleship into the fabric of our everyday lives.* South Carolina: 3DM Publishing, 2014.

Breen, Mike, and Steve Cockram. *Building a Discipling Culture: How to Release a Missional Movement by Discipling People like Jesus Did.* South Carolina: 3DM Publishing, 2011.

Buford, Bob. *Finishing Well: The Adventure of Life Beyond Halftime.* Tennessee: Integrity Publishers, 2004.

Chandler, John P. *Courageous Church Leadership: Conversations with Effective Practitioners*. Missouri: Chalice Press, 2007.

———. *Praying the Kings: Mining the Old Testament Judges, Kings and Unsung Heroes for Daily Leadership Guidance*. Virginia: Uptick Imprint, 2013.

———. *Praying New Beginnings: Mining the Torah for Daily Leadership Guidance*. Virginia: Uptick Imprint, 2013.

———. *Praying the Prophets: Mining the Old Testament Prophets for Daily Leadership Guidance*. Virginia: Uptick Imprint, 2013.

———. *Praying Wisdom: Mining Old Testament Wisdom for Daily Leadership Guidance*. Virginia: Uptick Imprint, 2013.

Charan, Ram. *The Leadership Pipeline: How to Build the Leadership Powered Company*. California: Jossey-Bass, 2011.

Collins, Jim. *Good to Great: Why Some Companies Make the Leap... and Others Don't*. New York: HarperBusiness, 2001.

———. *Good to Great and the Social Sectors: Why Business Thinking is Not the Answer*. New York: HarperCollins Publishers, Inc, 2005.

Collins, Jim, and Morten T. Hansen. *Great by Choice: Uncertainty, Chaos and Luck—Why Some Thrive Despite Them All*. New York: HarperCollins Publishers, Inc, 2011.

Cuddy, Amy. *Presence: Bringing Your Boldest Self to Your Biggest Challenges*. New York: Back Bay Books, 2018.

Dale, Robert D. *To Dream Again: How to Help Your Church Come Alive*. Georgia: Nurturing Faith, Inc, 2004.

———. *To Dream Again, Again!: Growing Healthy Congregations for Changing Futures*. Georgia: Nurturing Faith, Inc, 2018.

Drucker, Peter F. *Managing the Non-profit Organization: Principles and Practices*. New York: HarperBusiness, 2006.

Easum, Bill. *Unfreezing Moves: Following Jesus into the Mission Field*. Tennessee: Abingdon Press, 2001.

Friedman, Edwin. *A Failure of Nerve: Leadership in the Age of the Quick Fix, revised ed.* New York: Church Publishing, 2017.

Frost, Michael, and Alan Hirsch. *The Shaping of Things to Come: Innovation and Mission for the 21st-Century Church*. Massachusetts: Hendrickson, 2003.

George, Carl F. *Prepare Your Church for the Future*, 1st ed. Michigan: Revell Publishing, 1991.

Goleman, Daniel. *Emotional Intelligence: Why It Can Matter More Than IQ*, 10th Anniversary Edition. New York: Bantam Books, 2005.

Grace, Kay Sprinkel. *Beyond Fundraising: New Strategies for Non-Profit Innovation and Investment*, 2nd ed. New Jersey: John Wiley and Sons, 2005.

———. *The Hidden Dimension: An anthropologist examines man's use of space in public and in private*. New York: Anchor Books, 1990.

———. *The Silent Language*. New York: Anchor Books, 1990.

Heifetz, Ronald, Alexander Grashow, and Marty Linsky. *The Practice of Adaptive Leadership: Tools and Tactics for Changing Your Organization and the World*. Massachusetts: Harvard Business School Press, 2009.

Heifetz, Ronald, and Marty Linsky. *Leadership on the Line: Staying Alive through the Dangers of Leading*. Massachusetts: Harvard Business School Press, 2002.

High, William F., and Ashley B. McCauley. *The Generosity Bet: Secrets of Risk, Reward and Real Joy*. Pennsylvania: Destiny Image, 2014.

Hirsch, Alan. 5Q: *Reactivating the Original Intelligence and Capacity of the Body of Christ*. Georgia: 100 Movements Publishing, 2017.

———. *The Forgotten Ways: Reactivating Apostolic Movements*. Michigan: Brazos Press, 2016.

Hirsch, Alan, and Tim Catchim. *The Permanent Revolution: Apostolic Imagination and Practice in the 21st Century Church*. California: Wiley, 2012.

Hirsch, Alan, and Debra Hirsch. *Untamed: Reactivating a Missional Form of Discipleship*. Michigan: Baker Books, 2011.

Hirsch, Alan, and Mark Nelson. *Reframation: Seeing God, People, and Mission Through Reenchanted Frames*. Georgia: 100 Movements Publishing, 2019.

Hirsch, Debra. *Redeeming Sex: Naked Conversations about Sexuality and Spirituality*. Illinois: InterVarsity Press, 2015.

Hoffer, Eric. *The True Believer: Thoughts on the Nature of Mass Movements*. New York: Harper Perennial Modern Classics, 2010.

Hunter, James Davison. *To Change the World: The Irony, Tragedy and Possibility of Christianity in the Late Modern World*, 1st ed. Oxford: Oxford University Press, 2010.

Janssen, Jeff. *How to Develop Relentless Competitors*, 1st ed. North Carolina: Winning the Mental Game, 2010.

Jay, Meg. *The Defining Decade: Why Your Twenties Matter—and How to Make the Most of Them Now*. New York: Twelve, 2013.

Jeffries, Elizabeth. *What Exceptional Executives Need to Know: Your Step-by-Step Coaching Guide to Busting Communication Barriers, Keeping Top Talent & Growing Your Emerging Leaders!* North Carolina: Spark Publications, 2018.

Jenkins, Philip. *The New Faces of Christianity: Believing the Bible in the Global South.* Oxford: Oxford University Press, 2006.

———. *The Next Christendom: The Coming of Global Christianity, 1st ed.* Oxford: Oxford University Press, 2002.

Kelly, Gerard. *Retrofuture: Rediscovering Our Routes, Recharting Our Routes.* Illinois: InterVarsity Press, 1999.

Kubicek, Jeremie, and Steve Cockram. *5 Voices: How to Communicate Effectively with Everyone You Lead.* New Jersey: John Wiley & Sons, 2016.

———. *5 Gears: How to Be Present and Productive When There is Never Enough Time, 1st ed.* New Jersey: John Wiley & Sons, 2015.

Lukianoff, Greg, and Jonathan Haidt. *The Coddling of the American Mind: How Good Intentions and Bad Ideas are Setting Up a Generation for Failure.* New York: Penguin Press, 2018.

McNeal, Reggie. *The Present Future: Six Tough Questions for the Church, 1st ed.* California: Jossey Bass, 2003.

———. *Missional Renaissance: Changing the Scorecard for the Church, 1st ed.* California: Jossey-Bass, 2009.

Osterhaus, James P., Joseph M. Jurkowski, and Todd A. Hahn. *Thriving through Ministry Conflict: A Parable on How Resistance Can be Your Ally.* Michigan: Zondervan, 2005.

Prince, Russ Alan, and Karen Maru File, *The Seven Faces of Philanthropy: A New Approach to Cultivating Major Donors*, California: Jossey-Bass, 1994.

Putnam, Robert D. *Bowling Alone: The Collapse and Revival of American Community, 1st ed.* New York: Touchstone Books by Simon & Schuster, 2001.

Rath, Tom. *Vital Friends: The People You Can't Afford to Live Without, 1st ed.* New York: Gallup Press, 2006.

Rogers, Everett. *Diffusion of Innovations.* New York: Simon and Schuster, 2003.

Rognlien, Bob. *A Jesus Shaped Life: Discipleship and Mission for Everyday People.* South Carolina: 3DM Publishing, 2016.

Russell, Bob. *After 50 Years of Ministry: Things I'd Do Differently and Things I'd Do the Same.* Illinois: Moody Publishers, 2016.

———. *When God Builds a Church: 10 Principles for Growing a Dynamic Church.* New York: Howard Books, 2015.

Russell, Bob, and Bryan Bucher. *Transition Plan: 7 Secrets Every Leader Needs to Know, 1st ed.* Kentucky: Ministers Label Publishing, 2010.

Schaller, Lyle E. *Activating the Passive Church: Diagnosis & Treatment.* Tennessee: Abingdon, 1981.

Schein, Edgar H. with Peter Schein. *Organizational Culture and Leadership, The Jossey-Bass Business & Management Series, 5th ed.* New Jersey: Wiley, 2016.

Sherman, Amy. *Kingdom Calling: Vocational Stewardship for the Common Good.* Illinois: IVP Books, 2011.

Sweet, Leonard. *The Gospel According to Starbucks: Living with a Grande Passion.* Colorado: WaterBrook Press, 2007.

Weese, Carolyn and J. Russell Crabtree. *The Elephant in the Boardroom: Speaking the Unspoken about Pastoral Transitions,* 1st ed. California: Jossey-Bass, 2004.

Willard, Dallas. *Hearing God: Developing a Conversational Relationship with God.* Illinois: IVP Books, 2012.

———. *Renovation of the Heart: Putting on the Character of Christ.* Colorado: NavPress, 2012.

———. *The Allure of Gentleness: Defending the Faith in the Manner of Jesus.* California: HarperCollins, 2016.

———. *The Divine Conspiracy: Rediscovering Our Hidden Life in God.* California: HarperCollins, 1998.

———. *The Great Omission: Reclaiming Jesus's Essential Teachings on Discipleship.* California: HarperOne, 2014.

———. *The Spirit of the Disciplines: Understanding How God Changes Lives.* California: HarperOne, 1991.

Williamson, Beth. *Christian Art: A Very Short Introduction.* Oxford: Oxford University Press, 2004.

Willimon, William H. *Who Lynched Willie Earle?: Preaching to Confront Racism.* Tennessee: Abingdon Press, 2017.

Woodward, JR. *Creating a Missional Culture: Equipping the Church for the Sake of the World.* Illinois: InterVarsity Press, 2012.

Woodward, JR, and Dan White Jr. *The Church as Movement: Starting and Sustaining Missional-Incarnational Communities.* Illinois: InterVarsity Press, 2016.

Acknowledgments and Appreciation

This book would not have been possible without the help of many Vital Friends: builders, champions, collaborators, companions, connectors, energizers, mind-openers, and navigators. Without relational capital, we have little worth saying. But, by God's mercy, the work of Uptick is freely shared within and shaped by a beloved community of mentors, peers, and protégés. I am deeply indebted to sisters and brothers who have been, are, and will be part of this Uptick journey. Max DePree has said that the two jobs of the leader are to define reality and to say thank you. You'll have to judge on whether Uptick is "reality-defining," but at least I can be sure to say thank you.

Thanks to the Baptist General Association of Virginia and our fearless leader and executive director, John Upton. Without John's leadership and the BGAV's deep trust in his heart to clear the way for starting Uptick, it would never have come into being. Time and space are the media through which God creates, and thanks to John and the BGAV for giving both of those with generosity and encouragement.

I would like to thank some of the pioneers who set the stage for Uptick to flourish. Thanks to Jim Baucom and Sarah Burnett, each of whom have ably led the Uptick board. For over a decade, Sarah and Jim have provided hope and help in innumerable ways, calibrating invitation and challenge, and offering deep friendship. Bob Dale, mentor and friend, blazed the path for Uptick with his ground breaking work in creating the Young Leaders Program, of which I and many were beneficiaries. Laura McDaniel has been a steady partner in broadening the Uptick tent; I think she's joking when she says the goal is "world domination," but I'm not really sure! Carey and Gannon Sims now walk alongside us in the Uptick work and bring so much prophetic richness to the venture. Thanks to Carey, along with Paul Maconochie, for writing the Prophetic Prayer section—and for introducing that practice into the Uptick lexicon. Special thanks to past and current members of the Uptick board—high-caliber folk who know how to plot (and resource) a revolution while having a lot of fun. And I am humbled by the individuals who have been incredibly generous with financial capital to make Uptick fly. I would name you here, but it would blow your cover, so plan on getting credit in heaven! I certainly pray that I thank you often enough and well enough in person to honor who you are.

Then there are the folk who have not only assisted concretely with Uptick but have inspired its very vision of leadership through the lens of discipleship in the first place. Thanks to Mike Breen for 3DM's early and formative influence. Thanks to Steve Cockram and Jo Saxton for being such insightful apostolic teachers. Alan and Deb Hirsch were early champions, who to this day continue to inspire and shape not only Uptick but movemental work around the world. They have inspired so many—especially me. I am indebted to them for writing the foreword— and more so for their leading me, along with so many, toward "the shaping of things to come." And Paul Maconochie has uniquely helped to chart and stay the course with brilliance, grace, and insight. His contributions have been invaluable and irreplaceable—both to Uptick and to me. May his prophetic voice increase, and may he continue to shape the Uptick movement in wide and profound ways.

Eric Howell and Kathryn McElveen get the credit for inspiring the coaching track of Uptick, and folk like Dan Elash, Elizabeth Jeffries, and Ken Kessler continue coaching Uptickers into strong Future Stories. Each have told me the truth a few times when it wasn't fun, but it sure has been helpful. Thanks for such generous and wise listening and forthtelling.

Artist Kristen Peyton deserves special mention for capturing the ethos of Uptick in her cover art. Her generosity captures the Uptick spirit of "pay it forward," and her work conveys beauty, truth, and goodness by means beyond words.

It may sound cliché, but there is no way this book could have happened without the unique gifts of editor Anna Robinson. Early in the writing process, Anna shared helpful feedback with me in such a timely and astonishing format that I thanked her effusively. She replied modestly, "This is just what it's like to have an editor." However, I've never worked with an editor like her. Her skills are remarkable. She deserves immense credit for wherever this book is clear and helpful.

Thanks to the never-flustered Darcie Trexler for admin wizardry from Richmond.

Of course, I am grateful to my precious, steadfast, joyful, and delightful wife Mary; strong, hilarious, and godly sons Preston and Roland; and granddaughters Nora and Emily—the apples of my eye. They, along with the Uptickers, inspire me to pray:

> we will tell to the coming generation the glorious deeds of the LORD, and his might, and the wonders that he has done [...] to teach to their children; that the next generation might know them, the children yet unborn, and rise up and tell them to their children, so that they should set their hope in God, and not forget the works of God, but keep his commandments
>
> PSALM 78:4–7

Autumn, 2019
Chapel Hill, North Carolina

A Note from the Cover Artist

I painted "Homage to Bottles and Jars," thinking of the words of Hans Hofmann. As an artist and teacher Hofmann spoke of the "push and pull" in painting, a phrase he used to describe the rhythm he observed at play in nature: light/dark; forward/backward; positive/negative, etc. Woven intelligently together inside a painting's rectangle these juxtapositions create dynamism.

In its teaching and creation of community, Uptick presents a similar dynamism inside the container of the cohort. My cohort of twelve was diverse in thought, theology, context, and color; creating a dynamic snapshot of the Kingdom of God. Together, Uptick called us to move deeper inward as it challenged us to reach further outward in our unique ministry contexts. Together, we learned that life in Christ is rhythm and flow—rest and work, pruning and yielding, invitation and challenge—a dynamic "push and pull" experienced together in community.

Adding the element of color to Hofmann's "push and pull," I painted a portrait of John Chandler, our "Uptick Gramps," as part of an ongoing series, to illuminate upon canvas the inherent light I saw evident in each Upticker. Color is contained within light: the prism present within every ray. Our eyes perceive frequencies of varying light waves and our brains separate and interpret these as comprehensible color sensations. With light as color and color as light, a possible reading of Genesis 1:3 follows, "God said let there be light and there was *color*."

As light reveals color in our visual world, color reveals light upon the canvas. It is this color-revealing-light and the embodiment of the "push and pull" that I am after in my work and life.

Kristen Peyton is a painter, printmaker, and draftsman working from observation and invention. She is a native of Pittsburgh, Pennsylvania, and a resident of Richmond, Virginia. To see Kristen's work and CV, visit KristenPeyton.com .

About the Author

John Chandler, a North Carolina native, leads Uptick, a network which invests in building the leadership pipeline in BGAV life and beyond. Since 2007, Uptick has been the catalyst for starting over one thousand new networks serving over five thousand ministry leaders. Uptick is noted as a global Baptist leader for best practices in developing high-capacity young leaders, having discipled over three hundred of them so far, many of whom have started Uptick networks in their own contexts.

He has served as a pastor and church consultant, and holds degrees from the University of North Carolina, Princeton Theological Seminary, and Fuller Theological Seminary, and is author of six books.

John and his wife, Mary, live in Chapel Hill, North Carolina, have two great adult sons, Preston (and wife Maria), and Roland (and wife Julia). His favorite title is "Gramps," to his granddaughters Nora and Emily. John enjoys playing tennis, motorcycling, and passionately rooting for the Tar Heels.

In the Uptick spirit of "pay it forward,"
please visit uptick.org and consider
investing in the future of new Uptickers.

MOVEMENTS
PUBLISHING

100 Movements Publishing is a hybrid publisher, offering
the benefits of both traditional and self-publishing.

OUR AUTHORS ARE **RISK-TAKERS**,
PARADIGM-SHIFTERS, **INCARNATIONAL**
MISSIONARIES, AND **INFLUENTIAL LEADERS**
WHO LOVE THE BODY OF CHRIST AND
WANT TO SPUR HER ON FOR MORE.

Our books aim to inspire and equip disciples
to take hold of their God-given call to make disciples
and to see kingdom impact in every sphere of society.

Changing the Conversation

OUR BOOKS SHIFT PARADIGMS, EQUIP
LEADERS, AND INSPIRE MISSIONAL
DISCIPLES TO PLAY THEIR PART
IN CATALYZING MISSIONAL MOVEMENTS.

For more information please visit us at 100Mpublishing.com